THEATRE AT THE CROSSROADS OF CULTURE

THEATRE AT THE CROSSROADS OF CULTURE

Patrice Pavis

Translated by Loren Kruger

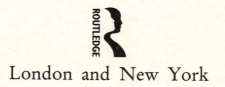

London and New York

First published 1992
by Routledge
11 New Fetter Lane, London EC4P 4EE

Simultaneously published in the USA and Canada
by Routledge
a division of Routledge, Chapman and Hall, Inc.
29 West 35th Street, New York, NY 10001

Phototypeset in 10/12pt Garamond by
Intype, London
Printed in Great Britain by T J Press (Padstow) Ltd
Padstow, Cornwall.

British Library Cataloguing in Publication Data
Pavis, Patrice
Theatre at the crossroads of culture
1. Theatre
I. Title
792

Library of Congress Cataloging in Publication Data
Pavis, Patrice
[Théâtre au croisement des cultures. English]
Theatre at the crossroads of culture / Patrice Pavis : translated
by Loren Kruger.
p. cm.
Translation of: Théâtre au croisement des cultures.
Includes bibliographical references.
1. Theater and society. 2. Drama. 3. Intercultural
communication. I. Title.
PN1643.P3813 1992
306.4′84--dc20   91–17519

ISBN 0–415–06037–0
ISBN 0–415–06038–9 pbk

CONTENTS

PREFACE

The essays brought together in this volume were written between 1983 and 1988, and focus principally on the question that semiotics has for too long avoided: the relationship between theatre and other cultures. At issue here is the proposal of a materialist theory of intercultural appropriation, which is intimidated neither by a sociologism that pays little attention to forms nor by an anti-theoretical terrorism. We may also venture beyond the French nation – a risky enterprise!

At a moment when, in Europe at least, theory seems out of date, when class struggle and conflicts are buried, when the relationship between culture and socioeconomic conditions has been forgotten, when anthropology is often brandished as a functional theory of harmony and consensus to further the doctrine of indifference and in-differentiation ('anything goes'), it seems salutary, even if intemperate, to react: I have attempted to retrace the path from text to stage, from a classical model that is relatively simple (the dramatic text and *mise en scène*) to a global model of interculturalism.

The fine-tuning of this sociosemiotic model of culture and of intercultural *mise en scène* was achieved – and the relationship and chronology of the chapters in this book bear the marks – by a series of investigations, from a model of the way in which the *mise en scène* functions (Chapter 2) to a theory of translation (Chapter 6) and interculturalism (Chapter 1). These studies have been presented in a variety of forms at international conferences and colloquia; these occasions have allowed me to adjust and focus my ideas, to carry over an intercultural project in a continuous state of development to other contexts for other listeners.

It is with great pleasure that I wish to thank those people who commissioned these texts and who have helped me with their advice and friendship. This gives me the feeling of undertaking a last journey beyond the all too narrow frontiers of France into the interior of Europe (where one may surely breathe more easily) and, further still, into the vast intercultural world, into which it is always good to venture. My thanks are due especially to Desiderio Navarro (Havana), Francisco Javier (Buenos Aires), Michael Issacharoff (London), Michael Hays (Ithaca), Wilfried Floeck (Giessen), José-Angel Gómez (Barcelona), Hanna Scolnicov (Jerusalem), Eugenio Barba (Holstebro), Erika Fischer-Lichte (Mainz), Gay McAuley (Sydney), Marianne König (Jegenstorf, Switzerland), Hyun-Sook Shin (Seoul). I am particularly grateful to Mary and Hector Maclean and Norman Price (Melbourne), Jill Daugherty (Pretoria), Alan Reed (London), Richard Gough (Cardiff) and Helena Reckitt (London) for discussing the final draft of the manuscript with me. Mary and Hector MacLean were also kind enough to edit the English version of these essays. The book is dedicated to Ježko-Bežko.

1

TOWARD A THEORY OF CULTURE AND *MISE EN SCÈNE*

The object of this study is the crossroads of cultures in contemporary theatre practice. This crossroads, where foreign cultures, unfamiliar discourses and the myriad artistic effects of estrangement are jumbled together, is hard to define but it could assert itself, in years to come, as that of a theatre of *culture(s)*. The moment is both favorable and difficult. Never before has the western stage contemplated and manipulated the various cultures of the world to such a degree, but never before has it been at such a loss as to what to make of their inexhaustible babble, their explosive mix, the inextricable collage of their languages. *Mise en scène* in the theatre is today perhaps the last refuge and the most rigorous laboratory for this mix: it examines every cultural representation, exposing each one to the eye and the ear, and displaying and appropriating it through the mediation of stage and auditorium. Access to this exceptional laboratory remains difficult, however, as much because of the artists, who do not like to talk too much about their creations, as because of the spectators, disarmed face to face with a phenomenon as complex and inexpressible as intercultural exchange. Does this difficulty spring from a purely aesthetic and consumerist vision of cultures, which thinks itself capable of dispensing with both socioeconomic and anthropological theory, or which would like to play anthropology against semiotics and sociology?

A SATURATED THEORY

When one seeks humanity, one seeks oneself. Every theory is something of a self-portrait.

André Leroi-Gourhan

1

Theory has a lot to put up with. It is reproached on the one hand for its complexity, on the other for its partiality. In our desire to understand theatre at the crossroads of culture, we certainly risk losing its substance, displacing theatre from one world to another, forgetting it along the way, and losing the means of observing all the maneuvers that accompany such a transfer and appropriation.

Any theory which would mark these cultural slippages suffers the same vertiginous displacement. The model of intertextuality, derived from structuralism and semiotics, yields to that of interculturalism. It is no longer enough to describe the relationships between texts (or even between performances) to grasp their internal functioning; it is also necessary to understand their inscription within contexts and cultures and to appreciate the cultural production that stems from these unexpected transfers. The term *interculturalism*, rather than *multiculturalism* or *transculturalism*, seems appropriate to the task of grasping the dialectic of exchanges of civilities between cultures.[1]

Confronted with intercultural exchange, contemporary theatre practice – from Artaud to Wilson, from Brook to Barba, from Heiner Müller to Ariane Mnouchkine – goes on the attack: it confronts and examines traditions, styles of performance and cultures which would never have encountered one another without this sudden need to fill a vacuum. And theory, as a docile servant of practice, no longer knows which way to turn: descriptive and sterile semiotics will no longer suffice, sociologism has been sent back to the drawing board, anthropology is seized on in all its forms – physical, economic, political, philosophical and cultural – though the nature of their relationships is unclear. But the most difficult link to establish is that between the sociosemiotic model and the anthropological approach. This link is all the more imperative as avant-garde theatre production attempts to get beyond the historicist model by way of a confrontation between the most diverse cultures, and (not without a certain risk of lapsing into folklore) to return to ritual, to myth and to anthropology as an integrating model of all experience (Barba, Grotowski, Brook, Schechner).

This keeps us within the scope of a semiology. Semiology has established itself as a discipline for the analysis of dramatic texts and stage performances. We are now beyond the quarrel between a semiology of text and a semiology of performance. Each has developed its own analytical tools and we no longer attempt to

2

analyse a performance on the basis of a pre-existing dramatic text. However, the notion of a *performance text* (*testo spettacolare*, in the Italian terminology of de Marinis (1987: 100)) is still frowned on by earlier semioticians such as Kowzan (1988: 180) or even Elam (1989: 4) and by cultural anthropologists (Halstrup 1990). This seems mainly a question of terminology because we certainly need a notion of texture, i.e. of a codified, readable artifact, be it a performance or the cultural models inscribed in it.

What is at stake is something quite different. It is the possibility of a universal, precise performance analysis and of an adequate notation system. It would seem that not only is notation never satisfying but that analysis can only ever be tentative and partial. If we accept these serious limitations, if we give up the hope of reconstructing the totality of a performance, then we can at least understand a few basic principles of the *mise en scène*: its main options, the acting choices, the organization of space and time. This may seem a rather poor analytic result, if we expect, as before, a precise and complete description of the performance. But, on the other hand, we should also question the aim of a precise and exhaustive semiotic description, if such a project arouses no interest. As Keir Elam puts it, 'the more successful and rigorous we are in doing justice to the object, the less interest we seem to arouse within both the theatrical and the academic communities' (1989: 6). For this reason, Elam proposes a shift from theoretical to empirical semiotics: 'a semiotics of theatre as empirical rather than theoretical object may yet be possible' (1989: 11). It is certainly true that we should consider 'reshaping' the semiology of theatre by checking its theoretical hypotheses and results with the practical work of the actor, dramaturge and director (Pavis 1985). But it would be naïve to think that one will solve the problems of theory just by describing the process of production. It is not enough to follow carefully the preparations for the performance, to be among the actors, directors, musicians, as we are during the International School of Theatre Anthropology (ISTA). We also, and first and foremost, need theoretical tools in order to analyse the operations involved. One has to be able to help a 'genuine' audience understand the meaning of the production (and the production of meaning). How can the production be described and interpreted from the point of a single spectator receiving the production as an aesthetic object? Instead of looking for further refinement of western performance analysis, we can

3

institute another approach, the study of intercultural theatre, in the hope that it will produce a new way of understanding theatre practice and will thus contribute to promoting a new methodology of performance analysis. In order to encompass this overflow of experiences, the theoretician needs a model with the patience and attention to minute detail of the hourglass.

AN HOURGLASS READY FOR EVERYTHING

> We count the minutes we have left to live, and we shake our hourglass to hasten it along.
>
> *Alfred de Vigny*

'An hourglass? Dear Alfred, what is an hourglass?' ask the younger generation with their quartz watches.

It is a strange object, reminiscent of a funnel and a mill (see Fig. 1.1). In the upper bowl is the foreign culture, the source culture, which is more or less codified and solidified in diverse anthropological, sociocultural or artistic modelizations. In order to reach us, this culture must pass through a narrow neck. If the grains of culture or their conglomerate are sufficiently fine, they will flow through without any trouble, however slowly, into the lower bowl, that of the target culture, from which point we observe this slow flow. The grains will rearrange themselves in a way which appears random, but which is partly regulated by their passage through some dozen filters put in place by the target culture and the observer.[2]

Figure 1.1 The hourglass of cultures

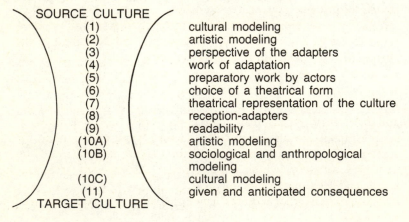

SOURCE CULTURE	
(1)	cultural modeling
(2)	artistic modeling
(3)	perspective of the adapters
(4)	work of adaptation
(5)	preparatory work by actors
(6)	choice of a theatrical form
(7)	theatrical representation of the culture
(8)	reception-adapters
(9)	readability
(10A)	artistic modeling
(10B)	sociological and anthropological modeling
(10C)	cultural modeling
(11)	given and anticipated consequences
TARGET CULTURE	

The hourglass presents two risks. If it is only a mill, it will blend the source culture, destroy its every specificity and drop into the lower bowl an inert and deformed substance which will have lost its original modeling without being molded into that of the target culture. If it is only a funnel, it will indiscriminately absorb the initial substance without reshaping it through the series of filters or leaving any trace of the original matter.

This book is devoted to the study of this hourglass and the filters interposed between 'our' culture and that of others, to these accommodating obstacles which check and fix the grains of culture and reconstitute sedimentary beds, themselves aspects and layers of culture. The better to show the relativity of the notion of culture and the complicated relationship that we have with it, we will focus here on the intercultural transfer between source and target culture. We will investigate how a target culture analyses and appropriates a foreign culture and how this appropriation is accompanied by a series of theatrical operations.

This appropriation of the other culture is never definitive, how-ever. It is turned upside-down as soon as the users of a foreign culture ask themselves how they can communicate their own cul-ture to another target culture. The hourglass is designed to be turned upside-down, to question once again every sedimentation, to flow indefinitely from one culture to the other.

What theory is, so to speak, contained in the hourglass? It has become almost impossible to represent other than in the meta-phoric form of an hourglass. It includes a semiotic model of the production and reception of the performance (Pavis 1985) in which one can particularly study the reception of a performance and the transfer from one culture to the other.

Can the most complex case of theatre production, i.e. intercul-turalism, be of any use for the development and *déblocage* of the current theory of performance? It certainly forces the analyst to reconsider his own cultural parameters and his viewing habits, to accept elements he[3] does not fully understand, to complement and activate the *mise en scène*. Barba's practice (at the ISTA), his trial-and-error method, his search for a resistance, his confrontation, with a puzzle-like use of bricolage, with several traditions at the same time, enable us to understand the making and the reception of a *mise en scène*, which can no longer be 'decoded' from one single and legitimate point of view.

The fact that other cultures have gradually permeated our own leads (or should lead) us to abandon or relativize any dominant western (or Eurocentric) universalizing view.

The notion of *mise en scène* remains, however, central to the theory of intercultural theatre, because it is bound to the practical, pragmatic aspect of putting systems of signs together and organizing them from a semiotic point of view, i.e. of giving them productive and receptive pertinence.

Mise en scène is a kind of *réglage* ('fine-tuning') between different contexts and cultures; it is no longer only a question of intercultural exchange or of a dialectics between text and context; it is a mediation between different cultural backgrounds, traditions and methods of acting. Thus its appearance towards the end of the nineteenth century is also the consequence of the disappearance of a strong western tradition, of a certain unified acting style, which makes the presence of an 'author' of the performance, in the figure of the director, indispensable.

CAVITY, CRUCIBLE, CROSSING, CROSSROADS

> Theatre is a crucible of civilizations. It is a place for human communication.
>
> *Victor Hugo*

Is the hourglass the same top and bottom? Yes, but only in appearance. For one ought not to focus solely on the grains, tiny atoms of meaning; it is necessary to investigate their combination, their capacity for gathering in conglomerates and in strata whose thickness and composition are variable but not arbitrary. The sand in the hourglass prevents us from believing naïvely in the melting pot, in the crucible where cultures would be miraculously melted and reduced to a radically different substance. *Pace* Victor, there is no theatre in the crucible of a humanity where all specificity melts into a universal substance, or in the warm cavity of a familiarly cupped hand. It is at the crossing of ways, of traditions, of artistic practices that we can hope to grasp the distinct hybridization of cultures, and bring together the winding paths of anthropology, sociology and artistic practices.

Crossroads refers partly to the crossing of the ways, partly to the hybridization of races and traditions. This ambiguity is admirably suited to a description of the links between cultures: for these cultures meet either by passing close by one another or by reproducing thanks to crossbreeding. All nuances are possible, as we shall see.

In taking intercultural theatre and *mise en scène* as its subject, this book has selected a figuration at once eternal and new: *eternal*, because theatrical performance has always mixed traditions and diverse styles, translated from one language or discourse into another, covered space and time in every direction; *new*, because western *mise en scène*, itself a recent notion, has made use of these meetings of performances and traditions in a conscious, deliberate and aesthetic manner only since the experiments by the multicultural groups of Barba, Brook or Mnouchkine (to cite only the most visible artists that interest us here). In this book, we will be studying only situations of exchange in one direction from a source culture, a culture foreign to us (westerners), to a target culture, western culture, in which the artists work and within which the target audience is situated.

The context of these studies can be easily circumscribed: France between 1968 and 1988, with some geographic forays. After maximal openness in 1968, there followed the 'leaden years' (*années de plomb*) of artistic and ideological isolation, elimination of dialectic thought and historicized dramaturgy, the last sparks of theoretical fireworks, the end of a radical way of thinking about culture which was still that of Freud and Artaud. From 1973 to 1981, the retreat of ideology and historicity became even more pronounced, communication advisers and sponsors gave us our daily bread, the economic crisis slowed down initiatives; foreign cultures were perceived more as a threat or an object of exploitation than as partners in exchange; this general numbness, this jaded lack of differentiation, this theoretical droning none the less did not prevent certain more or less subsidized artists from attempting a cultural exchange; geography and anthropology replaced a failing history. From 1981 to 1988, the French socialist experiment exploded a last taboo (so-called socialist chaos), but came up against the hard realities of management, tasted the social democracy of ideas; the debate on the relativity of cultures and on *La Défaite de la pensée* ('The defeat of thought') by Alain Finkielkraut (1987) managed to compress every historicizing perspective, but rediscovered geographical and cultural horizons, which it recuperated with a postmodern scepticism and functionalism. Culture is at the center of all these debates: everything is cultural, but where has theatrical culture gone?

CULTURE AND ITS DOUBLES

Never before, when it is life itself that is threatened, has so much been said about civilization and culture. And there is a strange parallelism between this generalized collapse of life, which is the basis for the current demoralization and the concern of a culture that has never merged with life, and which is made to dictate to life.

Antonin Artaud (*Theatre and its Double*)

Let us admit it (and not without apologizing to Antonin): our western culture, be it modern or postmodern, is certainly tired; theory aspires in vain to encompass all questions posed by the scope of the concept. The concepts it opposes are just as varied, whether it be life (Artaud), nature (Lévi-Strauss), technology (McLuhan), civilization (Elias, Marcuse), chaos, entropy or non-culture (Lotman). In theatre, the definition is still sharper and the exclusion more marked, since the first cultural act consists of tracing a circle around the stage event and thus of separating performance from non-performance, culture from non-culture, interior from exterior, the object of the gaze from the gazer.

Before following the flow of sand from one bowl to the other and tracing the series of filters and deposits, it is perhaps useful to mobilize for theatre and *mise en scène* some of the definitions and problematics which the notion of culture in anthropology and sociology offers. The excellent synthesis of Camille Camilleri (1982) is illuminating here: we will consider in turn culturalist conceptions and sociological approaches, before examining how we might find them again at each level of the hourglass, and whether it is possible to attempt to differentiate them.

Culturalist premises

Cultural anthropology, particularly in America (Benedict, Mead, Kardiner), investigates culture with regard to the coherence of the group within the sum of the norms and symbols that structure the emotions and instincts of individuals: it 'attempts to discover the characteristics of a culture through the study of its manifestations in individuals and in its influences on their behavior' (Panoff and Perrin). Globally, one might say that culture is a signifying system (a modeling system, in Lotman's sense), thanks

8

to which a society or a group understands itself in its relationship with the world. As Clifford Geertz has it:

> A culture is a system of symbols by which man confers significance upon his own experience. Symbol systems, man-created, shared, conventional, ordered, and indeed learned, provide human beings with a meaningful framework for orienting themselves to one another, to the world around them and to themselves.
>
> (1973: 250)

More specific definitions, inspired by Camilleri's reflections, will enable us to become aware of the ramifications of culture at all levels of the theatrical enterprise.

Definition 1

'Culture is a kind of bent, of foreseeable determinations, which our representations, feelings, modes of conduct, in general all the aspects of our psyche and even of biological organism, take on under the influence of the group' (Camilleri 1982: 16).

Transposed to the stage, one might observe that every element, living or inanimate, of the performance is subject to a similar determination; it is reworked, cultivated, inscribed in a meaningful totality. The dramatic text includes countless deposits, which are as many traces of these determinations, the actors' bodies, in training or in performance, are as though 'penetrated' by the 'body techniques' belonging to their culture, to a performance tradition or an acculturation. It is (almost) impossible to unravel this complex and compact body, whose origin can no longer be seen.

Definition 2

'This determination is common to members of the same group' (Camilleri 1982: 16). Actors also possess a culture, which is that of their own group and which they acquire especially during the preparatory phase of the *mise en scène*. This process of *inculturation*, conscious or unconscious, makes them assimilate the traditions and (especially corporal, vocal and rhetorical) techniques of the group. Because actors belong to a certain culture, they have convictions and expectations, techniques and habits, which they cannot do without. Actors are thus defined by 'body techniques'

(Mauss 1936), which can be got rid of only with difficulty and which are inscribed by the culture on their bodies, then on the performance. According to Barba, part of the actor's work consists of undoing this natural acculturation, or this everyday behavior, so as to acquire a new 'body technique.' Even naturalist actors, who ought to be free of this constraint by virtue of their mimeticism and supposed 'spontaneity,' are subject to a repertoire of signs, attitudes, 'authenticity effects.'

Definition 3

'Cultural order is *artificial* in the proper sense of that term, that is, made by human art. It is distinct from the natural order' (Camilleri 1982: 16). Culture is opposed to nature, the acquired to the innate, artifice and creation to spontaneity. This is the meaning of Lévi-Strauss' celebrated opposition:

> everything universal in humankind relates to the natural order and is characterized by spontaneity, everything subject to a norm is cultural and is both relative and particular.
> (1949: 10; 1969: 8).

> What heredity determines in human beings is the general aptitude to acquire any culture whatever; the specific culture, however, depends on random factors of birth and on the society in which one is raised.
> (1983: 40; 1984: 18)

In theatre, stage and actor play on this ambiguity of the natural milieu and the artificial, constructed object. Everything tends to transform itself into a sign, to become semiotic. Even the natural utilization of the actor's body is inscribed in a mechanism of meaning, which claims from the reluctant flesh its share of artificiality and codification.

Definition 4

'Culture is transmitted by what has since been called "social heredity": a certain number of techniques by means of which each generation makes possible the later generation's internalization of the common determination of the psyche and organism, which make up culture' (Camilleri 1982: 16–17).

10

In the *mise en scène*, one cannot establish the internalization of techniques quite so clearly. On the other hand, certain performance traditions in the most codified and stabilized genres transmit these techniques, and the players internalize, incorporate, a style of performance (such as the *commedia dell'arte* or Peking Opera).

Definition 5

Certain cultures are essentially defined by national characteristics, which are sometimes opposed to cultural minorities, the better to affirm themselves (see Chapter 7). These majority cultures are sometimes so powerful that they are capable of appropriating – in the negative sense this time – foreign cultures, and transforming them according to their own majority interests. We are so much caught in the network of our national cultural modelizations, Eurocentric in this case, that we find it difficult to conceive of the study of performance or of a theatrical genre within a perspective other than that of our acquaintance with the European practice of theatre.

From these definitions inspired by cultural anthropology flows a series of consequences linked to the following general hypothesis: 'Cultures are without doubt the principal means that humankind has invented to regulate its amorphous psychic form, so as to give itself a minimal psychic homogeneity that makes group life possible' (Camilleri 1982: 18).

A. This regulation by culture is both a repression of individual, instinctive spontaneity and an expression of human creativity:

> Civilization is built upon a renunciation of instinct . . . it presupposes precisely the non-satisfaction (by suppression, repression, or some other means) of powerful instincts.
>
> (Freud 1961: 97)

> There is no document of civilization which is not at the same time a document of barbarism.
>
> (Benjamin 1969: 256)

In theatre, this regulation is assured by the *mise en scène*, which prevents any one sign system from taking on unlimited or unilateral importance. The function of the director is relegated to a physical absence, to a superego that does not directly display itself. The real authority is thus *internalized* and 'civilized.' This is the 'discreet charm of good staging.'

B. The principle of internalization of authority consists in accepting the repressive and expressive function of culture. The *mise en scène* regroups directives in order to put on the performance, accepting the constraints of meaning. Likewise, actors internalize the sum of rules of behavior, habits of performance. They accept the ephemeral nature of theatre, the way it cannot be stored, grasped or memorized. These are the unwritten laws, which control everything and which are permanent: 'What is of short duration,' writes Eugenio Barba, 'is not theatre, but performance. Theatre is made of traditions, conventions, institutions, habits, which are permanent in time' (1988: 26). This is the phenomenon of internalization of authority, which should inspire a 'negative' semiotics capable of indicating what is hidden in the sign, what makes a sign without signaling it, what the actor or the stage shows while hiding it.

All these definitions accentuate the cultural unity of humankind, but they tend to isolate it from its sociohistorical context, grasping it only on a very abstract anthropological level. These definitions need therefore to be completed (and not replaced) by a sociological approach, better grounded in history and ideological context.

Sociohistorical premises

The ideological, especially the Marxist, approach tends to be undermined by the very fact of being opened up to foreign cultures and to the enlargement of the anthropological notion of culture. In the process, the notions of group, subgroup, subculture or minority tend to replace those of classes in conflict. Conversely, Marxist sociology has too often simplified the debate and proposed ready-made answers without a knowledge of all the implications of the cultural debate. To say, for example, that, 'in Marxist terms, culture is the ideological superstructure, in a given civilization, relative to the material infrastructure of society' (art. 'culture,' *Dictionnaire Marabout*), does not help to clarify the cultural mechanisms at work. It would be necessary to show that culture conditions and is also conditioned by social action, of which it is the cause and the consequence.

I have elsewhere proposed a theory of ideologemes and their

12

function in the ideological and fictional construction of the dramatic and performance text (Pavis 1985: 290–4). But that was within the perspective of the dramatic text's inscription within history rather than within culture. The phenomena are obviously still more complex when they are considered within very different, especially extra-European, cultural contexts. It is therefore necessary to imagine a theory of mediation, of exchange, of intercultural transfer, a 'culture of links' in Brook's sense (Brook 1987: 239), i.e. 'between man and society, between one race and another, between micro- and macrocosm, between humanity and machinery, between the visible and invisible, between categories, languages, genres' (1987: 239). The image of the hourglass emerges once again, as a means of understanding the dynamic of the flow and the successive deposits. We will examine each step of the cultural transfer, noting which conception of culture is presupposed by each operation at each level of the hourglass (see Fig. 1.1).

(1), (2) *Cultural and/or artistic modeling*. An initial difficulty, particularly in our western societies, consists in marking the points of modeling, whether in the source culture (1), (2) or in the target (10A), (10B), which are clearly specific either to an artistic activity or to a codification proper to a subgroup or given culture. With the multiplication of subgroups and subcultures, culture, especially national culture, can only with difficulty integrate and reflect the sum of particular or minority codifications. As Camilleri writes, culture tends 'to become what would be common to the subgroups that constitute society, once we have separated out the differences. But this common content becomes more and more difficult to define' (1982: 23). In contemporary *mise en scène*, it is practically impossible to understand what a commercial play, an operetta, an avant-garde play or a Bunraku performance have in common, not only because of the artistic codifications at work, which are extremely varied, but also because of their ideological and aesthetic function.

In short, the difficulty in all these examples is to grasp the connection between artistic modeling on the one hand and sociological and/or anthropological modeling on the other. We can observe that comprehension of specifically artistic codes generates an interest in the comprehension of cultural and sociological codes in general, and conversely the knowledge of general cultural codes is indispensable to the comprehension of specifically artistic codes. The fact of grasping the symbolic functioning of a society (1) invites one to perceive artistic codifications in particular (2). In tackling source and target cultures, we are on the other hand led to compare the relationship of (1) and (2) specific to each culture with the slippage which is produced when the source culture is received in the target culture, thus the relationships between (1) and (2) as well as among (10A), (10B) and (10C). We have thus to determine how we recognize a foreign culture, what indices, stereotypes, presuppositions we associate with it, how we construct it from our point of view, even at the risk of being ethnocentric.

(3) *Perspective of the adapters*. As soon as we are asked to take account of this segmentation of modeling – for example, when trying to convey a foreign culture to our western tradition – it becomes difficult to find a unifying point of view; the result is a relativism in concepts of culture and the real.

> We in industrial or at least western societies are witness today to a segmentation of systems of thought. As there cannot be several truths on the same point, one gets used to thinking that these systems (themselves often relative to the subcultures of different subgroups, in particular sociopolitical groups) are simply points of view on the real, and to reconnecting these systems to thinking subjects. Hence the appearance of the spirit of relativism, which goes hand in hand with the progress of disenchantment [*désacralisation*].
> (Camilleri 1982: 23)

Relativism is particularly evident in what has been called the postmodern *mise en scène* of the classics: the rejection of any centralizing and committed reading, the leveling of codes, the undoing of discursive hierarchies, the rejection of a separation between 'high' culture and mass culture are all symptoms of the relativization of points of view. We are no longer encumbered with the scruples of a Marx, who sees in classical (for example, Greek) art a high culture admittedly distorted by class, but above all a potential universality, which ought to be preserved. At the moment, the split between tried and tested classical values and modern values to be tested no longer exists; we no longer believe in the geographical, temporal or thematic universality of the classics.

Their *mise en scène* opts for a resolutely relativist and consumerist attitude, which is postmodern since their only value now resides in their integration into a discourse that is obsessed neither by meaning, nor by truth, nor by totality, nor by coherence.

(4) The perspective of the adapters and their *work of adaptation* and interpretation are influenced by 'high' culture, that is the culture of a limited subgroup, which possesses (or arrogates to itself) knowledge, education and power of decision. This 'concentrated' culture becomes a methodological code, an expertise the mastery of which enables us to deepen our knowledge: 'we acquire schemas of thinking, equipment which permits us to discover other information based on this initial knowledge and thus to deepen the analysis' (Camilleri 1982: 25). This conception is not far from Lotman's semiotic conception of culture: a hierarchy of partial signifying systems, of a sum of texts and an assortment of functions corresponding to them, and finally a mechanism generating these texts (Lotman 1976).

This methodological code, this expertise, is often a 'cultural cipher' (Bourdieu) which enables the act of deciphering: it is sometimes also the instrument of one subgroup against the others. As Michel de Certeau remarks, cultivated people 'conform to a model elaborated in societies stratified by a category which has introduced its norms at the point where it imposed its power' (1974: 235). The difficulty is often in guessing where expertise becomes power, in noting the fluctuations of the code and the powers it confers. Take the example of the treatment of the classics: during the era of Jean Vilar's 'popular theatre,' the classics were presented implicitly as a universal good, but in reality they represented a cultural good whose acquisition led to social promotion. At the moment, postmodern utilization of these same classical goods no longer attempts to give the audience cultural baggage or political arms, but to manipulate codes and to relativize every message, especially political messages.

(5) The *preparatory work of the actors* does not simply involve rehearsal or the *choice of a theatrical form* (6), but the actor's entire culture, 'theatrical knowledge, which transmits from generation to generation the living work of art that is the actor' (Barba 1989: 64). The actor accomplishes the semiotic project of culture conceived as the memory storage (*mise en mémoire*) of past

15

information and the generation of future information. According to Barba, culture is in this sense always 'the capacity of adapting to and modifying the environment, as a means of organizing and exchanging numerous individual and collective activities, the capacity to transmit collective 'wisdom,' the fruit of different experiences and different technical expertises' (1982: 122). The culture of the actor, especially the western actor, is not always readable or codified according to a sum of stable and recurring rules and practices. But even western actors are not protected by a dominant style or fashion, or by body techniques or specific codifications, but are impregnated by formulas, habits of work, which belong to the anthropological and sociological codifications of their milieu, imperceptible codifications which try to escape notice, the better to proclaim the original genius of the actors, but which are in reality omnipresent and can be easily picked up and parodied.

(7) *The theatrical representation/performance of culture* obliges us to find specific dramatic means to represent or perform a foreign or domestic culture, to utilize theatre as an instrument to transmit and produce information on the conveyed culture.[4] Theatre can resolve one of anthropology's difficulties: translating/visualizing abstract elements of a culture, as a system of beliefs and values, by using concrete means: for example, performing instead of explaining a ritual, showing rather than expounding the social conditions of individuals, using an immediately readable *gestus*. The *mise en scène* and theatrical performance are always a stage translation (thanks to the actor and all the elements of the performance) of another cultural totality (text, adaptation, body). When one remembers, following Lotman, that cultural appropriation of reality takes place in the form of a translation of an extract of reality into a text, one understands that the *mise en scène* or intercultural transposition is *a fortiori* a translation in the form of an appropriation of a foreign culture with its own modeling.

(8) The term 'appropriation' sufficiently indicates that the adapter and the receptor take possession of the source culture according to their own perspectives; hence the risk of ethnocentrism, Eurocentrism in this case. This Eurocentrism is not so much a rejection of eastern forms as a myopic view of other forms and especially conceptual tools different from those in Europe, an inability to

16

conceptualize cultural modeling, western and eastern, theoretically and globally. Until the conceptual tools (extremely problematic in their very hybridization) which would do justice to the western and eastern context become available, intercultural communication needs *reception-adapters*, 'conducting elements' that facilitate the passage from one world to the other. These adapters allow for the reconstruction of a series of methodological principles on the basis of the source culture and for their adaptation to the target culture:

> Discovering the secret of some fascinating exotic dance does not mean that one can easily import it: one would have grasped at most an inspiration, a utopia or more exactly a series of methodological principles subject to reconstruction in the context of our culture.
>
> (Volli 1985: 113)

Whatever the nature of this adaptation – character, dramaturgy (Shakespeare as dramaturgical model for the *Indiade* or for the adaptation of the *Mahabharata*), these adapters are always placed beside receptors simplifying and modeling some key elements of the source culture. In this sense, the adapters necessarily have an ethnocentric position but, conscious of this distorting perspective, they can relativize the discrepancy and make one aware of differences.

(9) *Moments of readability* are also responsible for relativizing the production of meaning and the level of reading that varies from one culture to the other. They respond to the crisis of the transcendental and universal subject which claimed, in the name of universal Cartesian reason and of centralized *raison d'état*, to reduce all differences: 'All *"general"* human formations rebound against humanity if they are not reappropriated every day by the concrete subject, in everyday operations' (Camilleri 1982: 29).

The theory of levels of readability explains how the receiver more or less freely decides at which level (for example, narrative, thematic, formal, ideological, sociocultural, etc.) to read the cultural facts presented by the *mise en scène*. This theory presupposes an epistemological concern to possess the cultural means of knowing the other, and which aspects of the other. Cultural transfer most often takes place due to a change in the level of readability, which profoundly modifies the reception of the work (10). The

17

change in the level of readability often corresponds to an ideological struggle between dominant and dominated cultures. In the transfer from (1), (2) to (10), certain elements are assimilated and disappear; these are what Dalrymple (1987) calls 'residual ideology,' the residue of ideas and practices in a culture which belong to another social formation. Other elements, on the contrary, emerge and are integrated into the dominant ideology in (10): this emergent ideology can become a normative model of sociological (10B) or more generally cultural (10C) codification (Dalrymple 1987: 136).

(10) Examining the cultural confrontation in (1)–(2) and (10), we choose to compare, to evaluate and to set up a dialogue between source and target cultures, but this confrontation has so to speak been attenuated by the filters from (3) to (9) which prepare the terrain and gradually transform the source culture, or referred culture, into the reception culture in which we find ourselves. Instead of avoiding this confrontation, it is useful to seek it out. It is necessary to pre-empt the demagogy that consists of rejecting comparison, in order not to risk imposing a hierarchy or setting a value on the confronted cultures, a demagogy that leads to cultural relativism and so to a lack of differentiation. Since Todorov has adequately criticized this rejection, it is unnecessary to return to it (Todorov 1986: 10–13). Encouraged by Todorov and Finkielkraut, Montaigne and Lévi-Strauss, in the excellent company of Brook, Barba and Mnouchkine, we have dared to compare two or more cultures in manifestly asymmetrical positions, where one appropriates the other and the target stage receives the whole mix at the crossroads of discourses and cultures. It is up to others to judge whether this theatrical confrontation leads to a generalized acculturation or mutual destruction, or rather to an amorous encounter (this deliciously vague metaphor has been deliberately chosen), a 'bricolage' (Lévi-Strauss), Eurasian theatre (in Barba's case), a 'culture of links' (Brook 1987: 239) or an 'influence' of eastern theatre (Mnouchkine 1982: 8). In reality, the hourglass is sufficiently complex to avoid a direct confrontation between peoples, languages or ethical values. Instead we compare theatrical forms and practices (between (2) and (10A), modelizations and codifications capable of being engaged and *intertwined* with each other (instead of merging together).

(11) *Given and anticipated consequences*. After the sand has filtered from one bowl of the hourglass to the other, the spectators are the final and only guarantors of the culture which reaches them, whether it be foreign or familiar. Once the performance is complete, all the sand rests on the spectator's frail shoulders. Everything depends on what the spectator has remembered and forgotten. Whence Edouard Henriot's perfect quip: 'culture is what remains when one has forgotten everything, what is missing when one has learnt everything'! After this continuous flow of the grains of culture, when the sand castles which are the *mises en scène* have collapsed, the spectators are finally compelled to accept the fact that the performance is transformed in them, that it succeeds or founders in them, and that it wipes itself out to be reborn. Spectators must welcome forgetfulness, which sifts everything for them, buries them alive in the sand; a forgetfulness which will eventually mitigate suffering. This forgetfulness is a savior and God knows what one can forget at the theatre (thank God)! Thus, the culture that the spectators reconstitute and which in turn constitutes them as spectating subjects is in perpetual mutation; it passes through selective amnesia: 'the essential dimension of the theatrical performance resists time, not by being fixed in a recording, but by transforming itself' (Barba 1988: 27).

It therefore becomes difficult to follow these transformations of memory, to predict how the spectators will organize their reading, whether they will accept or reject the series of filters that have predetermined and selected cultural and especially foreign material. It is still more problematic to determine what course the performance will take within the spectators: 'Spectators, as individuals, decide the issue of depth: that is, how far the performance has managed to sink its roots into particular individual memories' (Barba 1988: 27). Despite this relativity in the depth of the performance's penetration in us, it is always culturally pertinent to see what the spectators retain and what they exclude, how they define culture and non-culture, what beckons them, what they do not pick up. The receiver – whether envisaged as a customer-king, a pig of a paymaster, a flock of sheep ('tas de veaux') (*Cyrano de Bergerac*, I, 2) or, more seldom, a partner – is at present an object often pursued by the covetous eyes of theory and cosmopolitan producers. But this sudden concern, this discovery of the spectator's freedom of choice and productivity, often leads to an anti-theoretical and anti-explanatory conception of art. Meanings belong to the realm of self-service, we are continually told. Perhaps, but do we still have to go past the cash register? 'Theatre should not interpret, it ought to give us the opportunity of contemplating a work and thinking about it,' as the great Bob Wilson warns us (1987: 208). So, let us contemplate. . . .

All these testimonies apparently revalorize the function of the spectator and the receiver, but they also lead to relativism and theoretical skepticism. Reception theory cancels itself if it confers on the receivers the absolute power of following their critical course without taking the objective givens of the work into account, under the pretext that, exposed to the whims of the text, they can pick and choose in the self-service of meaning. We will have the chance, in the body of this book, to return to this postmodern relativism which often takes the guise of the intercultural, the better to disguise an anti-historical and relativist discourse, in which works and their contexts are no longer anything but pleasing pretexts for undifferentiated diversions, deferred rendezvous at the crossroads of a nebulous postmodernity.

NOTES

1. We should make the following distinctions:

the *intracultural* dimension refers to the traditions of a single nation, which are very often almost forgotten or deformed, and have to be reconstructed

the *transcultural* transcends particular cultures and looks for a universal human condition, as in the case of Brook's notion of 'culture of links,' which supposedly unites all human beings beyond their ethnic differences and which can be directly transmitted to any audience without distinction of race, culture or class

the *ultracultural* could be called the somewhat mystical quest for the origin of theatre, the search for a primal language in the sense of Artaud. In Brook's *Orghast* (1970), Serban's *Medea* and *The Trojan Women*, Ronconi's *Oresteia* (1972), we had such a quest for a universal language of sounds and emotions, as if all human experience sprang from the same source

the *precultural*, which Barba calls the *pre-expressive*, would be the common ground of any tradition in the world, which affects any audience, 'before' (temporally and logically) it is individualized and 'culturalized' in a specific cultural tradition

the *postcultural* would apply to the postmodern imagination, which tends to view any cultural act as a quotation of restructuring of already known elements

the *metacultural* aspects refer to the commentary a given culture can make on other cultural elements, when explaining, comparing and commenting on it.

2. It is therefore almost impossible to separate source culture from target culture. But one can, at least, observe how the source culture is appropriated step by step by the target culture. This does not mean, however, that we are using a model borrowed from the theory of communication which studies the transfer of information between sender and receiver. Each level of the hourglass (i.e. each 'layer') must be seen as also determined by the levels of the opposite bowl.

It is true, as Fischer-Lichte notes, that 'the foreign text or the foreign theatrical conventions are chosen according to their relevance to the situation in question; transformed and replanted' (1990: 284). But we would not draw the same conclusions, since, according to Fischer-Lichte,

> It makes little sense, therefore, to speak of the source text and the target text, even less of a source culture or target culture, as should be the case when the foreign is to be communicated in translation. This is due to the fact that the source culture and the target culture are one and the same thing, i.e. the culture.
>
> (1990: 284)

This would seem to lead all too quickly to giving up any theory of the transfer. The translation model itself is only a particular case of the general model of cultural transfer, which manifests itself in translation, *mise en scène*, intercultural exchange, etc. Moreover, in our culture, we are still quite able to make a distinction between native elements and imported elements. Source culture and target culture are never blended into one, other than in the case of complete annihilation (Marvin Carlson's second category where 'foreign elements [are] assimilated into the tradition and absorbed by it. The audience can be interested, entertained, stimulated, but they are not challenged by the foreign materials' (1990: 50). In this case we cannot speak of intercultural exchanges). For our hourglass model of intercultural exchange, we no longer need a theory of 'productive reception' (Pavis 1985: 233–96) and we should resist the temptation to reduce the exchange and the theory to a single pole of reception/target culture. Even if the source culture is almost assimilated and reconstructed by the target culture, we should still look for the means to describe its modelization and possible reconstruction. What we enumerate in the lower bowl of the hourglass ('layers' (3) to (11)) should therefore also be distinguished and studied – even if only in a tentative reconstruction from the viewpoint of our target culture.

3. I am using *he/his* since I am a male critic. I am aware that it could also be *she/her*, but I would like to speak from my own point of view

rather than repeat in each sentence *he/she* since the text would then become repetitive and hard to follow.

4. I use the notion of *representation* both in the meaning of a stage performance (*représentation* in French) and in that of 'being replaced or depicted by something,' as Marx uses it in *The 18 Brumaire of Louis Bonaparte* ('Sie können sich nicht vertreten, sie müssen vertreten werden'). The *representation* of a culture thus refers to all texts which depict it, in the sense of Said's notion of *orientalism*, i.e. of texts exterior to it, which are supposed to describe it adequately. The texts of the represented culture are 'found just as prominently in the so-called truthful text (histories, philological analyses, political treatises) as in the avowedly artistic (i.e. openly imaginative) text' (1978: 21). As in the case of orientalism, 'the things to look at are style, figures of speech, setting, narrative devices, historical and social circumstances, *not* the correctness of the representation nor its fidelity to some great original' (1978: 21). Thus, in order to describe/represent the foreign culture, we have to look for its conventions, codification, modelizations, i.e. for its forms and codes.

BIBLIOGRAPHY

Artaud, Antonin (1958) *Theatre and its Double*, New York: Grove Press.
Barba, Eugenio (1982) *L'Archipel du théâtre*, Cazilhac: Bouffonneries Contrastes.
—— (1988) 'Quatre spectateurs,' *L'Art du Théâtre* 10.
—— (1989) 'Le théâtre eurasien,' *Jeu* 49.
Benjamin, Walter (1969) 'Theses on the Philosophy of History,' in *Illuminations*, ed. Hannah Arendt, trans. Harry Zohn, New York: Schocken.
Brook, Peter (1987) *The Shifting Point*, New York: Harper & Row.
Camilleri, Camille (1982) 'Culture et sociétés: caractères et fonctions,' *Les Amis de Sèvre* 4.
Carlson, Marvin (1990) 'Peter Brook's *The Mahabharata* and Mnouchkine's as Examples of Contemporary Cross-cultural Theatre,' in Erika Fischer-Lichte (ed.) *The Dramatic Touch of Difference*, Tübingen: Narr Verlag.
de Certeau, Michel (1974) *La Culture en pluriel*, Paris: Union Générale d'Edition.
Dalrymple, Lynn (1987) *Exploration in Drama, Theatre and Education. A Critique of Theatre Studies in South Africa*, Durban.
De Marinis, Marco (1987) 'Dramaturgy of the Spectator,' *The Drama Review* vol. 31, 2.
Elam, Keir (1989) 'Text Appeal and the Analysis. Paralysis: Towards a Processual Poetics of Dramatic Production,' in Tim Fitzpatrick (ed.) *Altro Polo – Performance: from Product to Process*, Sydney: Theatre Studies Unit, University of Sydney.
Finkielkraut, Alain (1987) *La Défaite de la pensée*, Paris: Gallimard.
Fischer-Lichte, Erika (1990) 'Staging the Foreign as Cultural

Transformation,' in Erika Fischer-Lichte (ed.) *The Dramatic Touch of Difference*, Tübingen: Narr Verlag.

Freud, Sigmund (1929) *Das Unbehagen in der Kultur*; trans. J. Strachey (1961) 'Civilization and its Discontents,' *Standard Edition* vol. 21, London: Hogarth.

Geertz, Clifford (1973) *The Interpretation of Cultures*, New York: Basic Books.

Halstrup, Kirsten (1990) Unpublished talk given at the International School of Theatre Anthropology, Bologna, July, 1990.

Kowzan, Tadeusz (1988) 'Spectacle, domaine signifiant,' *Semiotica* 71, 1/2.

Lévi-Strauss, Claude (1949) *Les Structures élémentaires de la parenté*, Paris: Presses Universitaires de France; trans. James Bell and J. R. von Sturmier (1969) *The Elementary Structures of Kinship*, Boston: Beacon Press.

—— (1983) *Le Regard éloigné*, Paris: Plon; trans. Joachim Neugroschel and Phoebe Hoss (1984) *The View from Afar*, New York: Basic Books.

Lotman, Juri et l'école de Tartu (1976) *Travaux sur les systèmes des signes*, Bruxelles: Editions Complexe.

Mauss, Marcel (1936) 'Les Techniques du corps,' *Journal de Psychologie* 32, 3–4.

Mnouchkine, Ariane (1982) 'Le Besoin d'une forme,' *Théâtre Public* 46–7.

Morin, Edgar (1962) *L'Esprit du temps*, Paris: Grasset.

Panoff, Michel and Perrin, Michel Article on 'Culturalism,' *Dictionnaire de l'éthnologie*, Paris: Payot.

Pavis, Patrice (1985) *Voix et images de la scène*, Lille: Presses Universitaires.

Said, Edward (1978) *Orientalism*, New York: Vintage Books.

Todorov, Tzvetan (1986) 'Le Croisement des cultures,' *Communications* 43.

Volli, Hugo (1985) 'Techniques du corps,' *L'Anatomie de l'acteur*, ed. E. Barba and N. Savarese, Cazilhac: Bouffonneries Contrastes. English edition: *The Secret Art of the Actor*, Routledge, 1991.

Wilson, Robert (1987) 'Spiegel-Gespräch mit Robert Wilson über Hören, Sehen und Spielen,' *Der Spiegel* 10.

2

FROM PAGE TO STAGE: A DIFFICULT BIRTH[1]

Translated by Jilly Daugherty

PRELIMINARY REMARKS

For a text to give birth to a performance is no easy matter. What the first-night audience sees is already an end-product, for it is too late to observe the preparatory work of the director: the spectators are presented with a gurgling or howling infant, in other words they see a performance which is more or less successful, more or less comprehensible, in which the text is only one of several components, others being the actors, the space, the tempo. It is not possible to deduce from the performance the work that led up to it; *mise en scène*, as we understand it, is the synchronic confrontation of signifying systems, and it is their interaction, not their history, that is offered to the spectator and that produces meaning.

We shall therefore not speak of the director, a private individual instructed by a theatrical institution to put his or her name to an artistic product, but of *mise en scène*, defined as the bringing together or confrontation, in a given space and time, of different signifying systems, for an audience. *Mise en scène* is here taken to be a structural entity, a theoretical subject or object of knowledge. Since the director, the 'unknown father,' is not directly relevant to us here, he will be replaced (with apologies to practitioners) by the structural notion of *mise en scène*.

It is important to distinguish between:

The *dramatic text*: the verbal script which is read or heard in performance (a difference in status which we shall examine later); we are concerned here solely with texts written prior to performance, not those written or rewritten after rehearsals, improvisations or performances (see Margin 1)

24

The *performance*: all that is made visible or audible on stage, but not yet perceived or described as a system of meaning or as a pertinent relationship of signifying stage systems.

Finally, the *mise en scène*, the confrontation of all signifying systems, in particular the utterance of the dramatic text in performance. *Mise en scène* is not an empirical object, the haphazard assembling of materials, the ill-defined activity of the director and stage team prior to performance. It is an object of knowledge, a network of associations or relationships uniting the different stage materials into signifying systems, created both by production (the actors, the director, the stage in general) and reception (the spectators).

The distinction made between performance as an empirical object and *mise en scène* as an object of knowledge allows one to reconcile the aesthetics of production and reception (cf. Pavis 1985).

Indeed, *mise en scène* as a structural system exists only when received and reconstructed by a spectator from the production. To decipher the *mise en scène* is to receive and interpret the system created by an artistic team. The aim is not one of reconstructing the intentions of the director, but of understanding, as a spectator, the system elaborated by those responsible for the production.

In what follows, we aim to establish a theory of *mise en scène*, valid at least for our western tradition, being the enactment – supposedly aesthetic and subjective – of a pre-existing dramatic text. Western *mise en scène* can reveal how the creation of meaning is conceived by our civilization, notably as a relationship of meanings when several sign systems coexist.

DENIALS

We shall refrain from linking the semiotics of the dramatic text and of the performance, taking care to distinguish between their methodologies and fields of study so as not to place them on the same level or in the same theoretical space, to the detriment of either. Unless the distinction between them is kept in mind, one is tempted to equate the text/performance relationship with other traditional relationships such as signifier/signified, body/soul, content/form, literary/theatrical, etc.

In the study of a dramatic text, we shall always specify whether it is being examined before or apart from a stage production, or whether it is being analysed as a constituent part of a particular production, with due account being taken of the enunciation and color lent to it by the stage.

The two semiotics must keep their autonomy because text and performance adhere to different semiotic systems. *Mise en scène* is not the reduction or the transformation of text into performance, but rather their confrontation. Before defining the delicate relationship that exists between text and performance, it is necessary to affirm what *mise en scène* is not, and therefore to challenge some incorrect definitions that still persist. Instead of stating what *mise en scène* should not be (this being too normative a vision), we should like to determine what the theory of *mise en scène* cannot or is no longer able to affirm. We realize that in wanting to establish an abstract theory of *mise en scène* we run the risk of including, in our description of its principal operations, several normative judgments on their roles and functions, particularly as regards the resultant construction of meaning. Let us nevertheless formulate a series of denials or warnings.

1 *Mise en scène* is not the staging of a supposed textual 'potential.' It does not consist in finding stage signifieds which would amount to no more than a repetition, inevitably superfluous (see Corvin 1985), of the text itself. That would entail disregarding the signifying materiality of verbal and stage signs and positing theatrical signifieds capable of setting aside their signifying matter and eliminating any difference between the verbal and non-verbal (see Margin 2).

Any theatrical semiotics which presupposes that the dramatic text has an innate theatricality, a matrix for production or even a score, which must be extracted at all costs and expressed on the stage, thus implying that the dramatic text exists only when it is produced, seems to be begging the question. Those who hold that position would contend that every play has only one good *mise en scène* already present in the text (see Margin 3).

2 *Mise en scène* does not have to be faithful to a dramatic text. The notion of faithfulness, a cliché of critical discourse, is pointless and stems in fact from confusion. Faithfulness to what? (Cf. Fischer-Lichte 1984; Jacquot and Veinstein 1957) If to an acting tradition (often obscure in the case of French classicism), the criterion

26

is irrelevant to modern productions. Different things are understood by faithfulness: faithfulness to the 'ideas' of the 'author' (two very volatile concepts), faithfulness to an acting tradition, faithfulness to 'form or meaning' by virtue of 'aesthetic or ideological principles' (see Jacquot, quoted in Corvin 1985) and, above all, the very illusive faithfulness of the performance to what the text has already clearly stated. If producing a faithful *mise en scène* means repeating, or believing one can repeat, by theatrical means what the text has already said, what would be the point of *mise en scène* (see Margin 4)?

3 On the other hand, *mise en scène* does not annihilate or dissolve the dramatic text, which keeps its status as a verbal text even once it is uttered on stage, i.e. enunciated in accordance with a given situation and directed towards a much more specific meaning. Once a text is uttered on stage, it is no longer possible for the spectator to imagine the time span between text and performance, since both are presented simultaneously, even if the rhythm of each is peculiar to its own signifying system. The argument is valid both ways, and the question whether the *mise en scène* is faithful to the text is posed as seldom as its opposite, namely whether the dramatic text is faithful to its *mise en scène*, whether it corresponds to what is seen on stage, whether Molière's text is faithful to a *mise en scène* by Vitez (see Margin 5).

4 Different *mises en scène* of a common text, particularly those produced at very different moments in history, do not provide readings of the same text. The letter of the text remains of course unchanged, but the spirit varies considerably. Text is here understood to mean the result of a process that we shall call, with Ingarden (1931) and Vodička (1975), its concretization. Nevertheless the text is not a non-structured reservoir of signifieds, a *Baumaterial* (building material), as Brecht would say; it is indeed the very reverse: the result of a historically determined process of concretization: signifier (literary work as thing), signified (aesthetic object) and Social Context (shorthand) for what Mukařovský calls the "total context of social phenomena, science, philosophy, religion, politics, economics, etc. of the given milieu" (1979: 391) are variables which modify the concretization of the text and which can be more or less reconstructed.

5 *Mise en scène* is not the stage representation of the textual referent. Moreover, the textual referent is inaccessible: what we have is at most a simulation (illusion) of this referent by means of signs which conventionally denote it. Nor is *mise en scène* the visual concretization of the 'holes' in the text which need a performance in order to take on meaning. All texts, not just dramatic texts, have holes; in other respects, however, they can be 'too full' or overloaded.

Rather than try to find these empty or overloaded areas, one should try to understand the processes of determination and indetermination performed in/by the text and the performance: *mise en scène* highlights the function of 'emptying' or 'filling' structural ambiguities (cf. Pavis 1985: 255–60).

6 *Mise en scène* is not the fusion of two referents (textual and stage), nor does it strive to find their common denominator. Instead of a fusion of referents, one should imagine a theory of fiction – capable of comparing text and performance in their peculiar processes of fictionalization – made manifest for an audience by *mise en scène*. Fiction can be seen as the middle term, as the mediation between what is narrated by the dramatic text and what is represented on the stage, as if mediation could be achieved by the textual and visual representation of a possible fictional world, constructed initially by dramaturgical analysis and reading, and subsequently represented by staging. This hypothesis is not false if one is careful not to reintroduce surreptitiously the theory of the actualized referent. There is an undeniable relationship between text and performance, but it does not take the form of a translation or a reduplication of the former by the latter, but rather of a transfer or a confrontation of the fictional universe structured by the text and the fictional universe produced by the stage. The modalities of this confrontation need further investigation.

7 *Mise en scène* is not the performative realization of the text. Contrary to what Searle (1982: 101–19) believes, the actors do not have to carry out the instructions of the text and the stage directions as if these had the illocutionary force of a 'cake recipe', in order to produce a stage performance. Stage directions form a 'frame' around a text, giving instructions for uttering the text in such a way that the dialogue will take on a meaning more or less

'envisaged' by the author. *Mise en scène* is, however, free to put into practice only some, or even none, of these stage directions. It is not obliged to carry out stage directions to the letter, reconstructing a situation of utterance identical in every aspect to the one prescribed. Stage directions are not the ultimate truth of the text, or a formal command to produce the text in such a manner, or even an indispensable shifter between text and performance. Their textual status is uncertain. Do they constitute an optional extra-text? a metatext that determines the dramatic text? or a pretext that suggests one solution before the director decides on another? The evaluation of their status cannot be divorced from history; although one should not forget that they form part of authorial speech, it should be remembered that the director has the choice of either using them or not, as in the case of Gordon Craig who considered stage directions an insult to his freedom. To conclude, it would seem inappropriate to accept stage directions, within the framework of a theory of *mise en scène*, as absolute directives and as discourse to be incorporated without fail into performance.

After all these denials regarding the nature of the relationship between text and performance (see Margin 6), let us now be more positive and formulate a few hypotheses about how *mise en scène* can establish links between text and stage.

MISE EN SCÈNE AS A MEANS OF MODULATING THE RELATIONSHIP BETWEEN TEXT AND PERFORMANCE

Instead of defining the relationship between text and performance as one of conversion, translation or reduction of the one to the other, we prefer to describe it as a way of establishing effects or meaning and balance between opposing semiotic systems (such as verbal and non-verbal, symbolic and iconic), and as the gap, both spatial and temporal, between the auditory signs of the text and the visual signs of the stage. It is no longer possible to see performance (stage signs) as the logical and chronological consequence of textual signs (even if, in the majority of cases, they are actually derived from the *mise en scène* of a pre-existing text). Text and stage are perceived at the same time and in the same place, making it impossible to declare that the one precedes the other (see Margin 7).

Stage enunciation and the concretization circuit

Mise en scène tries to provide the dramatic text with a situation that will give meaning to the statements (*énoncés*) of the text. Dramatic dialogue therefore seems to be the product of (stage) utterance and at the same time the text used by the *mise en scène* to envisage a context of utterance in which the text acquires a meaning. *Mise en scène* is not a transformation of text into performance, but rather a theoretical 'fitting' which consists in putting the text under dramatic and stage tension, in order to test how stage utterance challenges the text and initiates a hermeneutic circle between the text and its enunciation (between *énoncés* and *énonciation*), thus opening up the text to several possible interpretations.

The change in context of utterance goes hand in hand with renewed concretization of the dramatic text; a two-way relationship is established between the dramatic text and the Social Context. With every new *mise en scène*, the text is placed in a situation, of enunciation according to the new Social Context of its reception, which allows or facilitates a new analysis of the text and so on, *ad infinitum*. This theoretical 'fitting,' this discrepancy between text and stage, the disparity between the reading of yesterday's Social Context and that of today, constitute the *mise en scène*. *Mise en scène* is a possibility for a stage enunciation, leading to a fresh text; it is always in a state of becoming, since it does no more than point the way, preparing the text for utterance while adopting a wait-and-see attitude. Therefore, not only does concretization-fictionalization take place, as is the case with any reading of a written text, but there is also a search for stage enunciators. The latter, gathered together by the *mise en scène*, produce a global performance text incorporating the dramatic text which takes on a very specific meaning. In no way does *mise en scène* resemble a piling up of visual systems on top of the text; it is, writes Alain Rey, neither "addition, nor an onion; it is (it should be) a collective project built around a language constraint, a structure made for communication" (1980: 188).

The concretization process is not only determined by the historical changes; it is also a result of the individual readings of the same text by different persons.

Verbal and non-verbal: Reading actualized

Mise en scène is reading actualized: the dramatic text does not have an individual reader, but a possible collective reading, proposed by the *mise en scène*. Philology and literary criticism use words to explain texts, whereas *mise en scène* uses stage actions to 'question' the dramatic text. *Mise en scène* is always a parable on the impossible exchange between the verbal and non-verbal: the non-verbal (i.e. staging and the choice of a situation of enunciation) makes the verbal text speak, reduplicating its utterance, as if the dramatic text, by being uttered on stage, were able to comment on itself, without the help of another text, by giving prominence to what is said and what is shown. Thus *mise en scène* speaks by showing, not by speaking, with the result that irony and denial (Freud's *Verneinung*) are its usual mode of existence. It always implicitly invites a comparison of the textual discourse and the staging chosen to accompany (follow or precede) the text. By speaking without speaking, *mise en scène* (more specifically the performance) introduces denial: it speaks without words, talks about the text thanks to a completely different semiotic system which is not verbal but 'iconic.' However, this does not imply that the stage image or picture (the visual and auditory signifiers of the stage) cannot be translated into a signified. The two alternatives proposed by Michel Corvin (1985: 256) therefore seems to us theoretically distorted from the outset:

> Our relationship with the stage image therefore remains ambiguous: if it is read in all its ideological fullness, it no longer exists as an image; if one is content to receive it ingenuously, and thank goodness nobody is obliged to be a semiotician, it remains a sterile shimmer of forms and colours.

The image can be transformed into a signified without losing its value as an image; conversely, it cannot remain a pure "shimmer of forms and colours" for very long, because even the most ingenuous theatre-goer ends up by transforming this pure signifier into a signified (in semiotizing the image). Michel Corvin is, however, right when he emphasizes the polysemy of the stage image which tends to produce ambiguous and polysemous semiotizations.

Stage representation – which is comparable to dream representation

– and the image parallel to the text enrich and give a reading to the text that is sometimes unexpected. *Mise en scène*, even at its simplest and most explicit, 'displaces' the text and makes it say what a critical commentary, spoken or written, could not say: it expresses, one could almost say, the inexpressible!

Although little is know at present about non-verbal processes of communication (kinesics, proxemics, perception of rhythm and voice quality), they can throw some light on the work of the actor, whose non-verbal behavior has so great an influence on the spectator's understanding of the accompanying text. *Mise en scène* and its reception by the spectator depend on the perception of the different rhythms of visual and stage discourse and the auditory and textual flow. As Michel Corvin correctly states (1985: 12), the spectator

> is submitted to a curious effect of *strabismus*: the text develops at its own rhythm with its meanderings and secrets, while the visual discourse of *mise en scène* accentuates, belies or anticipates it, introducing a direct dialogue between the director and the spectator without having to pass through the character or the words that compose the text.

Mise en scène always initiates a dialogue between what is said and what is shown and, Vitez adds, "theatrical pleasure, for the spectator, resides in the difference between what is said and what is shown . . . what seems exciting to the spectator springs from the idea that one does not show what is said" (1974: 42).

Change in perspective

Research into *mise en scène* and the theories thus evolved indicate a clear change in perspective, a desire to get away from a logocentric notion of theatre, with the text as the central and stable element and *mise en scène* necessarily an incidental transcription, representation and explanation of the text.

Until certain postmodernist experiments in which the text was considered to be asemantic material to be manipulated by such processes as ready-mades, collages, quotation and concrete poetry, both fiction and *mise en scène* seemed to pivot around the dramatic text. The most recent experiments in postmodernism (see chapter 3) on the non-verbal element and the new status these have accorded the text – that of a sound pattern and a signifying

32

rhythmic structure – have not been without repercussions on the conception of the classical dramatic text and its *mise en scène*, which no longer always turns on the semantic pivot of the text. But is it so simple to escape from the text and logocentrism? Has the text at least been freed, now that it has made a timid reappearance on stage, from a relation of authority or vassalage *vis-à-vis* performance? According to Jean-Marie Piemme (1984: 42)

> the text has indeed returned, but during its exile it lost any pretensions it had of being a fetish, a sacred or royal object. It questions us today without the burden of its old ghosts; our approach to the text is no longer dictated by that double-headed monster, faithfulness and betrayal.

The text resists any attempt to make it banal or to reduce it to "meaningless music" in the *mise en scène*. It continues to question the rest of the performance and to make its presence felt (Piemme 1984: 43). It is indeed a force to be reckoned with: reading a dramatic text is no longer regarded as an effortless pastime. *Mise en scène* makes it difficult, but essential, to distinguish between three kinds of reading:

the *reading of the text* as carried out by an *ordinary reader*, the kind of thing a spectator might do before going to see a performance; the problem here is to ignore the context of the text as a stage utterance, for any reading of a dramatic text calls for a concretization/representation which is a kind of imaginary pre-*mise en scène*

the *reading (by listening) of the spoken or enunciated text* as uttered in the performance; the text is here concretized, actualized in a specific context which confers on it a certain viewpoint and meaning. In actual fact, this reading is not possible without taking into consideration the third kind of reading, that of the performance text

the *reading ('decoding') of the performance text*, especially all the various stage systems, including the dramatic text. The reading of the performance text implies a perception of the way in which the text has been read by the *mise en scène*, for the reading of the text has preceded the *mise en scène* and the performance text is thus a stage actualization (an actualization by stage means) of

33

this reading. This third reading is the result of the first two readings, and is the one peculiar to *mise en scène*.

Metatext or discourse of the *mise en scène*

In order to understand the concretization of the dramatic text by the *mise en scène*, we must look for the metatext of the *mise en scène*, i.e. its commentary on the text or the stage rewriting it offers of the text. The problem lies in locating this metatext (or discourse) of the *mise en scène*. One must be especially careful not to confuse this metatext (or unwritten text of the *mise en scène*) with the series of commentaries written on a dramatic work, particularly a classical work, which sometimes 'attach themselves' to the original text, even becoming an integral or obligatory part of it (see Margin 8). Nowhere does the metatext exist as a separate and complete text; it is disseminated in the choice of acting style, scenography, rhythm, in the series of relationships (redundancies, discrepancies) between the various signifying systems. It exists, moreover, according to our conception of *mise en scène*, as the vital link in the production/reception chain only when it is recognized and, in part, shared by an audience. More than a (stage) text existing side by side with the dramatic text, a metatext is what organizes, from within, the scenic concretization; thus it is not parallel to the dramatic text, but, as it were, inside it, being the result of the concretization circuit (circuit involving signifier, Social Context and signified of the text).

A normative, and even political, question arises: must this metatext be easy to recognize and formalize, 'laying its cards on the table', offering a battery of explicit options and theses? Or should it rather be discreet and even secret, being mainly produced – completed and 'rewritten' – by the spectator? Whatever the answer is to this question, *mise en scène* as redefined here exists only when the spectator appropriates it, when it becomes the creative projection of the spectator (see Margin 9).

In order to conclude our examination of the text-performance modulation, a modulation carried out anew by every *mise en scène*, let us ask three related questions in an attempt to determine the circuit formed by the dramatic text and the Social Context:

1 What *concretization* is made of the dramatic text with every new reading or *mise en scène* and what circuit of concretization

is established between the work-as-thing, the Social Context and the aesthetic object?

2 What *fictionalization*, or production of fiction from text and stage, results from the combined effects of the text and the reader, the stage and the spectator? In what way is the interaction of the two fictions, textual and stage, essential to theatrical fictionalization? This question develops the first one by specifying the effects of fiction: the pretense of a referent, the construction of a possible world, etc.

3 What *ideologization* is applied to the dramatic text and the performance? The text, whether the dramatic or the performance text, can only be understood intertextually, when confronted with the discursive and ideological structures of a period in time or a corpus of texts. The dramatic and the performance texts must be considered in relation to the Social Context, i.e. other texts and discourses about reality produced by a society. This relationship being the most fragile and variable imaginable, the same dramatic text readily produces an infinite number of readings. This last question adds to our perspective the social inscription of the text, its link with history via the unbroken chain of other texts. *Mise en scène* can thus also be understood as a social practice, as an ideological mechanism capable of deciphering as much as reflecting historical reality (even if fiction claims precisely to negate reality).

Mise en scène as discourse on emptiness and ambiguity: Imaginary solution and parodic discourse

The confrontation of the two fictions (textual and stage) not only establishes links between texts and utterance, absence and presence, it also compares areas of indetermination in the text and in the performance. These areas do not necessarily coincide. Sometimes the performance can resolve a textual contradiction or, indeterminacy. Similarly, the dramatic text is able to eliminate ambiguities in the performance, or, conversely, to introduce new ones.

To make opaque on stage what was clear in the text or to clarify what was opaque: such operations of determinacy/interdeterminacy are typical of *mise en scène*. Usually, *mise en scène* is an interpretation, an *explication de texte*, bringing about a mediation between the original receiver and the present-day receiver. Sometimes, however, it is a *complication de texte*, a deliberate effort to prevent any communication between the Social Contexts of the two receptions.

In certain productions (particularly, but not exclusively, those inspired by a Brechtian dramaturgical analysis), *mise en scène* can show how the dramatic text is itself an imaginary solution to real ideological contradictions that existed at the time the fiction was invented. *Mise en scène* then has the task of making it possible to imagine and stage the textual contradiction. In productions concerned with the revelation of a Stanislavskian kind of subtext, the unconscious element of the text is supposed to accompany, in a parallel text, the continuous – and in itself pertinent – flow of the text actually spoken by the characters.

Whatever the reason, overt or otherwise, for wanting to show the contradiction in the fable or the profound truth of the text through the revelation of its subtext, *mise en scène* 'displaces' the text, it is always a discourse parallel to the text, a text which would remain 'unuttered,' in other words neutral and without meaning. It is therefore always marginal and parodic, in the etymological sense of the word.

A TYPOLOGY OF *MISES EN SCÈNE*?

The theory of *mise en scène* we are trying to establish allows us to eschew impressionistic discourse on the style, inventiveness and originality of the director who adds his so-called personal touch to a precious text regarded as closed and inviolate. However, the same theory is more or less incapable of answering two very frequent questions:

Is the *mise en scène* faithful?
What *mises en scène* could be given to a dramatic text?

The first of these questions is meaningless, as we have seen, for it is based on the presupposition that the text has an ideal and fixed meaning, free from any historical variations. In order to answer the second question, and to avoid resorting to the naïvities of the first, the semiotician must examine how *mise en scène* is determined according to the following modes: autotextual, intertextual and ideological (or, preferably, ideotextual). These three dimensions, which we have defined elsewhere (Pavis 1985, 1986b) as the three components or levels of any text, coexist in any *mise en scène*. The sole purpose of the proposed typology is to examine the effect of emphasizing one of these three dimensions (but not to the exclusion of the other two).

1 Autotextual *mise en scène* tries to understand the textual mechanisms and the structure of the plot according to an internal logic, with no reference to anything beyond the text to confirm or contradict it. In this category we find productions that try – in vain moreover – to reconstruct archeologically the historical context of the performance without opening up the text and the performance to the new Social Context, as well as productions hermetically sealed around a personal idea or thesis of the director and purportedly total re-creations with their own aesthetic principles. This was the case with Symbolist *mise en scène* as well as that of the 'founder directors' (such as Craig or Appia) who invented a coherent stage universe closed upon itself, concentrating their aesthetic options in a very readable and rigorous discourse of *mise en scène*.

2 Ideotextual *mise en scène* is the exact opposite. It is not so much the text itself that is staged, but the political, social and especially psychological subtext, almost as if the metatext – i.e. the analysis of the work – sought to take the place of the actual text. The dramatic text is regarded as nothing more than a 'dead weight,' tolerated as an indeterminate signifying mass, placed indiscriminately either before or after the *mise en scène*. Staging a text therefore means being open to the outside world, even molding the textual object according to this world and the new circumstances of reception. The text mimes its referent, pretending to be substituted by it. The text loses its texture, having preconceived, extraneous knowledge and discourse added to it, and takes its place in a global explanation of the world, a victim of what Michel Vinaver (1982) has called the tyranny of ideologies. This kind of *mise en scène* completely assumes the role of mediator between the Social Context of the text produced in the past and the Social Context of the text received in the present by a given audience; it fulfills the "communication function" (Mukařovský 1970: 391) for the work of art, making it possible for a new audience to read an old text. It is this kind of *mise en scène* that is being singled

out for criticism nowadays, for the director is blamed for setting himself up as a 'little god' of ideology.

3 Intertextual *mise en scène* provides the necessary mediation between autotextuality and ideological reference. It relativizes every new production as one possibility among others, placing it within a series of interpretations, every new solution trying to dissociate itself polemically from the others. Particularly as far as French classical theatre is concerned, a *mise en scène* cannot help but declare its position in relation to past metatexts. This 'interlucidity' applies to all compartments of the production: only by quoting can a stand be taken, *mise en scène* being, as Vitez (1974) said, the art of variation.

(PROVISIONAL) CONCLUSIONS

Taking a new structural definition of *mise en scène* as a starting point, we have been able to describe certain mechanisms of its reception. The theory of fiction with its two facets, concretization and ideologization, is the indispensable link in the production of meaning. It has not seemed feasible to extract from this theory any idea of what happens to dramatic texts when they are reread and produced once more; it is clearly impossible to foresee, for a given text, the complete range of potential *mises en scène*. The fault does not lie with an impressionistic theory, but with the large number of variables, especially as far as the Social Context is concerned. The necessity of linking the textual and stage concretizations to the Social Context of the audience – and therefore of relativizing any concretization/interpretation – has become apparent.

The difficulty at present seems to be that of expressing in theoretical terms the manner in which a text experiments with several possible utterances. Utterance and the overall rhythm of a performance are still inadequately defined, for it has only just been realized that these are not restricted to gestural and visual changes, but are germane to the whole *mise en scène*. It has now been understood and accepted that staging is not the mere physical uttering of a text with the appropriate intonation and 'seasoning' so that all can grasp the correct meaning; it is creating contexts of utterance in which the exchanges between verbal and non-verbal elements can take place. The utterance is always intended for an audience, with the result that *mise en scène* can no longer ignore the spectators and must even include them as the receptive pole in the circuit comprising the *mise en scène* produced by the artists and the *mise en scène* produced by the spectators.

Theatre – the dramatic text as well as *mise en scène* – has become a performance text, a spectacle of discourse as well as a discourse of spectacle (Issacharoff 1985). Theatrical production has become impregnated with theorization. *Mise en scène* is becoming the self-reflexive discourse of the work of art, as well as the audience's desire to theorize. They want to know just how the work of art functions: "no more secrets" is today's watchword.

The modern work of art, in particular the theatrical *mise en scène*, does not exist until we have explicitly extracted the system, traced the performance text, experienced the pleasure of deconstruction and uncovered the management of the whole stage operation (see Margin 10). 'Le charme discret de la bonne régie' ('the discreet charm of good staging'): such is the name of the practico-theoretical play we treat ourselves to when we go and see Planchon's *Tartuffe*, Strehler's *Lear* or Vitez' *Hamlet* (see Margin 11).

Who would still dare speak of the 'birth' of a performance from a text, thanks to the more or less artistic 'forceps' of an all-powerful director? 'What a childish business,' thinks the semiotics of *mise en scène*. 'Structural I was born, structural I remain!'

MARGINS

Margin 1

We have no intention of entering the debate on the status of the dramatic text, the question of whether a play can exist independently as a text or whether it can exist only in performance. We merely wish to point out that one can certainly read a dramatic text in book form, but that the reader is always encouraged to imagine the manner in which it could/should be uttered, to envisage therefore a possible *mise en scène*. Cf. Michel Vinaver's survey of seventy-three French authors who were divided into autonomists (of the text: 13 percent), fusionists (of text and performance: 22 percent), radicals (a play exists only in performance: 11 percent), and the vast majority, being the cohabitationists (a play is not reading matter *per se*, but may nevertheless be read: 43 percent) (Vinaver 1987: 83–8).

Margin 2

A point of view, to our way of thinking erroneous and idealistic, to which Danièle Sallenave (1987: 22) has reverted:

> The same text can give rise to productions of varying quality. These can be compared according to whether the text had been more, or less, actualized. ... *Mise en scène* has to do with trueness to the text, with what Gadamer calls actualization as a *manifestation of truth* (this was already in Aristotle's *Poetics*).

Margin 3

This position is best represented, and with a great deal of rigor, by Michael Issacharoff in *Le Spectacle du discours* (1985) and in an article 'Inscribed performance' (1986): he considers the performance to be more or less, but always to some extent inscribed in the dramatic text, very little in the case of Racine, very much so in the case of Beckett or Shaw. It is undeniable that elements of the didascalia or the text suggest a possible performance, but nothing, absolutely nothing (not even the Society of Authors), can oblige the director to conform to it. Usually the director produces the *mise en scène* that he or she wants; whenever reading and *mise en scène* take place, the process of *mise en scène* is extraneous to the text and not inscribed in it, at least not necessarily. To talk about performance (or *mise en scène*) implies that theatre is seen as the enactment of the text, not as a reading inherent to the text. In order to perform (or stage) a text, one has to approach it from the outside and 'break down the (textual) house' by having it enunciated in a specific period and place and by physical bodies.

Margin 4

Here one recognizes the self-effacing attitude of *mise en scène*: the director puts on a show of modesty, saying "I serve the author, not myself" and "I don't stage myself". In point of fact, such talk is sometimes a mixture of naïvety and cunning, sometimes indicative of an authentic search to induce in the actor and the spectator a 'wavering attention' (Freud). Two examples:

1 J. P. Vincent (1982: 20): "In the sense in which one generally uses the word, there was no mise-en-scène in *Peines d'amour perdues* . . . I tried to bring out the stage reality inherent in the text." This attitude of non-interpretation is often demanded by the authors themselves: according to them, directors should let the authors' texts speak for themselves. Thus H. Müller praises Bob Wilson's directing: "He never interprets a text, contrary to the practice of directors in Europe. A good text does not have to be 'interpreted' by a director or by an actor".

2 Now two examples of productive self-effacement: C. Régy:

> The principle of *mise en scène* that I try to put into practice is *not to do a mise en scène*; my work is rather like that of a midwife; I do not obstruct, I open up the inner walls so that the deep subconscious thoughts of the author and the actors can flow freely and reach, without having to surmount any barriers, the subconscious of the audience.
>
> Quoted in Pasquier 1987: 62)

Lassalle and what he calls 'toneless theatre' offer another example of self-effacement as a creative process laying bare the subconscious: "Seghers' text (*Remagen*), itself an incandescent, condensed and essential material . . . passes through the bodies of the narrating actresses and provokes a kind of shock by the very force of its utterance" (quoted in Deprats, 1987: 27).

Margin 5

Except of course in the case of well-known classical texts of which the spectator is seeing the nth production. Nor is it impossible for a very experienced producer to try to reconstruct the original text. Michael Langham (1983) recounts how the British director Sir Barry Jackson, when he saw a play on stage, always tried to imagine what the text was like. He adds, however, that Jackson was rather eccentric.

Margin 6

In a recent article, Marvin Carlson (1983) uses, in order to criticize them, some of our own categories that he calls *illustration, translation* and *fulfillment*. the theory of illustration wrongly presents

41

mise en scène as a visual illustration for those who do not know how to read (or who read badly and want illustrations) (cf. p. 26§2). The theory of translation is based on the incorrect assumption that the text is translated into visual signs (cf. p.28§6). The theory of fulfillment, presented as the opposite of the theory of illustration, explains performance as the realization or fulfillment of the text (cf. p.28§7), rather like Anne Ubersfeld who talks about the text with holes in it which is filled up or made complete by *mise en scène* 1977: 24). M. Carlson (1983: 10) proposes to describe the relationship between text and performance in the manner of Derrida in *Of Grammatology*, i.e. the one is seen as a supplement to the other and vice versa:

A play on stage will inevitably reveal elements which are lacking in the written text, which probably do not seem a great loss before the performance takes place, but which are subsequently revealed as meaningful and important. At the same time the performance, by revealing this lack, reveals also an infinite series of future performances, adding new supplements.

For Carlson this theory is an adequate explanation of the infinite potential richness of the dramatic text and the incompleteness of any *mise en scène*. This Derridean vision seems to us related to the idea of Vitez who sees *mise en scène* as an art of variation. In our opinion, this notion could lead to a relativism of readings and an unending game of mirrors, distracting the reader from research based more on history and explicable, after all, by the complex variety of the parameters of reception and of any particular concretization. It is true that Vitez has recently revised his theory of variation:

I find this art of variation all the more exhilarating for having recently discovered that in actual fact, in theatre, there cannot be many more than three or four 'families' of interpretation of the character Célimène. The number of possible interpretations is of course infinite, but they can be classified under three headings at the most. Likewise there are only a few basic ways to produce Chekhov's plays and not, contrary to what I myself believed formerly, an infinite variety of productions. . . . The pleasure of *mise en scène* or of theatre itself is to be found in this variation; it is what is inscribed in people's memories. When one sees a performance of *Le Misanthrope*, one can compare it with another performance one remembers, and this affords pleasure. This is the pleasure of theatre. It seems to me that the same is true for translation. Translation must of necessity be redone.

(Vitez 1985: 115–16)

Mesguich seems to share this 'Derridean' vision:

Appropriation – if it takes place at all – is always momentary; restitution is already present in it; in the very act of appropriation lies the act of cession, and, instead of 'Planchon has *taken possession* of Tartuffe', could one not just as well say, this is how he *gave him back*?

Le Symposium (1985: 245)

Margin 7

B. Dort (1985: 234–41) comes close to sharing this vision of a confrontation between text and stage, except for one important detail:

One must now try to see theatrical performance as a game between two distinct albeit related practices, as the moment when these two practices, confront and question each other, as their mutual combat of which the spectator is, in the final analysis, both the judge and what is at stake. The text, all texts have their place. Neither the first, nor the last, but the place of the written or permanent aspect of a concrete and ephemeral event. This confrontation, at least, is nowhere near complete.

In our opinion, the text has nothing permanent about it: it is of course materialized and fixed in writing and in book form, but it has to be constantly reread, and therefore concretized anew again and again, being therefore eminently unstable: it is impossible to count on it as something unchanging and durable.

For this reason, we should understand the staging of a text as a way of putting the text to work. The production, by enunciating the text in a certain manner, constitutes a possible text: "The character of the text will determine the nature of the production but conversely the production will determine the character of the text, will by a process of selection, organization and exclusion, define which text is actually being put to work" (Eagleton 1978).

Margin 8

Cf. the metaphor of dust, created by Vitez, which is very popular in modern critical discourse. For instance Mesguich (1985: 245) says: "A text is enlarged by being worked on, displaced, contaminated, re-evaluated by a director; it is 'swollen' by the affluents of its readers, its *mise en scène*. They are its dust, its blood, its history, its value, the course it takes."

Margin 9

This explains why we agree in this instance with Danièle Sallenave who, while giving the director his due, stresses quite rightly the activity of the spectator who plays the game:

> We can add here another reference to Gadamer's work [*Vérité et méthode*]: his notion that, in theatre, the real actor is the spectator. The actor *plays his role* in the play, but the spectator *plays the game*. In order for the spectator to play the game, somebody had to set up the game: this somebody is the director. But when the spectator plays the game, he does not play with the director, or even with the actor, but with the text, with the idea of the text. The director has to be suppressed and even the actor has somehow to be 'forgotten' so that the idea of the text can be generated.
>
> (1987: 18)

This 'game with the text' is what we call the perception of the *mise en scène* as a structural system, in complete isolation from the person of the director.

The notion of the author of the *mise en scène* disappears, just as did the idea of the author of the text; it is 'replaced' by the concept of the structure or discourse of the *mise en scène*. It is the notion of the *author*, "invisible yet ever present" according to Flaubert, that Sallenave cites further on (p. 23).

The same metaphor of the absent author is used by Mesguich (1985: 244):

> The main characteristic of this offspring who is not allowed

to be naïve, this child-born grown up, is never to find out his name, never to permit himself a single word. The strategy of this illegal immigrant, this unlawful worker, this gipsy in the kingdom of theatre, is to move on tirelessly as soon as he has spoken, never to be where one thinks he is, to cross and recross the frontiers, taking them with him. His behaviour is one of ruse.

Margin 10

G. Banu (1986: 50) wonders if the present-day director can still claim to be an artist, the author of a work:

> Does the director's desire to create a work still have a *raison d'être*? Yes, but he has changed his tone, for he is less aggressive, less obvious. . . . The presence of the director is acceptable only if it is mediatized, perceptible through the presence of others.

Nowadays the director no longer wishes to impose his reading of the text: "The director only wants the text to be heard in all its ambiguity, he watches over this. He no longer wants to treat it violently, imposing strong readings on it. Instead he slips into it gently, making its secret organization his own."

We cannot but agree with this account of the director's disengagement: he does indeed try to preserve textual ambiguities. However, this is the exact opposite of neutrality and his method does not consist in letting the text speak. It is definitely not a case of textual literalness, as is claimed by J. M. Piemme (1987). Piemme sees *mise en scène* oscillating "constantly between two poles, both dramaturgically based: the pole of deciphering and that of readability" (p. 76). He suggests that *mise en scène* can "produce for the spectator a mediation space where he will find displayed, not one specific interpretation, but the text in all its literalness" (pp. 76–7). We contest this display of the text's literalness. One cannot avoid interpretation; it is impossible not to breathe into the text an interpretation from the outside. Textual literalness does not exist, or else there are as many literal texts as there are readers. A text does not speak on its own, it has to be made to speak. But this presents no problem to the director, who, like the torturer, has the means to make it talk.

Watchwords often heard today – 'one must let the text be

heard,' 'one should not interfere' etc. – seem to us either very naïve or dishonest. It is not possible to neutralize the stage so that the text can speak on its own, or be heard without mediation or without distortion. Because *mise en scène* is repudiating itself does not mean that it is suddenly going to disappear, as if by magic, and let *the* text be heard.

Margin 11

What we call 'the discreet charm of good staging' is a delicate balance between what is and what is not visible in *mise en scène* as a system of meaning. Régis Durand correctly describes this phenomenon as follows:

> In order for a *mise en scène* to be perceived, the concept which inspires it must be grasped by the audience. This concept must be made visible in some way or other; if the spectator does not perceive it, he will get the impression that he has not seen a *mise en scène*, that he has seen things happening without any coherence or unity. On the other hand, if the concept is made too visible because simplistic, rudimentary or over obvious, the work will be systematic, giving the impression that once the system has been understood, all the rest follows as a matter of course.
>
> (1987: 19)

NOTE

1. I have borrowed the title 'From page to stage' from Gay McAuley's projects, in which she observes the work of professional actors during rehearsals as part of Performance Studies at the University of Sydney.
    A first version of this article appeared in Michael Issacharoff and Robin Jones (eds) (1988) *Performing Texts*, University of Pennsylvania Press, pp. 86–100.

BIBLIOGRAPHY

Banu, G. (1986) 'Dossier Mise en scène,' *Art Press* 101.
Carlson, Marvin (1983) 'Theatrical Performance: Illustration, Translation, Fulfillment or Supplement?', *Theatre Journal* (March).
Corvin, Michel (1985) *Molière et ses metteurs en scène d'aujourd'hui*, Lyon.
Déprats, J. M. (1987) 'Glissements progressifs du discours,' *L'Art du Théâtre* 6.

Dort, B. (1985) 'Le Texte et la scène: pour une nouvelle alliance,' *Encyclopedia Universalis.*

Durand, Régis (1987) *L'Art du Théâtre* 6.

Eagleton, Terry (1978) *Marxism and Literary Criticism.*

Fischer-Lichte, Erika (ed.) (1984) *Das Drama und seine Inszenierung,* Tübingen.

Ingarden, Roman (1931) *Das literarische Kunstwerk,* Tübingen.

Issacharoff, Michael (1985) *Le Spectacle du discours,* Paris.

—— (1986) 'Inscribed performance,' *Rivista di letterature moderne e comparate* 34.

Jacquot, Jean and Veinstein, André (1957) *La Mise en scène des oeuvres du passé,* Paris.

Langham, Michael (1983) 'Preface' in David Ball, *Backwards and Forwards,* Southern Illinois University Press.

Mesguich, (1985) 'La mise en scène ou le double jeu,' *Encyclopedia Universalis.*

Mukařovský, Jan (1970) 'L'Art comme fait sémiologique,' *Poétique* 3.

Pasquier, M. C. (1987) 'Claude Régy: garder le secret du livre,' *L'Art du Théâtre* 6.

Pavis, Patrice (1985) 'Production et réception au théâtre: la concrétisation du texte dramatique et spectaculaire,' *Voix et images de la scène,* Lille: Presses Universitaires.

—— (1986a) 'The Classical Heritage of Modern Drama: The Case of Postmodern Theatre,' *Modern Drama* 29, and chapter 3, this volume.

—— (1986b) *Marivaux à l'épreuve de la scène,* Paris.

Piemme, Jean-Marie (1984) 'Le Souffleur inquiet,' *Alternatives Théâtrales* 20/21.

—— (1987) 'Le sens du jeu,' *L'Art du Théâtre* 6.

Rey, Alain (1980) 'Le Théâtre, qu'est-ce que c'est?', in D. Couty and A. Rey (eds.) *Le Théâtre,* Paris.

Sallenave, Danièle (1987) *L'Art du Théâtre* 6.

Searle, John (1982) 'Le statut logique du discours de la fiction,' in *Sens et Expressions,* Paris.

Ubersfeld, Anne (1977) *Lire le théâtre,* Paris.

Vinaver, Michel (1982) 'Sur la pathologie de la relation auteur–metteur en scène,' *L'Annuel du Spectacle.*

—— (1987) *Le Compte rendu d'Avignon,* Actes Sud.

Vincent, J. P. (1982) 'Un théâtre de l'écoute,' *Théâtre/Public* 67.

Vitez, Antoine (1974) 'Ne pas montrer ce qui est dit,' *Travail Théâtral* 14.

—— (1985) 'La traduction: désir, théorie, pratique,' *Actes des premières assises de la traduction littéraire,* Arles.

Vodička, Felix (1975) *Struktur der Entwicklung,* Munich.

3

THE CLASSICAL HERITAGE OF MODERN DRAMA: THE CASE OF POSTMODERN THEATRE[1]

Whoever wishes to evaluate the classical heritage of modern drama is confronted from the beginning with the problem of defining notions which are either deliciously imprecise or archaic. This all too attractive opportunity tempts us to unravel the ambiguities attached to every one of these terms and to test their paradoxical meanings and semantic richness. For it is only by playing on these words, using the negative dialectic dear to Theodor W. Adorno, that we can unblock certain contradictions and shake up some old habits. Each of these notions recalls its opposite, or at least a corrective or a different point of view that relativizes its meaning.

1 *Classical* is opposed to *modern*, but also, more recently, to *postmodern*. I shall be examining these borderlines and this over-flow of modernity to justify the paradox that postmodern theatre cannot define itself without recourse to classical norms. I shall be referring to Roland Barthes' (1979) distinction between the classical *work* and the modern *text*.

2 *Heritage* is at once a bourgeois and a Marxist idea. With regard to theatre, it refers, in the case of *mise en scène*, to the traditions of performance and to the interpretation of texts; and it refers, in the case of dramatic texts, to dramaturgical forms available. Postmodern theatre seems unwilling to listen to talk about textual or theatrical heritage, which it treats as no more than *memory* in the technical sense of that word, as an immediately available and reusable memory bank.

3 *Modern, classical* and *postmodern* constitute three paradigms that

48

are often confused and difficult to define a priori. The criterion separating them most precisely in the case of theatre would be theatrical usage and *mise en scène*, rather than the origin of the staged text.

4 *Drama*, which refers to the written manifestation of theatre (i.e. the dramatic text), does not provide us with a satisfactory means of understanding what is modern about the theatre.

The notion of theatre, on the other hand, allows us to juxtapose classicism, modernism and postmodernism with respect to the concrete practices of the actor, the stage, the audience – in short, of a specific theatrical enunciation which varies considerably over time.

The title of this proposed reflection thus becomes – for the sake of dialectic as well as provocation – 'The textual memory of postmodern theatre.' In order to explain these terms, I shall take up each component of this title, defining the relationship between the modern and postmodern theatre on the one hand, and the classical theatre on the other, to justify the paradox that postmodern theatre recuperates by reworking the classical heritage and needs classical norms to establish its own identity.

CLASSICAL WORK OR MODERN TEXT?

The Work and the Text

Before sketching a definition of postmodern theatre – a term used rather frequently today without much methodological precaution[2] – we should examine the notion of *classical text* by returning to Barthes' idea of the *classical work* and the *avant-garde text*. The historical definition of the classical work or author has been habitually linked to the rather imprecise notion of ancient times, remote from the present. Difficulties arise the moment we look for any inherent structural properties of the classical text: we need, in effect, to evaluate the role of historicity in the signifying process of the text, in its concretization (see Pavis 1983, 1985a) at various historical moments in different contexts, especially with respect to the reception and establishment of meaning by the reader or spectator. Concretizing the text, establishing its meaning, depends on factors of reception, which cannot, however, exclude the production and the intrinsic structure of the text. At the end of the circuit of concretization, one is in a position to give meaning to the 'oldest' text (the most classical) or to the most recent (the most modern); this specific signification would tend to relativize considerably the distinction between *classical* and *modern*. We may indeed be tempted to treat the classical text either as a work like any other, only more temporally remote, or – as is often the case in contemporary *mise en scène* – as a text that is more open and productive than contemporary texts and whose context of enunciation determines and more precisely limits meaning. Barthes warns us of this temptation to distinguish between *classical work* and *modern text* on the grounds 'of their chronological situation':

> The text must not be thought of as a defined object. It would be useless to attempt a material separation of works and texts. One must take particular care not to say that works are classical while texts are avant-garde. Distinguishing them is not a matter of establishing a crude list in the name of modernity and declaring certain literary productions to be 'in' and others 'out' on the basis of their chronological situation. A very ancient work can contain 'some text,' while many products of contemporary literature are not texts at all. The difference is as follows: the work is concrete, occupying a portion of book space (in a library, for example); the text, on the other hand, is a methodological field.
>
> (Barthes 1979: 74)

The opposition, which Barthes refused to sanction, is established as follows:

work	text
classical	modern
readerly	writerly
linear text	spatial text
simple text	difficult text

This rather fragile set of opposites threatens at any moment to turn upside-down, since the *work* is modern and the *text* classical. Any search for the specificity of the classical work in textual terms is compromised. The *work* or the *text* is neither the opposition between ancient and modern nor the opposition between old-fashioned and avant-garde. Both conditions are above all *textual*, that is defined in relationship to other texts with respect to their different productive and receptive instances. Let us limit ourselves to a few criteria defining the classical *work* and the modern *text*.[3]

The readability of the classical text is based on the small amount of effort the reader needs to determine action, character and the logic of the narrative – of course, without taking into account the opacity of classical language which resists deciphering and the variations which the play undergoes in the determination of the plot. If the classical text appears *simple* on first glance, it becomes extremely complex when, dissatisfied with its primary and literal meaning, we undertake to reread it. Conversely, if we accept the idea that the modern text's meaning is only what can be reconstituted by the hypotheses and open tracks of the reading process, then this text can be read according to a schema entirely constituted by the recipient, and then both difficulty and polysemy vanish for ever. The 'spatiality' of the text – that is the tiny capillaries in its textual body – is no more than a univocal and simplifying readability.

Difficulty is a completely reversible and relative criterion; every text is difficult in so far as it demands that the reader recognize zones of indeterminacy, ambiguity and contradiction. This kind of difficulty is paradoxical in that it ceases to exist once it has been deciphered and made functional. What is at issue is the determination of what creates difficulty in a text. Is it the comprehensiveness of classical language? the shifting horizons of expectation of past and present readers? the possible logic of the narrative? the filling of zones of indeterminacy? The notion of difficulty itself – its function and evaluation – varies historically, because it depends on the Social Context[4] of reception and on factors often condemned as psychologistic – the desire or the willingness to read the text at one or another level, the resulting textual orchestration which ensures that the same text gives rise to divergent readings, the decision finally to read the text according to one or another end: following history and becoming distracted by immediately translating textual utterances into a fictional world, thus neglecting the (auto)textual makeup of the work; multiplying the openings of the plot and the text; reading for the purpose of writing a university thesis, a journalistic report or a contribution to a Marxist or Lacanian journal, for example.

Despite the relativity and even interchangeability of criteria specific to the classical text, despite the instability which makes a text of the work and which cannot exclude the possibility that a modern text might already be a classical work in the sense that it is reduced from the start to the classical moment of a self-evident meaning, it is not too risky to list a number of criteria which are in no way eternal or logically stable, but which simply bear witness to the ways in which the classical text is received and perceived today.

1 The classical text is spontaneously ideological: behind the homogenous façade of a clear and compelling plot, of writing which avoids any drop in tension within the various discourses of the speakers, it hides the codes and mechanisms that keep it going. The perfect and bounded qualities of classical writing make one forget the codes governing its production to the extent to which they become the purely evaluative criteria of classicism: a text whose formal perfection is such that one forgets that it is a text situated in history. Verisimilitude and techniques of persuasions are used in this kind of text to make us believe in a 'real story,' in flesh-and-blood characters; we forget that the text and its procedures fabricate all these reality effects. The response of a critical reading and also, in the case of theatre, of a *mise en scène* would be to unveil the codes, to accentuate, by means of the grotesque or of baroque irony, the fabricated and artificial character of these codes.[5]

2 The relationship between the classical text and its intertext is also significant, not only because poetics requires that authors refer faithfully to antiquity and invent only what is absolutely necessary, but also because the series of absent texts, which everyone is supposed to know, is very long. This intertextual reference is important in so far as it prevents the contemporary reader ignorant of these references from grasping the function of the classical text. What may happen is that certain philosophical texts, as well as literary ones, bring about a transformation and rereading of other texts in the field of knowledge.

This phoenix text that is the classical work cannot always be reborn in a way that renews our understanding of it. In fact, and rather more prosaically, its contemporary hearer is never quite sure whether he understands it as a text of the past or as a contemporary text. Straddling several centuries, this text is chronically *misheard* (*mal entendu*); its hearer (even more than its reader) experiences a feeling of strange familiarity when confronted with the language of Molière or Marivaux (while, on the other hand, the successive translations of Shakespeare and Goethe have the paradoxical power of adapting to the evolution and the image reservoir (*imaginaire*) of the French language). Classical French is like an opaque plate between us and the fictional world set up by the text. There is no longer a direct and transitive connection between the world and discourse. The hearer is obliged to lend a more attentive ear and to call into question continually the relationship between the text and the world, that is its ideological dimension. He arrives at this dimension only by way of perceiving the text as formal artifact. Thus, a connection is established between text and ideology (which is constitutive of the text's functioning). Once made aware of a form which resists efforts to make it transparent, the reader/spectator is likely to attribute to the text a profound and hidden significance of which a historicizing reading would not dream. All work on the form of theatrical enunciation – codes of baroque irony, speech that is exaggeratedly rhetorical or sung, the theatricalization of character – ends up by making classical French opaque and by inviting us to sound its dizzying depths. As a result, despite its traditional image, classical discourse does not shine with a clarity that makes of language a faithful mirror of the world.[6]

For a long time criticism of the classics and interpretation of *mise en scène* have acted as if time had done no more than cover the text with layers of dust; in order to make the text respectable, it was enough to clean up and get rid of the deposits which history, layers of interpretation, and hermeneutic sediment had left on an essentially untouched text. This phantasmic image of the classical text could develop not only into an attempt to reconstruct archeologically the historical conditions of performance, but also into a modernization of performance style (classics in modern dress, gadgets alluding anachronistically to contemporary life). In each case, 'dusting' the text entails an idealist assumption according to which correcting classical language is all one needs to do to reach the level of the fictional world and of the ideologemes reduced to an *objet fixe*, a mixture of ancient and modern times. The reaction of dramaturges and directors to this static image of criticism of *mise en scène* as 'cleaning house' (*ménage*) has luckily not been long in coming. Alain Girault (1973: 79) has noted that 'the dusting operation implies an idealist philosophical notion of the permanence of man. "Dusting" is finally "dehistoricizing," denying history(reducing it to surface reflection, to "dust").' Refusing to 'dust off' involves an assumption of historical displacement, shocking the audience with the consciousness of a formal separation which corresponds to a separation of distinct world views. Brecht (1967: 112) notes that, after the *mise en scène* of Schiller's *Robbers*, Piscator told him that 'he had looked for what would make people remark on leaving the theatre that 150 years were no small matter.'

Today dramaturgical reflection refuses to give way to the vertigo of dusting as the 'miraculous solution.' Antoine Vitez has suppressed the practice in his own work:

> If one speaks of 'dusting,' it is because one believes that dust has accumulated on something: an intact object which one has lost and which, after cleaning up and polishing, one can rediscover. That is precisely what happens to works of art. Either one leaves the dust and continues as before – the Comédie Française has been gathering layers of dust for a long time and masking the dust with a new layer of wax – or one can try something else. One can do more than simply remove the dust; one can alter the object itself. A vase that has been miraculously preserved can always be useful. A play is quite different. The object itself is fundamentally transformed, even if the text remains completely intact. We can no longer read it in the same way as those readers for whom it was written. What we read is a kind of memory; this consists of making distorted elements reappear to our present life – in fact, the correspondence between individual and social body.
>
> (Vitez 1977: 45)

What appears to be important in the reading of the classical text is the ability to historicize the dust, instead of ignoring it or covering it up. This practice is quite close to translation, which provides a version of the source text in the language of the new reader, who then has a choice: between a translation-adaptation that, in order to avoid slavishly copying the text to be translated, transposes the text into its new cultural context; and a more literal translation that, at the risk of a feeling of strangeness and idiomatic shortcomings, preserves something of the rhetoric and world view of the source language.

3 Like translation, reading the classics is always accompanied by a loss of meaning, or rather by the destruction of whole facets of signification. Rather than speaking of textual elements which remain after each new reading, it would be more accurate to speak of zones of indeterminacy or ambiguity which one can partly patch up or partly remove. Like the literary text in general, the classical text possesses on the one hand structural ambiguities which are programmed and necessary for the development of the fictional world, and on the other hand ambiguities due to changing concretizations of the same text. The first kind of ambiguity is to remain untouched. Dissolving such ambiguities would only destroy the mechanism of suspense and discovery. Above all it would simplify and, by taking a partisan position, expose the implicit ideologeme(s) which the text unknowingly articulates in accordance with its historical position. This may be a (very) useful task, but chiefly for the theorist of literature and ideology.

The second kind of ambiguity arises out of unforeseeable modifications in the circumstances of reception – the temporal and cultural shift from utterance to reception – in particular because of both the widening gap between the social contexts of reception and the length of time between the production and reception of the text. For example, it is difficult to ascertain a character's social milieu or group from his/her speech and behavior, and whether this speech conforms or not to the character's social origins. This difficulty is not a structural ambiguity, but the production of a new zone of indeterminacy which modifies our reading of the plot. Often a classical text, for which we no longer have reception guidelines, appears as a text constructed according to a strategy of mystery and ambiguity through which the text acquires unearned significance. Hence a further reason for the success of classical texts: historical, geographical or social distance; production of ambiguity and enigmas which change a work hitherto monosemic into one that is complex and undecidable. If the *mise en scène* can, in a new concretization of the text, suggest new zones of indeterminacy, organize possible trajectories of meaning between them, the classical dramatic text may recapture the glow tarnished by the passage of time and by banal interpretations. This phenomenon of recycling grants the classical text a perennial life by founding this life, not on permanent and unchanging significance, but on change and adaptation.

These characteristics of the classical work – in particular, the way in which they can be manipulated as in a modern text – lead the *mise en scène* to call into question the historical or theoretical difference between notions of *classical* and *modern*. The *mise en scène* of a classic may be modern or postmodern (as we shall soon see), whereas the *mise en scène* of a contemporary text may be out of fashion and, in some cases, may prevent the text from revealing its newness and modernity. What has radically changed since modernism and, *a fortiori*, since postmodernism and its theatrical practice, is the relationship between the director and the text.

The impossible unitary space

Today's authors seem incapable of making use of the classical dramatic text. They find it unthinkable to offer plays with dialogue exchanged by characters as in social conversation. The phenomenon is not a new one: as Peter Szondi (1956) has shown, it heralded the beginning of 'modern drama' in about 1880 and continued until about 1950. It is characterized by a rupture in theatrical communication and dialogic exchange; by the occurrence of a crisis in drama and further by rescue attempts (naturalism, conversation pieces or one-act plays, existentialism) or attempts to resolve the issue (expressionism, epic theatre, montage, Pirandellism, etc.). Even theatre of the absurd is a modernist (rather than postmodernist) manifestation, since its nonsense still makes sense and recalls an interpretation and conception of the world. As Adorno writes:

> Even so-called absurd literature – in the work of its best representatives – has a stake in the dialectic: that there is no meaning and that negating meaning maintains nonetheless the category of meaning; that is what both allows for and demands interpretation.
>
> (1970: 235)

Adorno goes on to remark that after the literature of the absurd (we might add, with the advent of postmodernism), meaning itself is no longer what is rejected as organizing principle, nor is nonsense presented as philosophy: 'The principle of harmony, although changed beyond recognition, continues to play a role, even in art that obeys whimsy without reservation, because these whimsical ideas count for something only when they present themselves in the artist's manner of speaking' (1970: 235–6).

One must take into account, in the new postmodern art, a new totality, not of utterances, but of their enunciation and arrangement in artistic discourse.

From the 1960s onward, theatrical conceptions changed radically again (a change which does not permit us to call the present definitively the new postmodern era). The question is no longer the debate between dialogue and monologue, communication and cacophony, sense and nonsense. Authors such as Peter Handke, Michel Vinaver, Samuel Beckett and Heiner Müller no longer attempt to imitate speakers in the act of communicating, nor do they lock themselves into indecipherable words. They present a text which – even if it still takes the form of words alternately expressed by different speakers – can no longer be recapitulated or resolved or lead to action. Their sort of text addresses itself as a whole to the audience, like a global poem tossed in the hearers' laps to be taken or left as they please. Searching for an impossible unitary space, this text attempts to return to a time before dialogue, to the 'earliest theatrical forms':

> Each word speaks alone, turned only towards those who have gathered together religiously to hear it; there is no lateral communication; he who speaks addresses the audience with a fullness that excludes any response, word from on high, in a relationship without reciprocity.
>
> (Blanchot 1969: 5)

But this religious gathering in a protected place, this global address to an undivided audience, and this sphinx capable of rereading scattered fragments no longer exist, even if authors such as Handke, Duras and Genet attempt to renew contact with a group linked by the desire to relive collectively – but not necessarily cathartically – their situation in a space which remains whole in the face of theatrical, familial, social or individual divisions. This quest for an aesthetic and social common ground, far from contradictions or conflicts, certainly implies (as we shall see) a close link with heritage and tradition, because the motivating force of theatre – of the actor, designer, director – is not only *cultural heritage* (great authors, great classical texts, fundamental myths of social and symbolic life), but *also* the heritage of *vocal, gestural* and *intonative practice*. We need to find the relationship between body and gesture, and the entire social and theatrical tradition. As Vitez remarks:

> The stage is the nation's language and gesture laboratory. Society knows, more or less clearly, that in these edifices called theatres, people work for hours to expand, purify, and transform the gestures and intonation of current life . . . to call them into question, into crisis. If the theatre is indeed society's gesture and language laboratory, it is then both the conserver of ancient expressive norms and the adversary of tradition.
>
> (1982: 8)

The unitary and unifying space masks the origin of words or relativizes their import. In *L'Ordinaire*, 'a play in seven pieces' by Vinaver, nine of the characters in the multinational *houses* take part in dialogue with their companions in misfortune. Without knowing it, each adds his stone to the edifice and the myth of the multinational, which consumes itself while they dream of survival and reconstruction. In *Quartett* by Müller, man and woman double and redouble into woman and man, as a result of which it is difficult, or even impossible, to determine which voice is speaking and to whom:

> We can no longer speak of psychologically identifiable characters or personae – nonetheless, they are emphatically set up as a conventional given of the play and are then developed in a way rather uncommon for Müller. 'Persona' means 'mask' originally, and in Müller's work, the mask is increasingly a privileged metaphor for possible faces and roles which have replaced the individual face, that phantasmagoria of bourgeois society and state Marxism.
>
> (Schulz 1982)

This discursive space, which refuses any clear-cut consciousness of character, can also be explained by a new relationship between directors and classical plays.

New relationship to the classical work

It is not so much the conception of man and his place in the universe that has changed, as the conception which directors have of classical *works*. In contrast to the time spanning both the

58

classical and modern periods, today nobody believes in the specificity of the dramatic text, or in the existence of rules and regulations governing dialogue, character, dramatic structure, etc. As proof, this search for texts not primarily written for the stage has given rise to theatre-narrative experiments (*Catherine*, based on *Les Cloches de Bâle* by Aragon, in the *mise en scène* by Vitez; *Louve basse*, after Denis Roche, staged by G. Lavaudant; *L'Arrivante*, based on *Là* by Hélène Cixous, spaced (*mise en espace*) by Viviane Théophilidès). The novelistic text has been taken up, not so much as a basis for plot and character, but as a point of departure for a theatrical reading more or less dramatized by the improvisations of its various readers. The text is neither a privileged collection of dialogues which 'make theatre,' nor construction material which the Brechtians would exploit without scruple, nor (of course) a novel read by a reader who imagines the narrated events.

New dramatic writing has banished conversational dialogue from the stage as a relic of dramaturgy based on conflict and exchange: any story, intrigue or plot that is too neatly tied up is suspect. Authors and directors have tried to denarrativize their productions, to eliminate every narrative point of reference which could allow for reconstruction of the plot. In recent texts such as *Les Cépheides* by J. C. Bailly, *Oeil pour Oeil* by L. J. Sirjacq, *Faut-il rêver, faut-il choisir?* by Bruno Bayen, *Rêves de Franz Kafka* by E. Corman and Philippe Adrien, it is impossible to retrieve the pleasure of narrative and plot.

The modern – written – text or the classical – shown – text have both been emptied of meaning, or at least of any immediate mimetic meaning, of a signified already there, readily expressed on the stage. Any search for the text's sociohistorical dimension, for its inscription in past or present history, is forbidden or at least delayed as long as possible: let her/him who can fictionalize. Meaning is kept in reserve or its variants multiplied, but not in order to explicate this meaning by what we think we know at the start of play, from the initial reading with the invincible armada of dramaturges, sociologists and directors.[7]

Instead of a dramaturgical analysis intended to determine probable signifieds, the signifying practices deal with the plurality of signification: they open the dramatic text up to theatrical experimentation without separating the reading of the text, the discovery of its meaning, and the stage translation that would explain the pre-existent textual meaning. The text is maintained as an object of questioning, the workings of codes, rather than a series of situations and allusions to a subtext which the spectator ought to feel. The text is received as a series of meanings which contradict and answer one another and which decline to annihilate themselves in a final global meaning. Signifying practice refuses to illustrate or confirm whatever analysis claims to discover in the first concretization through reading. The plurality of signifieds is maintained by multiplication of theatrical enunciators (actors, music, rhythm of presentation, etc.); rejection of hierarchy in stage systems; refusal to partition the latter into major and minor systems, to reduce them to a fundamental signified; and finally, refusal to interpret. Peter Brook has set himself up as the theoretician for this hermeneutic refusal, claiming that the forms of the great works, such as Shakespearean forms, are open to interpretation *ad infinitum*, 'forms as deliberately vague as possible, so as to avoid imposing interpretation' (1975: 87).

This desire for the text's infinite openness to significance seems, despite its association with Barthes or Kristeva,[8] to be nothing but an effective snare to hold back for as long as possible the issue of taking a stand and to leave this difficult task to the reader/spectator. At the point where theatre distinguishes itself from the text to be read, it may reveal or hide what the text has already said. Two strategies are possible: to show what is not said (this is what historicized representation suggests); or, following Vitez, to champion the text's openness, 'not to develop indiscriminately any point of view, but to give oneself over to infinite variations' which 'will provide a link between significations' (1981: 4). This kind of *mise en scène* establishes a perpetual game of hide-and-show, text and stage. Meaning is accessible to the spectator only if s/he submits to a practice that deciphers both theatrical signs and textual signifieds. Vitez is the best representative of this tendency: 'For the spectators, theatrical pleasure resides in the difference between what is said and what is shown . . . or rather what interest can they have for the theatre? What is interesting is the difference' (1974: 50). 'What seems to me stimulating is to have the spectator stick to the idea that what is said is not shown' (1974: 52).

With this approach, the dialectic between text and performance is definitely established (whereas beforehand the performance always flowed from the reading of the text). The *mise en scène* becomes the validation (*mise en valeur*) of what Jean-Loup Rivière calls, with reference to Vitez' work on Racine, the 'pantomime of the text':

> [the] successive shifts, the jumps between these two series, in order to make of the text (which is an ensemble of words) a gesture (movement which the *detailed* enunciation of each alexandrine accentuates) which at the same time as the bodily gesture of the actor, in its displacement (and in a dialectical/ playful relationship with it), contributes to the writing of this new text which is the performance.
>
> (Rivière 1971: 5)

Infusing, decentering, undoing the rhythm

This *mise en scène* of a classical work, or rather its vocal articulation (*mise en bouche*), is supposed to breathe a physical and respiratory meaning into the text, the consequence of its global enunciation. Current research on the rhythm of classical diction and versification, on vocal and gestural performance, tends – as Brook, Mnouchkine (the *Shakespeares*), Vitez (*Phèdre, Britannicus*) or Grüber (*Bérénice*) have shown – to undo the rhythm of the text in its first (habitual or self-evident) reading. Theatre and theatrical enunciation become, by way of the actor, the new priest of utterance, the mythic site where this undoing of rhythm imposes a new meaning on the classical work.

The text, even the classical text, is still used in the contemporary *mise en scène*, but in the light of postmodernism it is no longer the deposit meaning awaiting the *mise en scène* that will express, interpret and transcribe this unproblematic meaning that theatre (dramaturge, director or actor) may bring to light through erudition and patience. The text has become signifying matter awaiting meaning, an object of desire, one hypothetical meaning among others, which is tangible and concretized only in a situation of enunciation resulting from the combined efforts of audience and *mise en scène* (where the audience is the recipient of the enunciation).

Revaluation of the text, experimentation with the classical *work* treated as the crossroads of meaning – these strategies accompany a change in the dominant paradigm of theatrical and, in particular, classical representation. The text and the plot are no longer at the center of the performance, nor are the space and theatrical systems (stage writing) as they were during the classical period of *mise en scène*. At the moment, time, rhythm and diction are central. Rhythm and parody become the system of meaning in the *mise en scène* on which all others rest. As Vitez has – symptomatically – remarked: 'I like prosody, I like rhyme, and these seem more important to me than the shock of pure images in which contemporary poetry has been trying to hide since the surrealists (n.d.:82).

Currently, the great theatrical undertaking is undoing the rhythm of a so-called natural expressive reading to get beyond a purely psychologizing or philological reading, in order to try or to impose various rhythmic schemata 'external' to the text (see *Théâtre du Soleil*, Vitez' work on the French classics of the seventeenth century).

INHERITANCE OR MEMORY

Bourgeois or socialist heritage

It is well known that the idea of inheritance is taboo in the good families of the petite bourgeoisie, and not without good reason, since it is associated with the sudden acquisition of material benefits owing to the death of a close relative, and thus with the impression that one has gained unearned profits from the possessions of others. We can – tentatively – compare this bad conscience with that of contemporary *mise en scène* confronted with the forms and themes of classical works, as well as with their performance techniques and theatrical traditions. We must distinguish once more between two kinds of inheritances. The bourgeois heritage conceives of literature, especially classical literature, as a treasure house of experience, forms and styles which cannot but inspire every new age, since they represent a tried and universal model, and are characterized by formal perfection and an indubitable knowledge of man. This is the typical position of the Ancients reproaching the Moderns for not taking acquired experience into account, for not trusting to old recipes. In the theatre, this respect for heritage manifests itself as much in veneration and reproduction in the theatrical tradition as in the attempt to reproduce as faithfully as possible in the *mise en scène* the traditions established at the time when the play was first produced.

The Marxist heritage (according to Marx, Lenin, Plekhanov,

Lukaćs or Brecht) claims to make use of the bourgeois heritage and to reinforce the conception of a socialist culture which selects positive elements from the inheritance that were suppressed in their time by forces stronger than they were: thus, for example, the outline of bourgeois thought during the period of feudalism. The heritage is thus *selective*: one seeks out only those embryonic progressive elements to be found in a reactionary past. It is *admiring*: one appreciates the form and technique of a classic; one praises, as Marx did, those aspects of Greek art which can still move us today. It is *militant*: one takes up only what can be appropriated for the current political struggle (Piscator, Brecht); and *versatile*: the heritage and its 'progressive content' can be changed in accordance with short-term directives determined by the historical situation or issued by the party. This way of inheriting classical universalism or bourgeois power rarely leads to a formal regeneration or, *a fortiori*, to questioning the relationship between form and content. In the best case (Brecht), dramaturgy and *mise en scène* find a form which is not a simple inversion of signs of inherited bourgeois art, but which invents a critical method for judging, revaluating and transforming the past.

Tradition and traditions

The practice of theatre, as opposed to drama, is necessarily inscribed in a tradition, because the institution within which it develops is the sum of material constraints and the locus of influences by other theatres past and present. Certain institutions – in particular, the Comédie-Française – have as their mission the preservation of a repertoire and mode of performance to which they see themselves heir: the interpretation of French classics of the seventeenth century, for example. Every regeneration of the *mise en scène* of classics in France since Artaud, Copeau or Jouvet has arisen from a critique of the falsified tradition of the Comédie Française or official institutions in general. Copeau wanted to 'approach the works of the true tradition and deliver them from the attachments with which official actors have weighed them down for three centuries (1976: 73). In 1955, Vilar was already much more skeptical as to the possibility of reconstituting certain past theoretical forms:

Would you like to know if it is possible to reconstitute these forms, faithful to the presentation as it was when the author was alive? And if, in doing so, these reconstructions retain any artistic interest? And if these theatrical forms still have the power to seduce today's audience? Let us answer these questions *grosso modo*. This kind of activity, scrupulously realized, is always interesting, at least for theatre craftsmen. But I doubt that we have the means to make, for example, the explosive Comédie Italienne – its subjects, its *lazzi* – come alive for a contemporary audience. This specialized art of the actor died with the actors. It was created within a tradition whose oral transmission (apprenticeship, experiment, routines, etc.) seems to me to have been essential and much more instructive than any written transmission (the work of Gherardi, etc.)

(1969: 59–60)

The oral and gestural transmission, which is more reliable than written transmission in the theatre, still does not guarantee respect for heritage and tradition, for there is considerable risk that only scraps of information, only 'bits' and cheap business, will be transmitted. Jouvet (1951: 165) (and after him Vitez) rightly insists on the difficulty of inheriting the spirit of *the* tradition. He distinguishes between tradition*s*, that is 'business, bits . . . whims,' each copied and recopied from the one before, and the tradition, in other words, the history of the theatre, the 'continuity of its exercises, performances, works, actors.' In the same spirit, Vitez (1978: 51) would like to reinvent tradition by keeping it at a critical distance: 'We need to remake tradition, not to be its dupes. If we reinvent tradition, we present it critically at the same time; we accept its convention, but we do not believe in it.' Following Vitez, we may realize the resolutely (post)modern attitude of this kind of *mise en scène*. What is at issue is no longer preserving the tradition (an impossible task, even at the Comédie Française), nor grasping its essence (Copeau, Jouvet), nor, needless to say, twisting it to socialist-realist ends (Brecht), but rather inscribing modern activity into the classical tradition. The current, 'post-Brechtian' distrust of any sociological *mise en scène* completely covered by a dense economic-political-sociocritical commentary arises from the kind of project like Vitez' where the relationship between heritage and tradition is a question no longer of bourgeois appropriation or socialist absorption, but of intertextual use of codes and conventions. Both avant-garde *mise en scène*, working with classical works, and the postmodern work of Wilson, Foreman and Laurie Anderson have used codes in this way.

The heritage of postmodern theatre

We have already noted the difficulty of grasping tangibly the way in which inheritance works in the theatre. It is relatively easy to observe the relationship *in drama* between modernity and tradition, and likewise easy to examine, as Szondi has done, the way in which dramatic form is contradicted and reappropriated by expressionism or epic theatre. But what about *mise en scène*? The textual trace, that is its theatrical manifestation (stage directions, *lazzi*, dialogue, external descriptions, theatrical events), is always unsatisfying, because this trace is only the residue of performance, and who wants to inherit this residue? Thus, it is without great regret that postmodern theatre and *mise en scène* abandon their textual and dramaturgical inheritance, the better to absorb the performance tradition – in particular, the unique and ephemeral event of the theatricalization of the stage utterance which Helga Finter has called 'achievements of historical theatre practice' (1985: 47):

> This kind of theatre is postmodern insofar as it does not destroy the achievements of historical theatre practice in the name of a blind faith in progress and in the myth of origins, as was still the case in the historical avant-garde. Rather, it dramatizes the constituent elements of theatricality as signs. This process of negativity does not destroy but rather produces in its deconstructive gesture its own meta-discourse. . . .
>
> Postmodernism, understood as the practice of deconstruction, bears a semiotic relation to the historical tradition and to its own impact, i.e., its practice generates its own metadiscourse, in that it opens up to the infinity of signs and makes the conditions of its own impact perceptible.
>
> (1985: 67)

According to these definitions, the difference between the historical avant-garde (modernism) and postmodernism can be seen as follows: the latter no longer feels the need to deny any dramaturgy or world view (as opposed to the theatre of the absurd, for

65

example); it sets itself the task of effecting its own deconstruction as a way of inscribing itself, no longer in a thematic or formal tradition, but into an auto-reflexive self-consciousness of its enunciation and thus into its very functioning – as if all forms and contents had lost their importance in view of the consciousness of functioning, enunciation and the 'order of artists' discourse' ('die Redeweise der Künstler'), as Adorno (1970: 236) would have it. Thus, despite the thematic incoherence of its utterances, the postmodern *work* maintains a certain coherence in its enunciation; and it often retains great simplicity, even naïvety, and as its organizing principle a certain harmony that organizes the work 'at least at its vanishing point' (Adorno 1970: 236).

This process of narcissistic self-contemplation (Hutcheon 1980) in the postmodern work, which isolates it proudly from any influence or inheritance of contents by reducing it to the consciousness of its own homeostatic and perpetual mechanism, not only is the distinguishing feature of works created to signify this mechanism (such as Wilson's *I Was Sitting on my Patio . . .*), but also is often taken up again in the *mise en scène* of classical works. Thus, in Grüber's *Bérénice* (1980, Théâtre des Amandiers), Claude Lemaire's scene design indicates theatre's reflection on itself by the presence of a small stage on the larger one where certain actions take place. Sometimes, as in Vitez' *Britannicus*, the actor quotes himself, winks and pushes to their utmost limits baroque irony, bombast and the pathos of situations. In every case, the enunciation's self-consciousness goes so far as to determine meaning, to the point at which the enunciation becomes a parasite on the development of themes and motifs.

The relationship of postmodern theatre and *mise en scène* to the classical heritage goes not by way of repetition or rejection of theme, but by way of inventing another kind of relationship which we can compare with a computer memory. Postmodern theatre is capable of storing cultural references which have been reduced to banal and repetitive bits of information (the language of advertising, ideology or everyday conversation). Storing these bits in memory is accomplished by two speakers repeating exactly the same syntactic patterns (Wilson, *I Was Sitting on my Patio . . .*, *Golden Windows*). As a result, each new bit of information behaves like a rapidly stored and immediately available formula. To this phenomenon of a memory bank, which replaces the classical work's cultural allusions to a weighty heritage, we could add that of refusing notation with a view to preserving or repeating the performance. According to Adorno, the idea of the endurance of works is an element in the category of property; it is as ephemeral as the bourgeois period, and foreign to certain periods and to large productions:

> Beethoven is supposed to have said, on finishing the *Appassionata*, that it would still be played ten years later. Stockhausen's conception, according to which electronic pieces, which are not scored in the traditional way but rather immediately displayed in brute material form, can be erased together with this material is extraordinary as a conception of art which has grand pretensions, but which would nonetheless be ready to be thrown away.
>
> (Adorno 1970: 265)

Stockhausen's music, like Wilson's theatre, can be neither scored nor repeated. The only memory which one can preserve is that of the spectator's more or less distracted perception, or the more or less coherent and concentrated system of its reprises and allusions. The work, once performed, disappears for ever. Paradoxically, it is during the age in which technical reproducibility is nearing perfection that one becomes aware of the non-reproducible and ephemeral nature of theatre, and the futility of trying to reproduce the score so as to repeat the performance. Theatre not only inherits scraps of information churned out daily by the media or banal everyday discourse, but also lends itself to borrowing, association, inheritance. It has an implacable but short memory.

Cutting the umbilical cord linking the work with tradition or heritage has led to mention at the end of history, the 'end of humanism' (Schechner 1982) and of man who, according to Foucault (1966: 398), 'vanishes like a face in the sand at the sea's edge.' It is true that the people who appear in the texts of Samuel Beckett, Peter Handke or Botho Strauss seem to have lost their identities or at least their contours. The human being appears no longer as an individual, historically placed by a radical stage treatment, by a sociohistorical explanation which answers all questions. S/he is also not a number, a cipher, an alienated being or an absurd mode of behavior – as in the theatre of the same name – suffocated, epigonal and finally didactic, but rather a machine for discharging text without being involved in a plausible situation.

So, *Über die Dörfer*, the most recent Handke production at the Théâtre National de Chaillot, does not – despite appearances – present individuals in quest of roots and identity. By letting the discourse unfold, by having a series of speakers who seem incapable of speaking, even if they are gathered together in the same village in order to make one last effort at contact, the text becomes unreadable and incommensurable, like a river or an immense dramatic poem: 'Form is law and law is great and will lift you up . . . keep to this dramatic poem. Go out to meet it always. Go by way of the villages (Handke 1981).

Thus erasure of character, of inheritance, of memory, entails not the end of humanity, despite what misunderstood structuralist slogans may lead us to believe, but rather – and perhaps not any better – an avalanche of discourse which no longer claims to be linked to a visible action in the world, an inheritance which pours out on to its heirs without giving them the choice of accepting, rejecting or selecting the best of it.

MODERN OR POSTMODERN THEATRE

By transforming *modern drama*, by a sort of postmodern *Diktat*, into *postmodern theatre*, we have committed an act of risky imprudence. On the one hand, we no longer know where to place this ephemeral, amnesiac theatre whose written traces we had better find; and on the other, the boundary between modern and postmodern – if we want to get beyond the vague temporal metaphor of the *beyond* (*jenseits, au-delà*) – has no theoretical, generic, geographical or historical foundation. Postmodernism may as well be founded on a postcomplex[9] – everything that comes after me is postmodern; *après moi le déluge*.

The postmodernization of works

In theatre, we may take as a point of departure the hypothesis not only that the stage and performance give life to drama, but also that the practice of *mise en scène* allows us to categorize the dramatic text by treating it in a classical, modern or postmodern fashion.

To convince ourselves, it is enough to consider Chekhov's dramatic work and to distinguish three possible cases delineated by the intervention of the *mise en scène*:

1 *'Classical'* Chekhov would be the unknown Chekhov, the author who was never satisfied with the way in which his plays were produced, whether in the provinces or at the Moscow Art Theatre, and who thought of his works as comedies or vaudevilles. This (imaginary) *auto-mise en scène* would have given rise to a theatre tending towards classical procedure, a well-made plot, well-constructed characters and rigid style of performance, *à la française*, as it used to be called.

2 *'Modern'* Chekhov would be what Stanislavski revealed to us, despite the author's protests in the face of naturalistic excess. This would be *modern*, justified as an author's *mise en scène*; and while it would certainly open up the text and the various voices of the characters, it would promptly close them up again in obedience to the discursive coherence of the *mise en scène*.

3 *'Postmodern'* Chekhov would be the version outlined by Meyerhold (in his critique of Stanislavski) and, to take a concrete example, by Vitez' *mise en scène* for *The Seagull* (1984, Théâtre National de Chaillot). In this case, the work is treated as a text: decentered, without answers, performed no longer as an arrangement of intrigue and agency within the plot, but as a vocal and gestural enunciation. Even if the spectator certainly hears Chekhov's text, he no longer perceives a totality or a center of attraction which would give a clue to the scattered fragments.[10]

Postmodernism in the theatre, rather than postmodern theatre – a rather vague term – is characterized by a number of tendencies and, in listing them, I take the risk of systematization and simplification, which are not any the less problematic for being postmodern.

Some tendencies in postmodern theatre

1 *Depoliticization?* Postmodernism is often equated with the depoliticization of art, absence of a historical perspective, and return of the forces of neoconservatism:

> The *Neoconservatives* welcome the development of modern science, as long as this only goes beyond its sphere to carry forward technical progress, capitalist growth and rational administration. Moreover, they recommend a politics of

defusing the explosive content of cultural modernity. According to one thesis, science, when properly understood, has become irrevocably meaningless for the orientation of the life-world. A further thesis is that politics must be kept as far aloof as possible from the demands of moral-practical justification. And a third thesis asserts the pure immanence of art, disputes that it has an utopian content, and points to its illusory character in order to limit the aesthetic experience to privacy.

(Habermas 1981: 13–14)

According to Habermas' description, postmodernism can be linked to a tangible reaction in the 1970s and 1980s, to a movement of ideological retreat and depoliticization, to what Michel Vinaver (1982) has called the end of 'ideological tyranny which marked the post-war years.' One cannot deny the existence of this political retreat, in contrast to the 1950s and 1960s, this refusal to pose questions in terms of social contradiction; or the difficulty that Marxist philosophy, hitherto dominant among the intelligentsia, has had in regenerating itself in order to get beyond the slogans of brother parties in the east, the short-term instructions of the western Communist parties, and the loss of faith among the intellectuals, treated for too long as negligible and untrustworthy by both right and left. As a result, a 'new philosophy' has arisen, much more cynical and disenchanted, an expert (a bit like postmodern discourse) in the analysis of the cold mechanisms of power and social functioning – whence the extreme distrust in the face of all inheritances, especially that of Marxism, and the fascination with textual manipulation and the deconstruction of every work, classical or modern.

2 *Coherence and totality*. Defiance in the face of the work of art as totality did not come into being with postmodernism: Brecht's theory of epic theatre had already noted: 'there is nothing more difficult than breaking with the habit of treating a performance as a whole' (1974: 91). But this fragmentation can be accomplished only when one becomes accustomed to recentering the work, to completing it and grounding it in the illusion of totality. Only works which are repetitive or fragments of an anticipated whole (the different parts of Wilson's *Civil Wars*, for example) are strong enough to resist the desire for totalizing and reunification.

Nothing any longer seems capable of integrating the work into a larger whole, so great is postmodernism's 'disbelief in the face of metanarratives,' as Jean-François Lyotard (1979: 7) has it. Furthermore, totality is masked by the demand for coherence which reintroduces it and reinstates it on principle.

The apparent incoherence of the postmodern theatre object can be contrasted with the coherence of its mode of function and reception. This coherence has to do with its mode of construction and enunciation. 'Works of art are what is wrought, which would be more than merely made' ('Kunstwerke sind das Gemachte das mehr wurde als nur gemacht') (Adorno 1970: 267). The process of its making and its reception always exceeds the work. For Brecht – who stops at the very threshold of postmodernism – the making and the process are still predicated on what is made, on the meaning to be produced; after Brecht, in the work of Beckett, for example, making and enunciating form a signifier which cannot be reduced to a signified.

3 *Contamination of practice by theory.* In order to appreciate the work – given that we cannot grasp or explain it – we should understand its mode of function. Hence the systematic, conceptual and abstract character of many of these works. Theory overflows into practice; it becomes difficult to separate or distinguish the apparatus of production/reception from the spectator's hermeneutic activity. Postmodern art uses and reinvests theory in the process of producing meaning at every place and moment in the *mise en scène*. Text and *mise en scène* become the stake in a signifying practice, opening up a series of tracks which contradict and cross one another and then separate again, rejecting a central or global signification. The plurality of readings is guaranteed by that of the enunciators (actor, music, global rhythm of the presentation of sign systems), by the absence or the flexibility of the hierarchy of stage systems. The text to be read and the *mise en scène* to be deciphered are no longer the guardians of a meaning that has to be found, interpreted and transmitted. They are no longer construction materials which a committed Brechtian reader would shape in obedience to a specific ideological project. They have become this 'obscure object of desire' which the rhythm of theatrical enunciation constitutes according to a 'multiplicity of points of view' (Brook 1975), or according to the 'infinite variations linking them' (Vitez 1981). It is here that the theories of the text

71

and of the rhythm which affects stage practice coincide; this is the theoretical decision that is the point of departure for a rhythmic, vocal, intonational, choreographic schema which gives a practical meaning to the dramatic text and/or the performance. Theory is no longer nourished by an uncontested a-priori practice; rather theory generates that practice. Postmodern theatre raises theory to the rank of a playful activity; it suggests as the only inheritance the faculty of replaying the past, rather than pretending to recreate and absorb it.

NOTES

1. This chapter first appeared in *Modern Drama* 39, 1 (March 1986).
2. See, in particular, Benhamou and Caramello (1977); Féral *et al.* (1985).
3. The three following pages recapitulate part of my article 'Du texte à la scène: l'histoire traversée,' *Kodikas/Codes* 7 (1984).
4. By *Social Context*, I mean what Mukařovský (1970) calls the

   > relationship to the thing signified, a relationship which has in view, not so much a separate existence – because what is at issue is an autonomous sign – but the total context of social phenomena (science, philosophy, religion, politics, economics, etc.) of the given milieu.

5. According to Alain Girault's formulation (1973: 79). Girault's remedy consists of applying autotextual forms in order to liberate ideology from its effect of transparence:

   > While codes remain visible, while 'theatricality' retains its 'autonomy' with respect to (apparent or essential) 'reality,' the effect of transparence no longer functions. Theatrical – or artistic – form may become 'signifying practice' and thus cease to be the instrument of a revelation of a supposedly pre-existent meaning. It brings about a 'decentering,' by means of which ideology is made visible, put at a distance. To admit to the code amounts, in the same movement, to freeing them from the 'natural' envelope in which the ideology of transparence claims to lock them up.

6. See the debate on clarity in Barthes (1966: 27–35).
7. The following page recapitulates a section of my article 'Du texte à la scène: l'histoire traversée.'
8. 'Interpreting a text does not entail giving it a meaning more or less grounded, more or less free; on the contrary, it means appreciating its plurality' (Barthes 1970: 11). Kristeva defines 'signifying practice' as a 'stage on which is engendered what is understood as structure' (1969: 301).
9. The attachment to novelty for novelty's sake, the pleasure of renaming things, the desire for things *post* – that is, for detaching oneself

POSTMODERN THEATRE

from tradition, the wish to 'be in,' either to identify with groups
who enjoy a certain prestige, or to participate in 'different' activities,
without critically examining the prestige or the 'difference': these are
the traits which belong to the configuration 'fashion' and which have
encouraged the generalization of the semiotic.

(Moser: 1984)

10. See my comments in the Livre de Poche edition of *La Mouette (The
Seagull)* (Paris, 1985).

BIBLIOGRAPHY

Adorno, Theodor W. (1970) *Aesthetische Theorie*, Frankfurt.

Barthes, Roland (1966) *Critique et Vérité*, Paris.

—— (1970) *S/Z*, Paris; trans. Richard Howard (1977) *S/Z*, New York.

—— (1971) 'De l'oeuvre au texte,' *Revue d'esthétique* 3.

—— (1979) 'From Work to Text,' in Josue Harari (ed.) *Textual Strategies:
Perspectives in Post-Structuralist Criticism*, Ithaca, NY.

Benhamou, Michel and Caramello, Charles (eds) *Performance in Post-
Modern Culture*, Madison, Wis.

Blanchot, Maurice (1959) *L'Entretien infini*, Paris.

Brecht, Bertolt (1967) 'Wie soll man heute Klassiker spielen?' [How
should one perform classics today?], *Gesammelte Werke*, vol. 15,
Frankfurt.

—— (1974) 'Alienation Effects in Chinese Acting,' in *Brecht on Theatre*,
trans. John Willett, New York.

Brook, Peter (1975) Interview with Peter Brook, *Travail Théâtral* 18.

Copeau, Jacques (1976) *Régistres* vol. 2, Paris.

Féral, J., Laillou-Savona, J. and Walker, E. (1985) (eds) *Théâtralité, écrit-
ure et mise en scène*, Montreal.

Finter, Helga (1985) 'Das Kameraauge des postmodernen Theaters,' in
C. W. Thomsen (ed.) *Studien zur Aesthetik des Gegenwartstheaters*,
Heidelberg.

Foucault, Michel (1966) *Les Mots et les Choses*, Paris.

—— (1975) *The Order of Things*, London.

Girault, Alain (1973) 'Pourquoi monter un classique?' *La Nouvelle Critique* 69.

Habermas, Jürgen (1981) 'Modernity vs. Postmodernity,' *New German
Critique* 22.

Handke, Peter (1981) *Uber die Dörfer*, Frankfurt.

Hutcheon, Linda (1980) *Narcissistic Narrative, the Metafictional Paradox*,
Waterloo, Ont.

Jouvet, Louis (1951) 'Tradition et traditions,' *Témoignages sur le théâtre*,
Paris.

Kristeva, Julia (1969) *Semeiotikè*, Paris.

Lyotard, Jean-François (1979) *La Condition postmoderne: rapport sur le
savoir*, Paris.

—— (1984) *The Postmodern Condition*, Minneapolis, Minn.

Moser, Walter (1984) 'Mode – moderne – postmoderne,' *Etudes Françaises* 20, 2.

Mukařovský, J. (1970) 'L'art comme fait sémiologique,' *Poétique* 3.

Pavis, Patrice (1983) 'Production et réception au théâtre: la concrétisation du texte dramatique et spectaculaire,' *Revue des Sciences Humaines* 60.

—— (1984) 'Du texte à la scène: l'histoire traversée,' *Kodikas/Codes* 7.

—— (1985a) 'La Réception du texte dramatique et spectaculaire: les processus de fictionnalisation et d'idéologisation,' *Versus* 41.

—— (1985b) *Voix et images de la scène*, Lille: Presses Universitaires.

Rivière, Jean-Loup (1971) 'La pantomime du texte,' *L'Autre Scène* 3.

Schechner, Richard (1982) *The End of Humanism*, New York.

Schulz, Genia (1982) 'Abschied von Morgen. Zu den Müllers,' Frauengestaltungen im Werk Heiner Mullers,' *Text und Kritik* 73.

Szondi, Peter (1956) *Theorie des modernen Dramas*, Frankfurt.

Vilar, Jean (1969) *De la tradition théâtrale*, Paris.

Vinaver, Michel (1982) 'Sur la pathologie de la relation auteur-metteur en scène,' *L'Annuel du théâtre*.

Vitez, Antoine (1974) 'Ne pas montrer ce qui est dit,' *Travail Théâtral* 14.

—— (1977) 'Lecture des classiques. Entretien avec Antoine Vitez,' *Pratiques* 15, 16.

—— (1978) 'Molière: vers une nouvelle tradition,' *L'Ecole et la Nation* 287.

—— (1981) 'Conversation entre Gildas Bourdet et Antoine Vitez sur *Britannicus* de Racine,' *Journal Mensuel du Théâtre National de Chaillot* 1.

—— (1982) 'Le devoir de traduire,' *Théâtre/Public* 44.

—— (n.d.) 'Un plaisir érotique,' *Théâtre de l'Europe* 1.

4

ON THEORY AS ONE OF THE FINE ARTS AND ITS LIMITED INFLUENCE ON CONTEMPORARY DRAMA WHETHER MAJORITY OR MINORITY

Ever since Barcelona, I have kept asking myself, 'Where am I at?' – a question evocative of the 1960s, when theory flourished.[1] For unfortunately I do not belong to a national minority: I am neither Breton, nor Corsican, nor Basque, nor Catalan, nor even Parisian, and the minority which I feel vaguely obliged to defend – theoreticians and semioticians – has been rather overwhelmed (but who's complaining?) by a flood of theatre practices, performances and questions of cultural politics. Subsection no. 9, the last of the whole lot, may well insist that 'theoretical research can contribute something to the development of theatre'; it sounds to me like a gentle provocation and an ironic call to justify theory's right to life by virtue of the beneficial influence that it cannot but exercise on the development of theatre. In short, I find myself called upon in a friendly way to defend not only theory but also minority[2] theory. Thus challenged, and motivated by caution as well as by tactics, I can only begin by affirming that this influence is limited and that theory ought to aspire to the elevated status of an artistic practice. Thus, everything remains to be (re)constructed: a classic situation for a theoretician.

A difficult one too, because the very concept of *minority*, which the mass media employ with a zeal as suspect as it is heartwarming, can refer to many different objects: to a people or a culture, to an oppressed social group, to a limited audience, or to a marginally represented artistic genre. The common denominator of these minorities is doubtless the definition in negative terms of their relation to a dominant majority. Is this sufficient reason to

75

keep the term *minority*, which seems somewhat condescending, defeatist and too closely linked to a long history of bullying and repression? Probably not (and I note in passing the title of the Barcelona convention opposes 'majoritarian dramaturgy' not to '*minoritarian dramaturgy*' but dramaturgy 'of limited impact,' doubtless choosing to neutralize the term by alluding to its limits rather than to its numerical or symbolic inferiority). The very use of the word *minority* is obviously extremely emotionally charged. No point in repressing it, because it will inevitably return.

Having no experience of minorities beyond my daily domestic use of the Slovak language, cuisine and culture, and the interplay of languages which delights rather than distresses me, I have a dispassionate notion of minority. The only thing that matters to me in this experience of minority and majority is not to fall victim to either. To be a victim of the minority, in theory as in society, would mean not being able to do or think anything but minority values; to be a victim of the majority would mean being able to think only in terms of majority values.

I shall thus keep this vague concept – *minority* – because it allows me to treat this (rather folkloric) notion as a metaphor by applying it to my favorite object: theatre theory. Theatre theory is indeed necessarily in the minority, since it is practiced by a limited number of people and mostly after a performance, in a totalizing discourse that is always *a posteriori*, a supplement to the described artistic object.

Minoritarian theory for an art that is itself in the minority: what weight can 'living' theatre carry against the media: television, film and now video? And the theatre that interests us, directors' theatre or research theatre, is also in the minority with respect to commercial theatre. That theory, in particular semiotics, should narrow its field of investigation by specifying the questions asked of the performance and the critical discourse, is of little consequence for either theatre or theory, since both are approached in a marginal and minor way, as theatrical genre and as a particular perspective on this genre.

THEORY AND MINORITY

This objective link between a necessarily 'minor' theory and the minority that it seeks to theorize invites us to reflect on the connections and respective definitions of the terms.

Meaning of 'theory'

A theory implies a relatively coherent group of verifiable hypotheses on the functioning of text and performance. How do we
verify a theatre theory? It does not produce a clear, precise result,
but it does grant us an awareness of the largest array of properties;
in particular, it allows us to understand what is coherent and
planned. Of course, nothing prevents us from setting up partial
theories: about the text, the action, the use of space, the actor,
the global arrangement of the *mise en scène*, etc. Many theories,
at least those in use today, such as dramaturgical, anthropological
or semiotic analysis, borrow concepts and methods from the
humanities, which have refined a series of analytic and explanatory
procedures and formulated a descriptive metalanguage at one or
several levels of the text or performance. Theory tends to general-
ize and to integrate diverse languages into a coherent whole. By
way of hypotheses and hypothetical-deductive procedures, it constructs models that can be modified, often criticized, but are at
least coherent, and which investigate both an internal logic and a
link to a theory of knowledge. Constructing these models entails
a calculated risk, an expenditure and a stake that are justified only
if the discourse produces a coherent meaning and if it can be
transferred to other texts or *mises en scène*, in short if it can be
verified by future theatre practice.

Theory must be distinguished from critical discourse: the latter
demands an immediate, committed, evaluative reaction that cannot
often be verified by the performance; it allows for the right to
error, correction and polemic; it involves a judgment that is not
only aesthetic, but also ideological and moral.

Meaning of 'minority'

Like theory, the question of 'minority' can be grasped from a
number of perspectives: according to the culture and audience of
the theatre, that is according to its differentiation with respect to
a dominant norm, culture or language; according to the limited
audience (in the narrow sense) that this theatre admits, due to its
difficulty or particularism. All that these criteria have in common
is the impossibility of expanding or generalizing about the audience or work produced.

If we bring together the notions of theory and minority, we

obtain the notion of *minority theory*, of which theatre semiotics is a perfect example. We still need to understand how and why semiotics is excluded from majority theory. Majority theory is the theory of no-theory, i.e. the belief that global reflection is unnecessary for the conceptualization of theatre practice, and that intuitive appreciation, without any a priori assumptions, is all we need to understand and enjoy a performance. This theory of non-theory is majoritarian in so far as it rests on an apparent public consensus, often supported by the critics, and according to which performance is a commodity that can be immediately consumed without any preparation, without ordered analytic techniques, without an explicit metalanguage. Such a theory conveys an impression of common sense and innocence and allows itself to joke about theoreticians' abstract and wordy jargon. In short, it always succeeds in getting the laughs on its side.

But he who laughs last laughs longest; for within this anti-theoretical majority, pockets of resistance can be detected; these pockets of resistance, in the minority context, are keen to understand the fabrication of the text or the performance, and even to propose a rudimentary theory of the production of meaning. These theoretical advances appear first as scattered minority formations, but end up by forming a system that is better adapted to the performance and more and more locally consistent. Thus, during the 1960s, structuralism learned to adapt a narratological model to the study of plot. Then, during the 1970s, semiotics transferred – rather mechanically – the notion of the sign and the minimal unit of meaning to the analysis of performance. These theories have arisen from a need to grasp the performance as a whole, by finding some of its laws of composition and functioning. Moreover, they underwent a development similar to that of the avant-gardes: once known, codified, reduplicated, they often become the new norm, the system that allows for a standard conception of a practice that continues to evolve. Thus there is a risk that a sizeable theoretical minority may become majoritarian and normative, therefore in turn obstructing reflection on, and even the evolution of, artistic forms.

Thus structural analysis of narrative tended to limit a brand-new theatre semiotics to a narratological model, ill adapted to the polyphony of performance. A theoretical notion, hitherto in the progressive minority, may eventually lose its theoretical force to the point of slowing down the development of new theories and practices. The notion of director (*metteur en scène*) is an example: at the end of the nineteenth century, the director appeared, appropriately enough, as the central organizer of performance, the author of the *mise en scène*, the one responsible for the link between text and stage, the coordinator of the group working on the performance. Today, this same notion of *mise en scène* conceived as centralization and homogenization of performance takes little account of new acting experiences or open 'decentralized,' decentered *mise en scène*; it reinforces the erroneous idea that the director is the 'homogenous' and 'unitary' author of the performance, that he or she has a personal style totally under his or her control. Further, the notion of *metteur en scène* hides the much more useful notion of *mise en scène* as a structural and collective system of enunciation. One and the same theoretical notion, such as the notion of *mise en scène*, can also be considered as both majoritarian and minoritarian: majoritarian and problematic, when assimilated to the subject or individual genius 'director'; it is minoritarian when seen as as open structural notion, such as collective enunciation.

Theory: minoritarian or minor art?

In every discussion of minorities, we notice both the echo of a complaint in the face of majority imperialism and the compensatory presupposition that the bullied minority is superior to its oppressor. The same is true in my own valorization of minority theory. This partial, ideological attitude is no better at helping us understand the structural influence of a minority on culture or theory, which is our sole consideration here. It might be better to let the debate cool down and not to assume that small is (always) beautiful, but rather to show that the minority imposes on literature and theory a set of constraints that are not necessarily negative, but which give to both literature and theory a unique and original character.

Let us begin with Deleuze and Guattari's remarkable study of Kafka, *Kafka: Towards a Minor Literature*. The authors point out 'three characteristics of minor literature: the deterritorialization of language, the connection of the individual to the political and the collective assemblage of enunciation' (1975: 33; 1986: 18). They focus on three essential characteristics: (1) Prague German as a deterritorialized language; (2) the connection of every individual

79

concern – such as the Oedipus complex – to the political; (3) the arrangement of Kafka's networks of enunciation through the figure of K. From these three characteristics of any minor literature, we can establish three constituent parts of a minor theatre theory, which are both three reductive moments and three ways of 'dreaming the opposing dream to that of a state or official language,' i.e. 'being able to create a minor-becoming.' This 'minor-becoming' could found a minor theatre theory, on the basis of the acceptance of its constraints.

1 *Deterritorialization*: just as, according to Deleuze and Guattari, 'a minor literature does not come from a minor language; it is rather that which a minority constructs within a major language' (1975: 29; 1986: 16), theatre theory is not limited to a restricted group of those people concerned with theatre. It involves the use by a (more methodologically than numerically) limited group of tools, borrowed from semiology or the humanities, within the discourse of criticism there is no point in a new metalanguage, for example in a codified or formalized metalanguage; but a common language is needed to grasp the performance from a new angle. In this respect, theory in general, and semiotics in particular, takes note of the deterritorialization of every critical discourse, of its necessary isolation from the dominant discourse or from any ideology of the self-evident, of its coherence as discourse within discourse on theatre and within theatre itself. At the same time, this deterritorialization is only the first step, which – given every theory's claim to universality – becomes its opposite: a *reterritorialization* of theory within different discourse on theatre, a willingness not to isolate semiotic discourse as a coded language for initiates, but rather to make of it a language which encompasses the global nature of performance, instead of remaining a minority discourse: a *minor* theory, in that it both creates and refuses deterritorialization. In this sense, theoreticians are all 'German Jews' in Prague, or as Miró has it, 'universal Catalans.'

2 *Connection of the individual to the political* (Deleuze and Guattari 1975: 33) is equally valid for theory, at least for the kind that would connect every aesthetic observation, every apparently formal description of performance, to politics, that is to a reflection on the ideology of forms (Pavis 1983). Semiotics examines or should examine the sociocritical dimension of signs, their relation

to discursive and ideological formations, rather than being satisfied with large cosmogonies or typologies of signs (in the Peircian manner, such as Marty 1984).

As Kafka said, 'as a consequence of the interior autonomy of literature, the notion that its links with politics are not dangerous leads to the spread of literature throughout the land, by way of attachment to political slogans' (1951: 209). In the same spirit, Adorno notes the 'double character of the work of art: its social fact and autonomy' (1970: 334; 1986: 320). This convergence of Kafka's minor literature and Adorno's aesthetic theory encourages us to link – within a sociosemiotic of theatre – a theory inspired by psychoanalysis and a theory of ideology which points to the political and aesthetic dimension of performance (Pavis 1983).

3 *The collective enunciation* of every literature is also finally a favored object of theatre semiotics, for the *mise en scène* does not present a central subject, multiplied in several 'sub-subjects,' but a complex arrangement of enunciative instances. Here again, minor theory does not try to describe the individual talents which supposedly express themselves in the *mise en scène*; it rather reconstructs a polyphonic system of enunciation, refusing the distinction (recently reintroduced by pragmatics and speech act theory) between central and derived speech of the author versus individual, primitive speech of the characters (Pavis: 1985a). Instead of this simplistic split which maintains the illusion of the dramatist as a homogenous and coherent subject, semiotics, in the manner of Kafka's and Deleuze's minor art, deals with a collective enunciation whose arrangement must be reconstructed, without any voice taking up a position of mastery, especially not the dramatist or director.

Thus, all these criteria of minor literature can, *mutatis mutandis*, be applied to a *minor theory*, which is all the more likely since this search for a minority theory is not based on criteria of the quality and superiority of the minority as opposed to an oppressive majority, but on the criterion of the marginality of research. Minor theory has difficulty remaining so, as if new majorities might ceaselessly aspire to universality and to take control over a general theory, to move from a minor to a dominant mode of global explication, often not paying attention to their epistemological foundations. Let us describe three cases of this phenomenon of theoretical 'majority-building' in pragmatics, anthropology and semiotics, or at least a certain semiotics.

New majorities in contemporary theatre theory

1 *Pragmatics* has developed not only within linguistics, but also in relation to literature and the study of fictional acts. The universal model of verbal action predominates in theatre studies, particularly in the analysis of dialogue and symbolic action. The model of theatrical dialogue, or the 'dialogical' in Bakhtine's terms, has even been used by a semiotician like Ducrot (1984) to ground a theory of irony, intersubjectivity and the power of words in discourse. Unfortunately, this pragmatics has not succeeded in clarifying the organization of theatrical dialogue, because, despite the references to Bakhtine and to a linguistics of enunciation, it does not take account of the relationship between dialogue and ideology or the multiple subject of psychoanalysis. Ducrot remains too closely linked to a theory of argumentation, content to use a theatrical metaphor within which a speaker sets in motion dialogue among several enunciators (Ducrot 1984: 225). Through this example from pragmatics, we can see the inordinate ambition of a linguistic and rhetorical theory to become a majoritarian and absolute model of theatre discourse, without being able to define the exact relationships between text and intertext, whether ideological or psychoanalytical (see Pavis 1985a, 1985b).

2 *Theatre anthropology* also aspires to universalize an incontestable observation: the authentic involvement of the spectator in the ritual of the theatre phenomenon. Grotowski's anthropological approach, during his paratheatrical period, envisions a hermeneutic act, for instance, in which the stage interrogates the meaning of the spectator's and the actor's intimate experience, without worrying too much about the external details of performance, dismissed as irrelevant to this encounter between actor and spectator and too closely linked to the classification of sign systems. In all these theories of creativity and bodily expression, but also in anti-theoretical deconstruction à la Derrida, anthropology sometimes gives the impression of promoting an anti-theoretical theory, which tries to grasp the ineffable exchange and direct perception of actor and spectator. Answering this Derridean or postmodern approach with a counter-theory is not easy, precisely because it

rejects the external description of semiotics, as well as the intellectual reasoning or global system of the *mise en scène* (see Chapter 3).

3 But *semiotics itself*, our third example, is not exempt from this universalizing malady that undoes the cautious limits of a minor but at least coherent theory. At any rate, this applies to the kind of semiotics that concerns itself with the classification of signs, without contesting their dimensions or even the formation of arrangement of signifiers, and above all carefully avoiding any connection with the Social Context (Mukařovský), especially as regards variations in the situation of reception. Against this kind of semiotics (unfortunately in the majority within minor theory) we could oppose the project of sociosemiotics that rejects both a positivism of signs isolated without reference to the audience's ideological situation and a sociologism preoccupied with statistics on socioprofessional categorization of the audience, or an experimental psychology that describes the spectators' reactions without linking them to an aesthetic reflection on the production of meaning.

In these three new theoretical majorities – pragmatics, anthropology and semiotics – we can see the return of the positivism that Adorno attacked for its ravaging of sociology (1972), an emergence of a blinkered scientism, of a psychology without secure foundation, cancelling any theory that claims to analyse history and society and above all that characterizes the social in the forms and not the extractable content in the work. Theory turning its back on history paradoxically blocks the formation of (other) theories, minor or major: all this ahistoricism might be a Stalinist backlash, a Brechtianism without irony, and a militant but uncritical art.

4 *Theory or theories?* Semiotic theory thus finds itself in a very uncomfortable position, tempted in turn or even simultaneously to withdraw into the ivory tower of a metatheory or a general epistemology of 'performance studies,' to degenerate into a notation technique, and to disintegrate into scattered, partial and isolated discourses on the theatre. This position reflects the disarray of semiotics, accused simultaneously of being too scientistic and systematic, as well as essayistic and hardly reliable. Semioticians who, according to Pierre Bourdieu, were still, in the 1960s,

pursuing the 'old fight of literati and essayists against the "scientism," "positivism," and "rationalism" of the "nouvelle Sorbonne,"' (1984: 155), currently affiliate themselves with the prestige of science:

> this eternally renewed fight against the 'reductive materialism' of the social sciences, this time incarnate in an idealized caricature, is set up in the name of a science that, together with semiotics and structural anthropology, claims to be capable of reconciling the demands of scientific rigor and the worldly elegance of authorial criticism.
>
> (1984: 155)

Bourdieu wisely invites us not to entertain too many illusions about the scientific character of semiotics, which always runs the risk of degenerating into worldly chat or groundless technology. This is the drama of a minor theory aspiring to a majoritarian universalization that would articulate the collection of partial theories: in moments of weakness or theoretical naïvety, this metatheory sometimes claims to be postmodern, although a magic label like this cannot really encompass a new theoretical ensemble by describing the mechanisms that control it (all the same, we can see a difference and a boundary separating it from a modernist or classical model).

Indeed, the very identity of theatre theory is at stake here: is theory plural? Is there not one, but several theories, as Josette Féral (1984: 12) suggests? Can we thus divide theory up without risking the compartmentalization of knowledge, degrading it to the level of techniques of investigation into isolated aspects of performance? Nothing is less certain. What we gain in methodological effectiveness in the description of an element in performance or theatre activity, we lose in global comprehension and epistemological rigor. Theory no longer manages to be a reflection that avoids dividing up knowledge or coherence, but attempts to juxtapose apparently unconnected phenomena, such as gesture, vocal rhythm, the gest of the dramatic text, the apparatus of reception. To speak of *theory* rather than *theories*, to maintain theoretical unity, does not lead us to abandon diversified approaches and methods of analysis; it means maintaining links between results, not splitting off a formal analysis of signs or a sociological enquiry from their links to ideology, but articulating as a whole the functioning of the sign within and without the performance (Pavis

1985b), trying to understand the sign in its auto-, inter- and ideotextuality. The difficulty lies in unifying and homogenizing partial theories without standardizing them. At a time of standardization in cultural and ideological models, this is no easy task.

5 *Standardization of cultural and theoretical models*: the creation of new majorities within minor theory, with all the negative side-effects, is caused by the standardization of cultural and theoretical models, in eastern as in western Europe.[3]

In the west, multinational technocracy, fast-food in mind and print, is paradoxically very well tolerated and even favored by regionalism in local color, and by minority culture, much as one keeps a corner of the garden free of chemical fertilizers in the middle of the countryside otherwise taken over by pesticides. Capitalism has well understood that minoritarian phenomena can be consumed at every level: Breton or Alsatian booths in department stores, festivals for traditional folk music or for theatre of regional cultures, etc. Cultural minorities are spared for electoral reasons, in order to recuperate an ecological movement that by itself cannot find a place on the political chessboard. In Eastern Europe this tolerance for regionalism, folklore or national literatures is accompanied by an unprecedented ideological standardization which can even have a good environmental conscience about protecting minorities on the verge of extinction; these minorities have no rights other than to be folkloric and secondary with respect to the dominant culture (Russian in the Soviet Union for example). We can see in both systems a false concern for the minority phenomenon, which is both marginalized and controlled by a centralized system which rests, in the west, on market control, and in Eastern Europe, on that of the police state of pseudo-socialism.

We can note the same phenomenon – marginalization into folklore or gadgetry – in the role attributed to literary and theatre theory. In Eastern Europe, the obligatory reference to a worn-out Marxism, with a few allusions to structuralism or semiotics by courageous theorists particularly of the Prague School, can only produce a massively majoritarian and immovable theory that cannot adapt to new forms (which are usually identified and repressed). The west, on the contrary, suffers from a surfeit of methods, techniques, systems and theories, which are only partially applied and can no longer be globally conceptualized within a single epistemological frame: we can no longer understand the link between audience surveys, description of stage systems, the pragmatics of enunciation or anthropology, and we take refuge in a cult of efficiency, of fragmentary results, of eclecticism, of consumerism or know-how. In such a maze of theories the audience's confusion is understandable, whether at university or in theatre and media. We can grasp the fascination that Derridean deconstruction exerts on American universities where pragmatic impressionism manages to apply a fresh coat of paint to its battered façade.

But in saying all this in the name of the (good) cause of theory, I am simplifying somewhat. It is precisely in these extreme cases that theatre activity[4] reclaims its rights and discounts (even) the least simplifying theories. I have two encouraging examples, which prove that theatre practice can still deal with the question of minorities, in Eastern Europe – without falling into the condescending tone of state or party – and in the west – without limiting itself to an ethnographic or folkloric conception of minorities.

Performed for the first time in Trnava, in a small town in Slovakia, in 1983, the play *Ako sme sa hladali* ('How we have searched for each other') recounts in a series of tableaux the troubles of the Slovakian nation, covering successive invasions, the Habsburgs in the fifteenth century, the Turks in the seventeenth, Austria-Hungary during the second half of the nineteenth and the Czechs during the first republic. The scenes show the rise of national consciousness, the ruses deployed to preserve language and culture, the endurance of a people whatever the circumstances. Nothing is said about the recent history of the last forty years, but the model of national identity and defence mechanisms of survival make any allusion to the Russians – comrades who came to 'free' the Czechoslovakians – quite unnecessary. The performance can only be understood if one is aware of the unsaid and the implicit: the question of the minority nation (rather than a national minority) is treated without concessions and thanks to spare, simple and concrete stage work that obviates the need for long (and in any case impossible) speeches about oppression.

The second example, western this time, is a recent production by Philippe Adrien, *Franz Kafka's Dreams*, based on the dreams in Kafka's *Diaries*, collected by Felix Guattari and arranged by Enzo Corman. The question of national minority is presented here in allusions to Jewish culture, to Yiddish, to the German spoken in Prague, and to Czech. But it is above all in the relation of the character of Kafka to K., in his confrontations with his father, his mother, his fiancée and certain bureaucratic and police authorities, that the performance engages with the three character-istics of minor literature mentioned above. What stands out is the fragmentation of the dreaming subject's ego, the recurrence of dream images presented by the actors, the music, the text of the diary uttered on stage or off. The *mise en scène* resists the temp-tation to mention the unconscious in terms other than that of the unconscious, to organize the dream material of the *Diaries* accord-ing to a rational logic. The performance takes the position of constituting these materials according to the laws of the uncon-scious itself, placing the spectators, in the minority despite them-selves, in a situation of psychological dispossession so that, when they leave the theatre, they do not know which pertinent element has escaped and what its meaning is: something has happened and I am the witness only after the fact. Thanks to this missing and always partial figuration of the dream, the performance offers an image of this deterritorialization of character and culture, due to the impossibility of appropriating a single homogenous language, of living within a major language without feeling at ease in the minor language. The dream becomes the stage metaphor of this expropriation of character, of meaning, of individual enunciation. It imposes a way of reading and thus a theory of reception, which do not depart from a predetermined grid but which try to grasp the *mise en scène* in the *minor mode*: with Kafka, Deleuze and Guattari as theoretical guides along this journey of initiation, a reterritorialization of theory, a critical reference point in the brute matter of dream and minority language is permissible. This brings theory closer to a creative activity which could be seen as one of the fine arts.

THEORY AS ONE OF THE FINE ARTS

The pleasures of theory

I would like to present this paradox, then, not without provo-cation. The separation of disciplines is supposed to be unques-tioned: practice and creation are supposed to be self-sufficient and only then is theory supposed to graft itself as an accessory, a parasite on creation. I will spare you the familiar connotations that plague theoreticians, 'pompous,' 'verbose,' 'impotent' and 'useless' creatures. As a complement, let me refer you to Barthes' description of the intellectual as seen by Poujade: a mercenary professor, lazy, dry, vain, sterile, cynical and derisive, in short *Parisian* (Barthes 1957: 182–90). (May I remind you that I am not Parisian?) More seriously: if the connections between practice and theory are often experienced in conflict and contradiction, this is the result of a largely romantic conception of art that favors the dramatist/demiurge as alleged genius and creator, that makes the actor a *monstre-sacré* and currently venerates the tyrant-director who incarnates simultaneously the theatre institution and the monopolistic production of meaning. This aesthetic and institutional recognition gives him unique powers, in particular the absolute power – which he is not eager to share with anyone else – to have both ideas and theories about the text to be performed and the means to realize this conception. The apparently natural articulation of knowledge and power, of theory and practice, in the person of the director, has become problematic at every other level, especially when the performance is over. Their reconciliation is henceforth possible only if we stop separating production from reception, in particular in the preparation of the *mise en scène* (with the intervention of the dramaturge before and during rehearsals) and also in the audience reception of the performance (by encouraging the connecting, generalizing power of the spectator, for example) (Pavis 1983, 1985b).

What is at issue is not the mixing of theory and practice in some newfangled practico-theoretical kind of writing, but to show how each activity needs its complement. There have been attempts to mix the different genres by theoreticians (mostly) and also by practitioners. There is a tendency in theoretical (and even more in critical) writing to rival theatrical creation, to make of the commentary a moment of writing with aesthetic or aestheticizing finality, whose stylistic devices attempt to render iconically the work of the *mise en scène*. This 'belletristic' writing has a rather unstable relationship with its object, since it does not use the same medium and is necessarily less convincing because, as critical discourse, it has never quite managed to cut its umbilical cord with the practice of which it is supposed to give an account. Thus it is not really possible to erase the boundary between the two discourses, quite simply because creation and reflection are two different modes of knowledge, which may coincide in a single individual, but not in the same discourse, or only at different moments of the same discourse.

The place of theory

The place – as well as the nature – of theory is at present difficult to determine, because it is ceaselessly displaced in theatre activity: its place is neither exclusively before the performance on stage – in preliminary work on the text – nor exclusively afterwards in a reflective account, but rather at every step of the way. Dramaturgical preparation, if it still occurs, is immediately faced with the actor's activity, testing what is practicable in his or her work; scenographic experimentation is set in motion at the first rehearsal; the actor's activity is continually interrupted by critical assessments and references to the whole stage enunciation. Hence the apparent theoretical withdrawal of many practitioners, the end of references to Brecht and of dramaturgical analysis, do not indicate the elimination of theory, but its displacement and ramification at every level of creation.

Theory is now more intimately associated with practice; it is conceived of as an irreplaceable component of *theatre work (Theaterarbeit)* – that expression of Brecht's that suggests the entwinement of practical reflection and theoretical activity. In order to follow this development of theatre work, we must establish a dialectical model of the production and reception of the dramatic text and performance which goes beyond the classical scheme of communication in terms of emission/reception. As I have already shown elsewhere (Pavis 1983), the production of performance presupposes a theory of the reception situation, and the reception of performance takes on meaning in relation to the Social Context of that reception and the continual revaluation of signifiers and signifieds, as a result of the continual change in the Social Context. In this way, reception and theory are no longer simply dragged in the wake of production and practice. The *mise en scène* is presented at the start – on its productive as well as its receptive side – as the apparatus (*dispositif*) of enunciation, which generates possible meanings, according to the orchestration of the relation theory/practice, production/reception. If minor theory – such as semiotics – was at first deterritorialized and thus isolated in a doctrine that grasps the performance as a whole and from the outside, it now sets in motion – in theory as in practice – a process of *reterritorialization*, while it infiltrates at every level and every moment of the performance.

This reterritorialization is not a compartmentalization of knowledge into partial theories; on the contrary, it means a ramification of this knowledge at several levels of practice. It claims to influence practice, instead of merely being its passive a-posteriori trace. Is this a new version of the tale of the frog (theory) who wants to get bigger than the bull (practice)? Maybe! But simply note that the crisis of minority theory, its deterritorialization and its attempts at reterritorialization, its rhizomatic (in the sense of Deleuze and Guattari) infiltration into theatre work that is a mixture of theory and practice are welcome responses to a crisis in the kind of semiotic theory considered as a simple, somewhat mythical technique of formal description of the performance text.

Crisis of semiotics

The solution to this crisis can be radical: Marco de Marinis speaks of 'the suicide of semiotics as an autonomous discipline' and of its 'reduction to a propædeutic support (or merely to cosmetic terminology)' (1983: 124), a 'closing-down sale of most of its theoretical patrimony and the specificity of the discipline' (1983: 124). The temptation is indeed great, if not to commit theoretical suicide, at least to 'throw out the baby with the bathwater.' This is more or less what Artaud, Derrida, Barthes and Lyotard have done, each in his own way, in the critique of the sign (Pavis 1984). Attacks on the part of traditional positivist criticism (on the rise again) as well as the ghetto situation of semiotics research (even if it is an expansible ghetto) encourage us to do the same. As a discipline with currency only in the gold-plated ghetto inhabited by specialists, semiotics attempts to survive by denying its existence as a discipline and *a fortiori* as a science, and now defines itself as a method. It often becomes a pedagogic activity, a way of sensitizing students to the practice of signs: Anne Ubersfeld does exactly that in *L'Ecole du spectateur* (1982). The publication and subsidy industry have manuals of applied semiotics on their program. I have provisionally resolved my problem of theoretical suicide by distributing to my students a questionnaire on the functioning of the *mise en scène*, without a word about signs or semiotics (see Appendix, pp. 95–7). Is this a pedagogical retreat in the face of terroristic anti-theory? Probably.

90

Obviously, the challenge issued by pedagogical discourse to the performance in pedagogic questions from the spectators' vantage point quickly degenerates into a check list for analysts in a hurry.

Paradoxically, the crisis, in a theory that has been brought down to the level of a recording technique and given up any epistemological pretensions, is not negative; it can even be useful, especially to practitioners who, tired of a weighty, elaborate theory located beyond text and theatre in a socioeconomic dramaturgical analysis (on the Brechtian model, for example), would like to treat the text or performance as multiple and minority theorizing, as plurality of signification, as signifying practice. We will look at only one example of theory flowing over into practice.

Theory overflowing into practice

A. The old dramaturgical analysis that tried to determine the text's signifieds and to display them in performance has been replaced by signifying practices which open up the dramatic text to stage experimentation, not to privilege any interpretation but to sustain a series of tracks that contradict, overlap and again move away from one another, resisting the production of a central or global signification. This plurality of readings is ensured by the multiplication of stage enunciators (actor, music, global rhythm in the presentation of sign systems), by the absence of hierarchy among stage systems (or the continual renewal of this hierarchy). The status of the dramatic text is thus radically changed. It no longer contains the meaning that the *mise en scène* has only to express, interpret, transcribe; it is no longer the 'building material' that a Brechtian reading might shape in the service of a particular ideological project; it has become that 'obscure object of desire' that the rhythm of the stage enunciation constitutes according to 'a multiplicity of points of view' (Brook 1975: 87) or according to the 'infinite variations . . . linked to one another' (Vitez 1981: 4). Obviously, this theory of rhythm (Pavis 1984) has indeed influenced practice; it is in fact the *theoretical* decision by way of a rhythmic vocal, intonational and choreographic scheme that in turn gives *practical* meaning to the text.

B. This example of theory overflowing into practice, this desire to stop separating the machinery (*dispostitif*) of production/reception from the spectator's hermeneutic activity is characteristic of an

91

avant-garde which distrusts any a-priori or univocal theorizing and renews theory and the process of meaning production at every moment of the *mise en scène*. This overflowing is none the less limited to the avant-garde, to a dramaturgy in a minority position within the whole of production. The influence of theory on dramaturgy varies considerably according to the dramatic genre and the majority or minority character of the performance. We will end this discussion with a brief account of theory's visible and hidden influences.

LIMITED BUT PERCEPTIBLE INFLUENCE

If this influence is thus limited, it is first because theory is thought of and sought after in places where we do not expect it: from the first reflections of practitioners on their activity, in their examination of their practice, out of a wish for systematization, effectiveness or the absolute, or out of simple intellectual curiosity. Artists' relations with theory are always indirect, mediated by discourse, debate, by ideas 'in the air' that they cannot escape. I would not go so far as to claim that the desire to create comes from theory, since every desire is defined by its object, not by its origin; creative desire, like theoretical desire (yes, it does exist), emerges from the wish to situate oneself in the world by assuming a point of view, by taking part in the debate of ideas, but also and above all in the debate of forms. Even if theory does not change institutional structures or artistic forms – which develop slowly as a result of long-range ideological and political changes – it is one of the structuring and destructuring factors, especially as regards the always suspended definition of what *makes sense* in theatre.

We ought none the less to state more precisely what dramaturgy we are talking about and state that the term, at least in French usage (*dramaturgie*), does not refer simply to dramatic writing, but includes the work of staging as well, 'stage' meaning more than the physical boards. The influence of theory on stage practice seems more evident than its influence on dramatic writing, since the collective activity of theatre is more exposed to a global reflection on the practical realization of performance. In so far as all dramatic writing truly exists only when produced on stage and received by the audience, it too is influenced by theoretical reflection.

Influence on majority dramaturgy

Commercial majority

In theatre's whole private sector, in the sphere of 'boulevard' or 'bourgeois' theatre, theory has almost no influence, or perhaps even negative influence, in so far as commercial theatre hates any intellectual pretensions to theory and to doubts cast on its ideological and economic mechanisms. Such pretensions have even been the subject of satire (as in *Le Tournant* by François Dorin, which takes issue with intellectuals and the avant-garde). Dare we say that theory's influence on this kind of theatre is no more limited than this theatre is anyway? An elitist remark, no doubt, but why bother to theorize about a kind of theatre that gets by with tried and tested recipes, that only takes any interest in sociological reflection so as to find out how the market and audience tastes are developing?

Ideological majority

The case of an ideologically dominant dramaturgy is much more delicate. Unfortunately, it is most easily found in Eastern Europe, where state control and censorship of the repertoire are absolute.[5] The paradox is that technical and acting standards are generally very high, but the imposed range of themes does not interest the public. The only theoretical innovation that can take place consists of a formal renewal or technical perfection; it never challenges the institution or the society beyond. As a result theory has the perverse effect either of attaching itself to an external discourse that has no place in the *mise en scène*, or of contributing to an empty virtuosity in the actor and all the artists involved in the production.

National majority in the mise en scène of classics

The subsidized theatre sector, at least in France and (West) Germany, is supposed, among other things, to preserve the classical repertoire. Theory had its hour of glory with Brechtianism and more generally with the critical approach to great myths, themes or texts. Brechtian theory corresponded not only to a vast process of democratizing theatre, but above all to the apotheosis of a

93

visual conception of theatre: everything – especially contradiction – had to be more 'readable' than 'visible,' and had to be imposed on the actor's body, on the arrangement of groups, on the stage. Reality had to be indicated in self-critical signs: 'dramatic art should not express the real as much as signify it' (Barthes 1964: 87). The conjunction of Marxism (its assimilation of economic, sociological and affective structures) and a semiotics of the visible made readable has provided dramaturgy with a theoretical and practical model for the analysis of society and its theatricalization. This means a considerable advance, which none the less owes its steady decline only to the monolithic ideology of regimes that continue to refer to Marxism and to a critical theory of society, while practicing imperialistic and dogmatic politics. But the decline and fossilization of this theorizing can also be explained by the arrival and competition of other disciplines – psychoanalysis, anthropology, linguistics, 'nouvelle histoire,' etc. – which have invaded critical discourse, but which can no longer get along or coexist within the discourse of the *mise en scène*. We have already noted the reaction of 'signifying practice' that claims to take account of these new languages without, however, permitting influence on or closure of the interpretation.

This reaction to global theorizing, like the reaction to Brechtian dramaturgy, may seem to be a rejection of theory, and of the too-precise directives of sociosemiotics, a transfer of power to the salesmen of the ineffable. In fact, the issue is rather that of the relocation of theory to other levels, of the unhappy irony of a *mise en scène* determined to deprive itself of illustration, commentary or explanation. The reterritorialization of theory within a theory of rhythm and stage enunciation creates a new paradigm, which owes nothing to the representation, readability or exteriority of sign or plot, but grounds itself on a more intuitive and internalized reading of the text considered as symbolic action and temporal flow.

Influence on minority dramaturgy

Minority of the avant-garde

It is precisely in this paradigm change, in this crisis and doubt about the power of semiotics, that theory's influence is most evident, as we have seen. In this case too, we need to distinguish between minority in a cultural and ethnological sense and the minority audience for the avant-garde. Let us leave aside the latter, having commented on it at length, and focus on the collusion between theatre and creation. It has even been suggested that the avant-garde no longer distinguishes or even separates the production from the reception of performance.

Cultural minority

Minority cultures can take advantage of their numerical inferiority and the solidarity reflex of a group under threat:

> The memory of a small nation is no shorter than that of a large one; it reworks the available material all the more thoroughly. It will not concern literary historians much, but this literature is less the concern of literary history than that of the people, and is thus preserved, if impurely. For the demands that national consciousness makes to individual members of a minor nation requires the readiness of each to get to know that part of the literature that is his lot, to support and defend it, to defend it even if he neither knows nor supports it.

> (Kafka 1951: 208)

We could – and perhaps should – take what Kafka magnificently describes, i.e. the profound (re)working of minoritarian material, and make this the emblematic figure of every culture of limited range and the goal of our theatre theory and our responsibility as intellectuals. For, even if they are in the minority and even minor, misunderstood or despised, this culture and this theory are none the less our *raison d'être*.

APPENDIX

1. Mise en scène:
a) what holds elements of performance together
b) relationships between stage systems
c) coherence or incoherence (of the reading of the text, of the *mise en scène*): on what is it founded
d) aesthetic principles of the production
e) what do you find disturbing about the production: strong moments and boring moments

2. *Stage design*:
a) forms of urban, architectural, stage, gestural space
b) relationship between audience space and acting space
c) system of colors and their connotations
d) principles or organization of space: relationship between what is on stage and what is off stage; connection between space used and fiction of play staged; relationship between what is shown and what is hidden

3. *Lighting system*: nature, link to fiction, performance, actors

4. *Objects*: nature, function, relationship with space and body; system of their use

5. *Costumes*: function, system, relationship to actor's body

6. *Actors' performances*:
a) individualized or typical acting style
b) actor's relationship with group: moves, blocking, trajectory
c) text/body and actor/role relationships
d) gesture, mimicry, makeup
e) voice: quality, effect on hearer, relationship to diction and singing

7. *Function of music, sound, silence*:
a) nature; relationship to fabula, to diction
b) when does it occur

8. *Rhythm (pace) of performance*:
a) rhythm of signifying systems (exchange of dialogues, lighting, costumes, gestuality)
b) overall rhythm of performance: continuous or discontinuous rhythm, changes, connection with staging

9. *Reading of the story (fabula) by this* mise en scène:
a) what story is being told
b) what are the dramaturgical choices
c) what ambiguities are there in the text and how does the *mise en scène* clarify them
d) how is the fabula structured
e) how is the story constructed by the actor and the performance
f) what genre of dramatic text is this, according to this *mise en scène*

10. *Text in performance*:
a) characteristics of translation (if applicable)
b) what place does the *mise en scène* give the dramatic text
c) relationship between text and image

11. *Spectator*:
a) within what theatrical institution does the production take place
b) what were your expectations of performance (your wishes, knowledge, information given in the program)
c) how did the audience react
d) spectator's role in the production of meaning; is the suggested reading univocal or plural

e) what images, scenes, themes have you retained

f) how is the spectator's attention manipulated by the *mise en scène*

12. *How to notate (photograph or film) this show*

13. *What cannot be semiotized (i.e.) put into signs):*

a) what, in your interpretation of the *mise en scène*, makes no sense

b) what cannot be reduced to sign and sense (and why), what escapes notation

14. *What special problems should be looked at*

15. *Any other comments on this production or the questionnaire.*

NOTES

1. This is the text of a lecture in Barcelona during the *Congrés internacional de teatre a Catalunya*, 1985.
2. Translator's note: Following current (Anglo?) American usage, I have used the noun and adjunct 'minority' wherever the meaning is 'of the minority.' Only on the occasions when the meaning is explicitly 'advocating the power of the minority' do I use the (necessary) neologism 'minoritarian.'
3. Translator's note: The text has 'à l'ouest comme à l'est.' To avoid confusion with the 'Orient' (the more immediate connotation in English), I have translated 'à l'est' as 'in Eastern Europe,' so as not to obscure Pavis' ideological point.
4. Translator's note: In most cases, I have translated 'travail' by 'activity' to convey the text's sense of dynamic as opposed to finished work.
5. This, obviously and happily, is no longer true in 1992!

BIBLIOGRAPHY

Adorno, T. W. (1970) *Ästhetische Theorie*, Frankfurt: Suhrkamp; trans. C. Lenhardt (1986) *Aesthetic Theory*, London: Routledge & Kegan Paul.
—— (1972) *Der Positivismusstreit in der deutschen Soziologie*, Berlin: Luchterhand.
Barthes, R. (1957) *Mythologies*, Paris: Seuil; trans. Annette Lavers (1973) *Mythologies*, New York: Hill & Wang.
—— (1964) *Essais critiques*, Paris: Seuil; trans. Annette Lavers (1968) *Critical Essays*, New York: Hill & Wang.
Bourdieu, P. (1984) *Homo Academicus*, Paris: Editions de Minuit.
Brook, Peter (1987) *The Shifting Point*, New York: Harper & Row.
Deleuze, G. and Guattari, F. (1975) *Kafka: pour une littérature mineure*, Paris: Editions de Minuit; trans. Dana Polan (1986) *Kafka: Towards a Minor Literature*, Minneapolis: University of Minnesota Press.
Ducrot, O. (1984) *Le Dire et le dit*, Paris: Editions de Minuit.
Féral, J. (1984) 'Pourquoi la théorie?' Unpublished manuscript.
Kafka, F. (1951) *Tagebücher, 1910–1923*, Frankfurt: Fischerverlag.

Marinis, Marco de (1983) 'Semiotica del teatro: una disciplina al bivio?', *Versus* 34.

Marty, R. (1984) 'Bases pour une théâtrologie,' Paper given at the Association internationale de sémiologie du spectacle, Royaumont.

Pavis, P. (1983) 'Production et réception au théâtre: la concrétization du texte dramatique et spectaculaire,' *Revue des sciences humaines* 60, 189.

—— (1984) 'Reflections on the crisis in postmodern theory and theatre,' Paper given at a conference on 'The Question of the Postmodern, Cornell University, April (trans. Loren Kruger).

—— (1985a) 'Einige Bemerkungen zur Konkretisation am Beispiel von Čechov's *Die Möwe*,' *Semiotik der Theaterrezeption*, Tübingen: Narr Verlag.

—— (1985b) 'La Réception du texte dramatique et spectaculaire: les processus de fictionnalisation et de l'idéologisation,' *Versus* 41.

Ubersfeld, A. (1982) *L'Ecole du spectateur*, Paris: Editions sociales.

Vitez, Antoine (1981) 'Conversation entre G. Bourdet et A. Vitez,' *Journal du Théâtre National de Chaillot* 1.

5

THEATRE AND THE MEDIA: SPECIFICITY AND INTERFERENCE

THEATRE WITHIN A THEORY OF MEDIA

Mediatization of theatre

Inscribing theatre within a theory of media presupposes – rather hastily – that theatre can be compared with artistic and technological practices like film, television, radio or video. That involves comparing theatre with what is usually opposed to it: (mass) media, technical arts, the techniques of the culture industry. We would do theatre a disservice by measuring it against media grounded in a technological infrastructure that it has done without; we would also endanger its specificity. On the other hand, however, theatre practice happily moves into other areas, either by using video, television or sound recording in the performance, or responding to the demand for television, film or video recording, reproduction or archival preservation. Exchanges between theatre and the media are so frequent and so diversified that we should take note of the ensuing network of influences and interferences. There is no point in defining theatre as 'pure art,' or in outlining a theatre theory that does not take into account media practices that border on and often penetrate contemporary work on stage. But can we go so far as to integrate theatre in a theory of media and so compare it to technical arts and practices? Besides, what are *media*?[1] The notion is not well defined. Media might be defined by a sum of technical characteristics (possibilities, potentialities) according to the technological way in which the artistic product is produced, transmitted and received, reproducible to infinity. The notion of media is thus not linked to content or theme, but to the current apparatus and state of technology,

99

None the less, this technology of technical reproduction and production of the work of art implies a certain aesthetic, which is useful only when concretized in a particular individual work, aesthetically or ethically judged. Discussing novelistic technique, Sartre said that every technique points to a metaphysics. We could say the same thing of the technology of media; it makes sense only when linked to aesthetic or metaphysical reflection on the passage from quantity (reproduction) to quality (interpretation). Technically describing the properties of media such as radio or television is not enough; we must appreciate the *visible* dramaturgy as we see it in a given broadcast or as we foresee it for a future production. I would like to invite the reader on this journey, which requires no particular knowledge of computer science.

The study of media is part of our main project of cultural studies. In western society one usually defines three types of culture (Abastado 1982):

1 *A culture defined in anthropological terms*, which is direct and oral: knowledge and wisdom are closely linked to experience; culture is transmitted by word and action; it is a relation between individuals, which consists in exchanges and often reciprocity.

2 *A written culture*, which is created by the writing, the culture of the 'Gutenberg galaxy' (McLuhan) which

> introduces a type of ambiguous social relationship, a simulacrum of dialogue, a false dual relation. Whoever owns this culture, or writes about it, pretends to talk to another speaker; in fact, it addresses readers whom he does not know and from whom he does not expect any reply: this communication is unidirectional, without any feedback; the book culture isolates the individual, makes of him a reader locked up in his silence.
>
> (Abastado 1982: 7)

3 *The media culture*, which is controlled by private or state institutions; it produces and diffuses all kinds of messages for a large audience. We will limit ourselves here to the study of film, radio, video, television in their connection with 'living theatre.'

Media in relation to theatre

One could write a chronological history of inventions in the media, showing their connections and technical improvements. It would be possible to situate theatre in relation to these technical stages, before the advent of the media and afterwards, in reaction to technological development. This is too difficult a task, so I will only show the opposing tendencies of theatre and media. Theatre tends towards simplification, minimalization, fundamental reduction to a direct exchange between actor and spectator. Media, on the other hand, tend towards complication and sophistication, thanks to technological development; they are by nature open to maximal multiplication. Inscribed in technological but also in ideological and cultural practices, in a process of information and disinformation, media easily multiply the number of their spectators, becoming accessible to a potentially infinite audience. If theatre relationships are to take place, however, the performance cannot tolerate more than a limited number of spectators or even performances because theatre repeated too often deteriorates or at least changes. As a result, theatre is 'in essence' (i.e. in its optimal mode of reception) an art of limited range.

Quantification and massification

The possibility of indefinitely repeating and diversifying mass media production affects the audience's tastes and expectations much more actively than the occasional visit to the theatre. We could thus distinguish between media or arts which have to be sought after and actively constructed such as theatre or video (in so far as we have to go to the theatre or preselect a video cassette) and those media that are *immediate*. ready-made, and almost compulsory, present almost without being summoned (we switch on the TV or radio as automatically as an electric light). This active/passive criterion is none the less rather tenuous and does not prejudge the spectator's activity in the necessary process of reception and interpretation, whether one is deciphering the performance of a classic or following a western. Media do not in themselves – by way of their technological possibilities – favour activity or passivity. Rather it is the way in which they structure their messages and utilize them according to a dramaturgy and a

101

strategy that stimulate the spectator's activity to a greater or lesser extent.

Theatre, media and the spectacular

In what system of the arts, in what classification, in what theory of art or the media can we place theatre? To say that these practices are linked to a theory of performance does not mean much since, if all human activity can be turned into a performance (*spectacularisable*) for a spectator, not everything is spectacular in the ordinary sense of the term. We will use the French terms.

Arts du spectacle (*performing arts*) is the most general and neutral designation; it allows for the inclusion of any new practice in which an object is submitted to the gaze of a subject (thus including peepshows, striptease, lectures, debates, etc.). Other groupings exist, which do not always allow for a differentiation of theatre and media:

arts de la représentation (*representational visual arts*): this term underlines the representational function of theatre and cinema, but also painting or any activity that produces a representation of the world

arts de la scène (*the arts of the stage*) are linked to the live unmediated used of the stage

arts mécanisés (*technically reproduced arts*) comprise all techniques of recording and reproduction that produce the same artistic message on every occasion, with the proviso that a product (a symphony or film) reproduced x times loses some of its substance when it is received innumerable times, the experience of vision being in inverse proportion to its repeated presentation and perception.

The double game of the media . . . and theatre

At first glance, what differentiates the media from the theatre is the double status of their fictionality: a television or radio broadcast presents itself sometimes as real (as in news broadcasts) and sometimes as fictional (telling a story). Airwaves are thus used for needs which we normally separate and spectators must continually work out the status of what they see on the screen or what they hear: fact or fiction? Different media have distinct markers that indicate their fictional status; theatre likewise plays on the two levels of fact and fiction, since its story is continually supported by reality effects and remarks that give this discourse credibility. Conversely, we could also note that TV news has its own story-line, its own narrativity, as well as zones of pure fiction and invention.

In order to sketch a theory of media that would grant space to theatre practice, we have to confront a few specific features of several media, comparing them to a minimal(ist) theatre. Establishing a general theory of the media and performing arts depends on the possibility of this confrontation and comparison.

DRAMATURGY AND SPECIFICITY OF THE MEDIA

Table 5.1 on pp. 104–7 invites us to compare media and theatre on the basis of their relationship to the spectator, their conditions of production and reproduction, their dramaturgy, specificity and fictional status: criteria which have in view the evaluation of technological potential and semiotic use.

Without commenting on every element in the schema, we will return to several particular key points, such as dramaturgy, specificity and fictiveness.

The damaturgy of radio

Character exists only through voice. Radio voices must be unusual and inimitable. The characters' voices must be very distinct, chosen according to a system that typifies the speakers. This casting procedure is a fundamental step in preparing a radio broadcast.

Time and space are suggested by changes in vocal intensity, distancing effects, echo and reverberation. A frame is created by sound or music that opens and closes the sequence; the place of action is immediately situated, then 'removed' at the end of the sequence. This framing device, the position of the microphones, volume control, sequence of characteristic sounds provide spatial-temporal orientation for the hearer. The possibility of intensifying

103

Table 5.1 Theatre and media: a comparison of their specificity

	Theatre	*Radio*
1. Relationship between production and reception	relatively stable and based on human body	body reduced to voice and ear: impoverishment but also enlargement
1.1. Voice	delivered and received 'naturally'	body reduced to voice
1.2. Audience	present during production	live but remote
2.1. Signifier	varied and live	limited and mediated
2.2. Mode of representation	stylization despite appearances	metonymic representation
3. Conditions of production	simplified, tends to use elaborate technology	mass medium: stable technology, diversified institution
3.1. Reproduction	live and non-technical	technical but live if desired
3.2. Distribution and reception	live, in unique time and place; necessarily active construction of meaning	ubiquitous distribution of listeners; inattentive reception possible – radio as background
4. Dramaturgy	extreme variety in historical forms	reuses theatrical dramaturgy with some specific research (voice, sound-frame, etc.)
4.1. Specificity	sought after through history, currently in doubt	technological specificity but hybrid thematics and usage

continued on next page

Cinema	Television	Video
photographed body gives a reality effect	immediate broadcast but no immediate feedback; phatic communication to keep viewer on one channel; extreme mediated relation to advanced technology	significant mediatization, but can be reinserted into live performance
reality effect of voice, but delocalized sound	voice has limited effect	limited effect
maximum mediation	variable mediation; possible live broadcast	extreme mediation
signifier of signifier	possible confusion between signifier and referent	signifier subject to infinite modification
representational enlargement	representational reduction	extreme reduction of representation; loss of information
advanced technology closely linked to commercial institutions	mass medium *par excellence*: complex production apparatus weighty institution	needs advanced technology but still accessible to individual use
technical, detached from productive instances, tied to institution	technical, linked to institution, live or delayed broadcast	technical support for TV, private technological sophistication
in diverse locations, absolutely distinct in time and relatively in space	in private interiors, choice determined by available programs; TV set has significant place in daily life	linked to TV (recordings), live, in theatre or installation
problematic search for 'cinematic language' based too rigidly on image	little specific research for TV dramaturgy, audiovisual adaptation for TV use	identity crisis in relation to TV image, experiments without clear theorization, especially for fiction
problematic search for 'cinematic language' based exclusively on image	hardly any; often adapts theatre dramaturgy to screen production	takes up research abandoned by TV; simple technique enables experimenting with montage and rhythm of image

Table 5.1 Continued

	Theatre	Radio
4.2. Framing	fixed by stage/house relation and semiotic framing of events	sound framing
4.3. Norms and codes	historically known and categorized	limited number of norms, as regards radio play as opposed to music
4.4. Repertoire	dramatic texts according to author and period; different *mises en scène* of same text possible; repertoire of exemplary *mises en scène*	not well known, often no trace of script of a radio play; product is complete, can be rebroadcast in entirety only
5. Fictional status	presents itself as fiction, despite reality effects	coexistence of 'pure' fact and 'pure' fiction, with mutual contamination
5.1. Indices of fictional status	no	yes

or reducing the sound, of having an actor speak closer to or further away from the microphone, lets us know immediately of a change of frame or movement within the same frame.

A series of 'shifters,' of musical or acoustic leitmotifs between sequences or spaces, allows for the identification of speakers and location in time and space. Often, the editing suggests an erasure of different time frames, composing an interior monologue. Rhythmic patterns, repetitions and almost musical variations can produce an effect of physical interiority, setting up exchanges between the visible and the audible. The pleasure of this perception rests on the hallucination of the hearer, who hears everything and see nothing: the text's enunciation by actors and transmission give the hearer the impression that the action takes place elsewhere.

More than any other medium, radio is the art of metonymy, of convention, of meaningful abstraction. It is left to the author

Cinema	Television	Video
framing fundamental to image-making before and after narrative montage	as in cinema, with supplementary constraint of small screen	as in TV, with even more impoverished image
specific and non-specific norms	norms not yet well known	pop video norms not well known; norms rejected in video art; no distance for definition
published scripts pale shadow of film; possible (teaching or specialist) repertoire of classics	INA* archives closed to public; vast, but unreliable memory bank	difficult to establish repertoire, because of unclassified diversity
distinction between documentary and fiction film	as in radio	information (control with closed circuit) or fiction (music video/MTV)
yes	yes	yes

* Institut National de l'Audio-visuel

to provide those indispensable points of reference that will allow the listener to grasp the coherence of the narrative and the organization of the fictional world without any great effort of memory.

The dramaturgy of television

Let us leave aside the issue of the live or deferred broadcast of a pre-existing theatre performance: such a procedure is still a form of reporting, and meaning is quoted but also lost (although, in the case of a live broadcast, it keeps some authenticity). Dramaturgy for the TV film (or the play made for TV) rests on a few general principles:

The image must be framed precisely, composed carefully so as to be easily read, given the small dimensions of the screen. Hence a stylization, an abstraction of elements in set and costumes, a systematic treatment of space. The miniaturization of the image leads to an increased importance of the sound-track.

The sound, by virtue of its quality and proximity, ensures the greatest reality effect. Language carries well on television, better than in cinema, and often better than on stage, since it can be modulated, transmitted 'off-screen,' adapted to the situation and the image: the 'delocalization' of sound in the image is much less noticeable than on a large screen. Television is often nothing more than visual radio: we listen to it in a way that is both private and distracted, as if to a close and convincing voice, whose image is only the confirmation of vocal authenticity.

The sets are usually noticed only piecemeal, as they appear behind the actors, except when the camera provides a close-up or a panorama so as to emphasize a detail or establish atmosphere. The sets for shows filmed in studios (up to *c.* 1965 in France) remained close to theatrical stylization; since then, work on location has provided an environment similar to that of film, and the reality effect has been attained at the expense of clarity and stylization.

Lighting is rarely as varied or as subtle as in the theatre or cinema; it has to accommodate black-and-white televisions, and so accentuate contrasts and treat luminous areas carefully.

Editing plays on the effects of heavy punctuation, dramatic breaks, lingering moments. The narrative must be readable, coherent, and quick-paced to maintain suspense.

Acting: the camera focuses on the speaker-actors, usually in medium-long shot (*plan américain*), so as to show their psychological and physiological reactions. Too many close-ups in color risk revealing skin imperfections. Like the other elements of film and screen, the actor is nothing more than an element integrated into the director's industrial and signifying apparatus. Hence a certain 'disembodiment': the actors exist only in their fragmentation, their metonymy and their integration into filmic discourse.

Plot and theme are certainly variable, but usually refer to social reality, to journalism, to daily life. This kind of narrative lends itself to serials. Inheritor of the trivial literature of the chapbook and melodrama, TV drama sticks to stories along safe lines, with unhappy heroes, unstable destinies. Television drama is consumed the same way as television news, weather or commercials. News takes on the appearance of a show on a large scale, with blood, deaths and marriages as in soap opera. Conversely, TV fiction maintains a basic realism and the feel of daily life; it lends itself best to a naturalistic repertoire and to an aesthetic of reality effects.

Mise en scène for television arises out of the preceding elements; it is the vast assembly line on which framing and editing determine the hierarchy and correlation of all components of the TV film. The more perceptible the coherence, the closer form moves toward identity with content and the more TV dramaturgy proves its specificity, thus moving successfully from *theatron* to *electron*.

The dramaturgy of video

We notice in video the same double status of fact and fiction as in radio and TV. The medium is used, on the one hand, to observe, note, record facts; on the other, to produce fictions, as in cinema or TV. Pop video sets up a narrative based on image sequences, which place the singer or illustrate the lyrics with shots that have a vague thematic connection with the words or musical atmosphere. The dramaturgy of these videos is based on a spatio-temporal anchoring of the song and on the attempt to link enunciator (singer) and utterance (song), so as to make the image alternately a visual commentary on the words and an anticipation of what the following words will say.

Specificity of radio

Words: the audience rarely just listens to the play. The transistor multiplies the locations where theatre penetrates. Radio restores an intimate, almost religious quality to the word; it returns us to the Edenesque state of a purely oral literature. Without being completely stuck in one place (as when watching theatre or TV), the radio listener is in something close to a daydream or fantasy. Listeners to a radio play conduct a sort of interior monologue; their bodies are as though dematerialized as they receive the amplified echo of daydreams and drives.

The fiction: the radio play is linked to a fiction, even if this aspect is not always clearly recognized by the audience (cf. the panic caused by Orson Welles' broadcast in 1938). As opposed to reporting, news and discussions, radio fiction uses voices impersonating characters and creating an imaginary world. It gradually frees itself from journalism, from linear information, from the dialogic form and realism in voice and action.

Studio production: unlike the stage, the studio is an immaterial space which supports the fabrication of sounds, the montage of voices or the synchronization of voice, noise and music. The listener has the illusion that the aural performance is manufactured and broadcast at the moment of its reception.

Types of radio plays:

1 live theatre broadcast: during the early years of radio, plays were often broadcast live from theatres in Paris. The set and stage business were described by a commentator. This practice continues with live broadcasts from the Comédie-Française. Neither theatre nor radio, this kind of broadcast is more a documentary than an original work

2 dramatized reading from the studio

3 radio play with recognizable character voices, dialogue, conflict, as in naturalist drama.

4 epic radio play: dramatizing a character or a voice

5 interior monologue

6 collage of voices, noises or music

7 electronic simulation of human voices using synthesizer and musical work on voice and noises.

Specificity of television

Defining the specificity of television is as difficult as looking for the essence of theatre. Let us begin with Patrick Besenval's proposition:

If we look for the real specificity of television, we quickly come to the following definition: 'Television is nothing other than the *domestic reception of audiovisual messages* that appear on the screen *at the very moment* that they are transmitted.' That is: something that pertains simultaneously to serials and film, as well as actual perception. In other words, television is first of all *a program*, second *'film in one's own living room*,' and last, the feeling of *immediate contact* with 'the world,' culminating in the live broadcast.

(Besenval 1978: 14)

But, once again, the subject is so vast that we will focus more precisely on the issue of television filming theatre, so as to observe the shock of their conflicting specific qualities.

The situation of reception: the television set occupies a central place in the home; it is the magnetic point and the umbilical cord connected to a 'somewhere else' that is difficult to locate. Voluntary or involuntary interruptions of the broadcast are possible and TV viewers, wooed by a number of other programs, are fundamentally unstable beings; hence the difficulty of fixing them to their seats and interesting them in a performance that is more rapid than the stage version which lasts three hours or more. The *mise en scène* of a performance made for TV must never be boring or lose its narrative power.

The mediations between producers and receivers are infinite: not only technological mediations, but also interference and semiotic transformation of meaning in the different phases of the actors' work, first in the theatre, then in the studio, then in the framing and editing of the film or video, finally in the adaptation and miniaturization for the small screen.

The erasure of theatricality: the TV director of a pre-existing theatre performance or of a TV movie can choose either to erase the most visual and stagy aspects of theatricality by looking for 'cinematic effects,' and naturalizing the acting style and sets, or to display this theatricality, underlining it with an abstract set and half-sung diction, as if the camera were reporting from the theatre itself.

Principles of the transposition of theatre to television: in theatre,

111

the spectators themselves sort out the signs of the performance, but in television (as in cinema) a meaningful indication has already been set up through framing, editing and camera movements. In the transmission of a theatrical *mise en scène*, this means that the cinematic *mise en scène*, has the 'last word' on the meaning of the performance. The most compact and complete theatrical object is thus deconstructed and reconstructed in filmic discourse, during filming and editing, and in television discourse (miniaturization, private and deferred reception and so forth). All this supports the notion of a dramaturgy that is specific to television.

Specificity of video

Because of its recent origin and the diversity in its use, video cannot be reduced to a series of specific features. We would have to specify the definition of the image used in video: 300–450 lines for portable video, 625 for TV. Video can also paradoxically produce the effect of a theatre event: closed-circuit video can have an effect of presence and eventfulness; it becomes the theatre of a technical event. Hence the dual relationship to theatre: in theatre, the performance is ephemeral, but the text is permanent; in video, the performance is permanent, but the discourse, meaning and text are ephemeral.

Fictional status of the media

Theatre presents itself as fiction, but this fiction is comprehensible only because perceived reality-effects intervene to authenticate it. Radio and television programming do their best to separate fact from fiction. To do this, they make use of fictional indicators: the anchor's announcement of the program and its content, the credits, the fact that we already know the journalists, their repeated allusions to the deictic situation of non-fictional communication, the assurance that the journalists are trying to get to the truth and so on. The use of voice, the foregrounding of aesthetic devices signaling fiction or fact enable us to recognize the fictional status of the broadcast. The fact that the listener or viewer rarely makes a mistake here, even when tuning in in the middle of a program, proves the effectiveness of this discrimination.

112

INTERFERENCES BETWEEN MEDIA

We have established that a unified theory of the performing arts, including theatre and the media, is very problematic. It is as difficult to understand the mechanisms of interference and contamination among various media and between theatre and media.

Leaving aside the fundamental question of the economic factors determining media development (see Busson 1983, 1985; Mattelart 1979; Flichy 1980), we will concentrate on evaluating the interdependence and interaction of the media. We can distinguish two types of influence.

1 *Technological influence* (==›). Development in one medium can affect others, by making available new technical possibilities which can also modify other media. We begin with the hypothesis that there is a technological and aesthetic struggle among the various media, that each evolves and is contaminated by another. As Alain Busson notes,

> the new medium offers broader possibilities for programming and broadcasting than hitherto existing media. The cost of production is much less if one relates it to the potential audience and the means of purchase are simpler and financially more attractive to the consumer.
>
> (Busson 1985: 103)

The aesthetic consequences of this rearrangement are our concern here: 'the dominated medium is not only obliged to redefine its social and economic role with respect to the new medium that dominates it, but is equally required to reposition itself aesthetically' (Busson 1985: 103).

2 *Aesthetic influence* (——›). Technological progress has aesthetic consequences for the media, either by modifying their meaning or their potential, or by creating new meaning. New possibilities of diffusion influence the aesthetic quality of the product. This influence can take the form either of a direct confrontation (such as 'filming theatre') or an indirect modification of its laws and potential (the development of film or radio, for example, which affect theatre writing). We will focus above all on this indirect aesthetic influence, on this mutual contamination of the media. Grasping this interaction is not easy, since it is never tangible and

cannot be reduced to technological influence (even if it certainly depends on this influence at the start). We will attempt to retrace this aesthetic interpretation of the media in the specific way in which artists use the media in their work. Paradoxically, although reciprocal influences between the various media and the theatre are at work, certain artistic practices are based on a rejection of those influences and the resulting competition means a renewed quest for their own specificity. This leads theatre people like Brook, Grotowski and Patte toward a *poor theatre* that does not allow itself to be 'impressed' by the all-powerful media.

So as not to obscure too much a media landscape that is already cluttered, I have limited this discussion to radio, cinema, television and video. Obviously, not all the theoretically possible combinations of these media, including theatre, are equally relevant, but we will examine them systematically, with respect to both technology and aesthetics.

Theatre ==› Radio

Theatre 'makes its entrance' in radio with the broadcasting, live or delayed, of a theatre performance conceived for and taking place in a theatre in front of an audience. The first recordings were made in this way and today we can still listen to live broadcasts of the Comédie-Française on Sunday afternoons on the program 'France-Culture.' The absence of the visual dimension is more or less compensated for by a description of the stage at the beginning of each act. The 'commentator' provides a rather discreet report of the stage business, especially at key moments. Sometimes, the commentator merely reads the stage directions, which have not always been kept to by the *mise en scène*. The listener can hardly hear the audience reaction, laughter, applause, response, but can still get a rough idea of the relation of real audience to performance; the perceived reactions seem more embarrassing than illuminating.

Theatre ——› Radio

At first, theatre imposed its own dramatic structure on radio plays, particularly reproducing the notion of character, action and plot attempting to structure 'radio drama' as a stage play, lacking 'only' the *mise en scène*. The history of the radio play is a series of

114

moves toward greater freedom, a search for its own minimal specificity. The best radio playwrights know how to meet the demands of the situation of production and reception, so as to differentiate their work radically from theatre. In a letter to his American publisher (August 27, 1957) for example, Beckett refused to allow a theatre performance of his radio play *All That Fall*:

> *All That Fall* is a specifically radio play, or rather radio text, for voices, not bodies. I have already refused to have it 'staged' and I cannot think of it in such terms. A straight reading before an audience seems to me barely legitimate, though even on this score I have my doubts. But I am absolutely opposed to any form of adaptation with a view to its conversion into 'theatre'. It is no more theatre than *Endgame* is radio; to 'act' it is to kill it. Even the reduced visual dimension it will receive from the simplest and most static of readings will be destructive of whatever quality it may have, which depends on the whole thing's *coming out of the dark*.
>
> (Beckett 1985: 38)

Radio ==› Theatre

Radio influences theatre's means of production in the slant of the texts, music, prerecorded noises 'inserted' into the performance. The audience perceives the recording through loudspeakers, just as a radio listener might. The use of portable microphones produces the same effect of delocalizing the sound and disembodying the performance. This introduction, subtle or not, of a mechanized voice threatens to 'denature' theatre, to deprive it of its spontaneous, vulnerable and unpredictable quality, so that the body is no longer the natural conveyor of the theatre event.

Radio — —› Theatre

Radio dramaturgy exercises a little-known influence on contemporary dramatic production. Dramatic writing today tends toward simplification, ellipsis, epic elements, rapid montage of sequences, collage of diverse materials. Thus radio contributes (just as cinema and television do) to the dematerialization of the stage, to the reduction of the actor to a mere vocal presence, to the banishment of visual signs in favour of the aural dimension of the text. This is the case with Beckett (*Happy Days*, or *Not I*) or Handke (*Through the Villages*): in these plays, everything is focused on the projection of the word deprived of the support of visual representation.

Radio ==› Cinema

Technological transfer occurs in adding sound to silent film. Even if the technicalities of radio and the film sound-track are not the same, the result is what counts: the possibility of technically reproducing a fragment of reality, specifically the aural environment, which gives rise to the most powerful reality-effects. Improvements in sound recording techniques (stereo, Dolby, etc.) allow the film audience to experience the illusion of a second reality.

Radio ——› Cinema

The aesthetic and/or ideological influence of radio on film is very difficult to pin down. Consider two apparently contradictory hypotheses.

1 The capacity for documenting reality and informing the radio listener about the external world is enhanced and even surpassed by the documentary film and particularly by television reporting since cinema rarely shows documentary films any more. Cinema has become the documentary medium *par excellence*.

2 But, on the other hand, experimental cinema may be tempted to question the imperialism of the image, by reducing the 'usual' (rather than 'natural') qualities of the medium: the power of the image. 'Divesting' the image of its representational function, avoiding changes in the frame or the shot, expanding and multiplying sound effects, creates a cinema – for instance, the work of Marguerite Duras – that reverses 'normal' perspective and highlights the constitutive properties of sound and the radio voice in relation to the spectator/listener.

Cinema ==› Radio

Technologically speaking, the influence is negligible, due to the different machinery of transmission in each case.

Cinema ——› Radio

Radio cannot match up to film's (or television's) greater capacity for capturing and showing reality; it has to defend itself against its new rival, television, which has cornered the market for news in the first forty years of its existence. Radio has an inferiority complex in relation to TV, even to the point of being advertised as 'radio en couleur,' 'radio in color" it knows that the consumer prefers soccer on TV and that films take away listeners. Radio does not always dare to develop its own specific dramaturgy beyond a pale shadow of theatre or cinema; it is content to announce films shown on TV and to discuss recently released films. It dare not 'speak' of soccer or theatre in a different way and tries to compensate for the lack of images with a flood of words and emotions. Such defensive and mimetic attitudes paralyse the search for specific solutions.

Cinema ==› Video

The format of the video cassette intended for viewing on a TV monitor miniaturizes and individualizes film. This transfer and reduction no longer pose any technical problems, but entail a reduction and decline in the quality of the image.

Cinema ——› Video

In the beginning, especially with the use of large TV cameras, video was constrained by the models of TV drama and cinematographic techniques: similar framing, shots, zooms, the same attention paid to narrative coherence. Under the influence of pop videos, the tendency has been reversed.

Video ==› Cinema

It is now possible to use portable video equipment that greatly simplifies the film-maker's task, speeds up editing, and thus reduces costs. After aping film for a long time, video has become the dominant medium imposing its own laws on others, thus affecting new cinematic dramaturgy. The results are not great, especially as regards the quality and definition of the image. Nothing can (yet?) replace good old 35 mm Eastmancolor.

Video ——› Cinema

Although video is a new and expanding medium, it has already affected the narrative structure of cinema, which had become less linear and more subject to manipulation, deconstruction, fantasy and the fascination of video's brilliant technique for filming commercials. J. J. Beineix, the director of *Diva* and *Betty Blue*, was inspired by the techniques of commercial clips. He also claims that clips have greatly influenced the narrative form and content of contemporary cinema:

> By definition, the clip is all or nothing, the best or the worst. One thing is certain; we are moving away from the beaten narrative track . . . we are witnessing an explosion of norms and forms, exactly as in painting years ago, when artists turned to abstraction.
>
> (*L'Evénement du Jeudi* November 22–8, 1984)

This kind of representation – in rock videos for example – the visualization of emotion and other visual tricks, the emphasis on surface impression, all this leads to the dissolution of the narrative, the rejection of causality, of a philosophical, social or psychological background, as if phantasms formed a surface totally detached from reality.

Video ==› Television/Video ——› Television

The increasingly frequent use of video cameras for television is justified in terms of simplifying the process of manipulating, storing and transforming the image.

In aesthetic terms, this leads to overly rigid or imprecise use of the video camera, producing a TV film that is too choppy and badly controlled:

> R. Jacquinet: 'We often hear that the continuity of the fixed video take allows the actors to present themselves much better than in the fragmentation of film shots.'

118

J. C. Averty: 'Above all, this allows them to enjoy their own way of speaking and to perform at a snail's pace. We get the slow pace of the performance at the Buttes-Chaumont: walking, then speaking, then walking without speaking, then stopping, then speaking, it's terrible.

(Quoted in Besenval 1978: 126)

Television ==› Video/Television — —› Video

Constant research on TV equipment has immediate effects on video equipment and vice versa. The osmosis between these two technologies is almost total but their aesthetic functions are radically different. They both use the same TV image. The relationship between video and television is both natural (with the same equipment) and conflicting. Jean-Paul Fargier, himself a video artist, describes their interaction in this way:

Right now, if I think about the video pieces that strike me as the strongest, the specifically strongest, and the most strongly specific, what almost always comes to mind are the tapes and installations that attack television in one way or another, that take television as their target, adversary, rival, alter ego, referent, primary material, exemplary model, negative, scrap, in short as other. An other from which video must separate and distinguish itself, but which it cannot not oppose, simply to be what it must be. It seems that video can only give of its best by directly or indirectly, knowingly or not, violently or diplomatically, spontaneously or in a calculated way attacking its links with television.

(Quoted in Bloch 1983)

Video gets from television a sense of the ephemeral and the evanescent together, however, with the possibility of replaying this emphemerality and thus denying it. Since television has a vast audience, its aesthetic procedures must be comprehensible and more or less transparent. Video, when it is not being used as a simple means of reproducing film or a TV broadcast, addresses an audience of connoisseurs, and experimentation appears to be the rule of the game; hence an abundance of experiments with image, narrative, rhythm and the relationship to sound. For the moment video art is in the position of a dominated medium, reduced to experimentation and limited by reason of cost and

119

complexity to a group of *aficionados*. Even here, socioeconomic conditions of production determine artistic specialization and the search for aesthetic specificity: 'the unavoidable abandonment of universality leads dominated media to *suggest more specific productions*, better adapted to their hitherto limited targets – the young (film) and the intellectuals (film, theatre)' (Busson 1985: 103).

Television = => Theatre

Television technology does not seem to have had an impact on theatre production, except negatively: the public, captured in the domestic space and by the irresistible sirens of the TV screen, neglects theatre, because of the effort required to choose a play, buy a ticket, go out, etc. The television spectator becomes one who looks without speaking, the opposite of theatre spectators who 'speak' to the stage by attending to it with eyes and ears, modifying it with their attention. They also 'speak' to their neighbours in the audience even without saying anything, because they know that while at the theatre they belong to a group which is *volens nolens* in solidarity, in the same boat, and whose members thus cannot but communicate. Jean Baudrillard has shown that the media

> *are what always prevents response*, making all process of exchange impossible (except in the various forms of response *simulation*, themselves integrated in the transmission process, thus leaving the unilateral nature of the communications intact). . . .
>
> TV, by virtue of its mere presence, is a social control in itself. There is no need to imagine it as a state periscope spying on everyone's private life – the situation as it stands is more efficient than that: it is the *certainty that people are no longer speaking to each other*, that they are definitively isolated in the face of a speech without response.
>
> (Baudrillard 1981: 170, 172)

That people are isolated and no longer speak to each other does not mean, however, as perhaps Baudrillard and a secular tradition of 'book literacy' suggest, that the TV spectator is passive, dominated by foreign emotions and lacking any imagination. One should not suppose that words are necessarily liberating, whereas

120

images are enslaving forces. In a way, this prejudice only repeats the logocentric pretensions of theatre which tend to view the dramatic text as more important and central than the performance.

Television — —› Theatre

The qualitative competition of television does not affect theatre; it feels itself superior to television and unhindered by the psychological realism so beloved of TV movies. In this sense, the formation (or rather the *deformation*) of audience taste by television necessarily rebounds on the future audience for theatre, particularly in the demand for realism, verisimilitude and the desire to be soothed, rather than disturbed, by the performance. On the other hand, we should not forget that an enormous part of theatre production, at least in France, is seen only on television, whether by way of broadcasts such as 'Au théâtre ce soir' or by way of cultural magazine programs. Television and its 'filmic discourse' (that is its way of filming theatre) have become the normal form of presentation. Therefore the potential audience is unprepared for avant-garde theatre even though its members may think they are familiar with theatre.

Obviously this merely describes the situation in France and does not reflect the work in Britain, where real talent is often involved:

> Both the BBC and the larger commercial companies (Thames and London Weekend Television in London, Granada in Manchester, Yorkshire TV in Leeds) make use of the best writing talent in the country for the production of dramatizations of novel and original plays specially written for the medium. During the last thirty years, almost every major dramatist has contributed to the substantial body of this literature.
>
> (Esslin 1985: 105)

In France, on the contrary, no 'televisual literature' has appeared in an audiovisual form of expression with its own aesthetics, rhetoric and poetics. The symbolic power of literature and of 'high culture' was too strong to tolerate the emergence of a new genre. It seems that a television culture could not constitute itself because it was unable to define itself in the terms of the three categories of culture described on p. 100 (anthropological, written, media).

The only concession of the television establishment was to promote in the 1960s film adaptations of classics. These were shot as films and cast by television: *Don Juan*, *Le Jeu de l'amour et du hasard* and *La Double Inconstance* in 1965, 1968 and 1969 by Marcel Bluwal; *Ubu Roi* and *Alice in Wonderland* by Jean-Christophe Averty. No attempt has been made so far to film the complete works of Molière as the BBC did for Shakespeare.

Again, the situation is quite different in a context where television commissions playwrights to write directly for the medium and to use TV-specific techniques, as in Britain where television has identified a number of specific characteristics:

> It requires a small screen, and its images lack a certain amount of sharpness or definition because of the current state of the technology. Large, spectacular panoramic long shots are not very effective on the television screen; close-ups and medium shots – scenes involving no more than two or three people – are most effective.
>
> Television drama thus tends towards a form of chamber play: close-ups of the characters' faces appear on the screen at the distance and on the scale of people to whom the spectator might himself be talking in an intimate context, a feature making television drama an ideal medium for this type of intimate dialogue. In contrast, large numbers of scattered groups are difficult to manage (one of the reasons why Chekhov does not televise well: the tension between different groups of characters is lost when one group disappears from view while the other moves into the foreground).
>
> (Esslin 1985: 106)

The editing of a TV production is capable of dynamizing the original play, but it is also in danger of eliminating the pauses, the silent moments which are so important on a stage and which the spectator needs to be able to reflect on the play. The TV production of a Shakespeare (BBC) also tends to use simple and standardized 'filmic language': none of the usual use of frames, few travelings or panoramics, relatively long shots (25/30 seconds) (Maquerlot 1987: 113–14).

Theatre = => Television

Despite its relative technological weakness with respect to television, theatre has none the less influenced television by offering itself as such to the inflexible and doubly frontal eye of the camera. This was and still is the era of the live or delayed broadcast of theatre and the now almost defunct era of slow and heavy shows filmed live with TV cameras at the Buttes-Chaumont studio.[2] Once theatre and cinema had entered the realm of television as they were, they could not but lose their original form and power, while contaminating and sterilizing television at the same time, preventing it from finding its own language. Theatre's clandestine entry into television has been criticized often, as here by J. C. Averty, for instance:

> It is a mistake to use fixed video cameras only to make filmed theatre. That is bound to disappear more and more. I am thinking of what we generally call the dramatic art of the Buttes-Chaumont, that is: a play written, specifically or not, for television, filmed in a set created by four cameras, either live or recorded in long half-hour sequences. In my opinion, this is a fundamental mistake. This is not really theatre; it has all its faults and none of its virtues. Nor is it cinema, because it is very heavy. It is certainly not television, since it merely uses television as a means of reproduction. It consists of hemming in the actors with the set and the microphones. It is the idea of cinema, without the analytic finesse of the cinematic camera whose multiplicity of shots allows for an in-depth investigation of the characters' psychology. In the case of live broadcasts, on the other hand, we are stuck with medium shots, close-ups, group shots. Moreover, the technique is rudimentry, because we have no choice: television cameras are not flexible, at least in the context of live recording. The actors perform badly because they are very tense. Even though they are performing live, they perform less well than in a theatre, without the aura of theatre, and less well than in a film where a director can guide them from shot to shot and inspire them with energy. Finally, this is in no sense television, because television is something else entirely: playing with electronics. To reproduce reality, to do the job of an usher in the studio has

123

completely ruined the TV drama that has been produced for the last twenty-five years.

(Quoted in Besenval 1978: 124)

Theatre — —› Television

In France the most disastrous consequence of this eruption of theatre on television has been the failure to adapt theatre dramaturgy to that of television life. This refusal to adapt has taken antithetical forms: thus in the dramaturgy of Buttes-Chaumont, the unities of place and time were respected under duress for texts that should have been performed in a variety of places and temporalities; on the other hand, filming on location with portable video cameras, television deliberately attempted to avoid being 'theatrical' by multiplying places, objects, points of view and changes in rhythm, thus completely losing the unity of tone and action necessary for drama (and not only *classical* drama). In both cases, what was lacking was a reflection on the means of coherently translating from one form of performance to another.

The evolution was completely different in Britain (see Esslin 1985: 99–100) where the BBC commissioned plays as early as 1924. (The first radio play was Richard Hughes' (1900–76) *Hanger*.) Plays were broadcast live from a number of studios so that different accoustic effects could be created. British radio drama remained very active:

> The BBC'S radio-drama department is thus a veritable nursery of writing talent. Although only about two per cent of the scripts received, on the average, ever meet a standard that can be broadcast, some fifty new playwrights receive their first productions each year on BBC radio – and many of these progress to television, the stage and cinema.
>
> (Esslin 1985: 103)

As early as the mid-1950s, authors in England managed to write for drama on television in a specific manner.

Theatre ==› Video

Theatre has no technological influence on video. Only *video performance art* enjoys manipulating machines theatrically, confronting human and machine, reducing the most sophisticated electronic technology to the level of the living actor, whose body always triumphs over the machine, despite appearances.

Theatre — —› Video

Video is obviously inspired by cinema and television (from which it tries to differentiate itself), but not really by theatre, unless in the banal sense of filming characters engaged in action.

On the other hand, theatre seems to have become easy prey for video recording. Theatre people seem no longer able to resist media pressure to film their performances, more or less to adapt them and thus produce a video version. Vitez has filmed his four Molière productions; Brook, the advocate of the immediate and ephemeral, prolonged the career of *Carmen* by recording three different versions for film and television. He also made a film of his *Mahabharata*. As La Fontaine might have said: 'They would not all die, but all were struck.' Indeed, this desire to control everything electronically also affects theatre, which risks losing its identity only because it hopes to reach millions of spectators and to preserve the performance for future generations and theatre researchers (a race threatened with extinction). But theatre people are not duped by this video market: they know that this electronic memorialization displaces and reconstructs what was originally a theatre event. As Vitez' poem suggests:

> The pleasure of theatre is linked to the fact . . .
>   – indestructibly linked –
>   – indissolubly –
> . . . to the fact that it does not last.
>   It is funny to think
>   of the efforts of notation
>   the efforts of archives
>   of videos, in canning plays:
> 'We must notate, gather up, store.'
> (Copfermann and Vitez 1981: 138)

These theatre people also understand that video cannot destroy theatre, but rather reaffirm that its uniqueness, its ephemeral quality, will emerge strengthened by suggestions from video.

Video = => Theatre

Video's technological influence is hardly perceptible in current theatre practice, except for experimental injections of preregistered video sequences into the theatre performance. None the less, the living, fragile, unpredictable and thus incorruptible character of theatre can only emerge reinforced. Video performance is first of all a performance, the artist's concrete activity for an audience, however reduced that audience may be; only afterwards is it a manipulation of video machines.

Theatre resorts more and more to video recording: for rehearsal, to make the actors aware of their acting style and their image in space; to record a *mise en scène* in order to remember moves, intonations, rhythm (this is current practice at the Comédie-Française of the Théâtre National Populaire (TNP) at Chaillot).

Video — —> Theatre

If technological transfer from video to theatre is more or less impossible, due to unequal technical development, their mutual aesthetic contamination is remarkable. By using video monitors on stage or in the house, the director inserts visual materials, documentary, film extracts, montage, closed-circuit images of stage or house. The function of this insertion varies considerably: redirecting attention, contradicting the stage and the living actor, treating the stage sculpturally with walls of screens, as Nam-June Paik does, destabilizing the spectators' perception by obliging them constantly to change the status of fictionality and representation. Sometimes living actors enter into dialogue with their video image or with other characters present only on video (such as in Ligeon-Ligeonnet's version of *Woyzeck*. Joseph Svoboda was the first to introduce closed-circuit television into his productions: *Prometheus* by Carl Orff (1968) and *Intoleranza* by Luigi Nono (1965)).

We may none the less doubt the success of this electronic injection into the living tissue of the performance, as does Evelyne Ertel:

> The conditions of spectator reception in theatre and television are radically opposed to each other. Sometimes the idea is to transform the theatre spectator into a television viewer, in order to play on this very opposition so that the

126

division produces a fissure, from which emotion or consciousness emerges. But this very division is not produced.
The theatre spectator cannot be divided – he remains entirely
a theatre spectator, in a community of spectators and actors;
he is not completely alone, or isolated with the family in a
small apartment, two feet away from and completely
absorbed by this familiar object that is almost a member of
the family. We may multiply the monitors, bring them closer
to the audience, but the difficulty remains: the spatio-temporal given of theatre is such that TV monitors can only
function as a global sign at the heart of the performance and
not as an autonomous medium transmitting its own signals.

Journal du Théâtre National de Chaillot 12 (June, 1983)

Evelyne Ertel clearly regards the video image in these examples
as an intruder in the theatre performance, an interloper that the
spectator finally rejects. Conversely, performance video plays with
the simultaneous utilization of the performers' bodies and the
images they produce or manipulate. What comes first is the artists'
performance and the *corps-à-corps* that they engage in with the
medium of video. In the work of Nam-June Paik and Charlotte
Moorman, video becomes a partner, making possible an active
meditation on the interaction between the human being and the
recording machine (cf. Bloch 1983: 24–30):

In T.V. Bra, Nam-June Paik studies the direct links established between the body of the young woman [Charlotte
Moorman] and the technical equipment: two small monitors
attached to her bra. In *T.V. Cello*, he has a complex apparatus consisting of several monitors piled on top of one
another. . . . According to Nam-June Paik, Charlotte is in
control since she generates images that she can direct while
playing her cello. . . . Charlotte is not within the video
apparatus; the apparatus is within her.

(Bloch 1983: 116)

Theatre ==› Cinema

No influence, since theatre lacks the technological infrastructure
necessary for the cinema.

Theatre — —› Cinema

Theatre's dramaturgical influence on early cinema was enormous during the last years of the nineteenth century: the weak development of cinematic technique and the habits of stage writing affected the very 'theatrical' – i.e. frontal, static and redundant – acting style in the first films by Méliès, that 'creator of the cinematic spectacle' and of a cinema that is still under the influence of theatre performance (acting, segmentation of the action, frontal rather than disorienting camera angles, recourse to playwrights for scripts).

In reaction to this embarrassing filiation, cinema quickly found its own specificity, set against a rather partial and limited image of theatre: it insisted on multiplying shots, perspectives and locations so as to bind the viewer to the editing rhythm, to play counterpoint on the sound and image, on the movements of objects and the camera. Only recently have we abandoned those vast cosmogonies in which theatre and cinema were opposed according to criteria that were 'specific' and metaphysical rather than historical and material. We no longer try to define them once and for all but we are interested in the exchange of procedures that characterizes their incestuous relationship and in the relativity of notions of 'theatricality' or 'filmicity' (as the neologism might go). Eric Rohmer remarked jokingly: 'The worst insult used to be calling a film "theatrical." Today, the worst is that it is "cinematic".'

(*Cahiers Renaud/Barrault* 96 (1977): 11).

Cinema = =› Theatre

The technological impact of cinema on theatre becomes obvious as soon as one tries to film theatre. There are certainly countless ways of capturing theatre on celluloid or videotape, but two major ones: (1) filming theatrical performances that existed prior to and independently of requirements for shooting; (2) instead of the pre-existing performance, filming something specifically prepared for the camera, but with some of the properties of a theatre event.

Filming a performance

We could legitimately claim that once we bring cameras into the auditorium, however discreetly, the acting is disturbed and changed; therefore we cannot film theatre without destroying it. The argument cannot be dismissed, but we can allow for a minimal degree of disturbance while a performance is being filmed live.

A. This is the case with *1789* by the Théâtre du Soleil, which was filmed over twelve performances, and which has the advantage of showing the audience, the wings, the performance in the making, not a hypothetical, typical and perfect performance. Mnouchkine's film captures the theatrical relationship, shows the space, multiplies the points of view on an already fragmentary scenography, restores the simultaneity of the narratives. (See, for example 'Taking the Bastille' in *1789*.)

B. Quite different is the case of *Le Bal*, filmed by Ettore Scola and based on the performance of the Campagnol company, 'coordinated' by Jean-Claude Penchenat. Here we have an adaptation for the cinema, not a film of an actual performance, with more or less the same actors, made in Cinecittà studios. The actor's performances, inspired by the original *mise en scène* but tailored to the new space, are directed at the camera and edited as in a normal film. In this sense, the film belongs in the second category; prior to the shooting, it did not exist – at least in this form and place – as a live performance directed at an audience in a theatre.

C. *Carmen*, filmed by Peter Brook, based on his opera at the Bouffes du Nord, is close to the second case. The essential difference is that Brook directs both opera and film and that he shot the film at the Bouffes du Nord, transformed into a closed studio without an audience. This is not the only difference. The stage set involves a sand-covered arena bounded by the orchestra pit at the back, the back wall, the side walls and the audience very close to the singers. The shots of the film point to several sublocations and focus on the singer or the two singers at the center of the drama, underlining the psychological details of their behavior.

Filming fragments of theatre

In this case, theatre no longer exists prior to being captured on film (as in *1789*), nor is it adapted to the technical demands on filming. The film rearranges the dramatic text and makes an extremely partial choice of fragments. In *Falstaff* by Orson Welles, the only remaining theatrical element is Shakespeare's text, which has been cut, edited and rearranged to make it say almost anything Welles required. The theatrical dimension is concentrated in certain scenes: for example, when Falstaff and Hal parody the conversation between the king and his son in the manner of psychodrama. For the rest, the filmic discourse owes absolutely nothing to any theatre performance of Shakespeare. The rapid editing, based on the contrasts of faces and places and on a segmentation of the texts, gives the film its dynamic montage.

Cinema ——› Theatre

Since the 1920s, cinema has been used on stage to illustrate the action or provide the spectator with documentation (Piscator, Brecht). Its function has been to disturb traditional perception, to provide background or ironic comment on the stage action. Today directors such as Richard Demarcy (in *Disparitions* or *Parcours*) and Henri Gruvman (in *Gru-Gru*) play with this disturbance of theatrical perception, making the actor react to an animated image.

The dramaturgical influence of cinema on theatre language has been much more profound and lasting. The introduction of epic elements or the montage of the plot in Brecht, the manipulation of time or space have become tried and tested techniques in dramatic writing. As in the cinema, *mise en scène* can frame an actor or a group, focus or de-emphasize a point on stage, effect a close-up or a 'traveling shot' on an actor. Eisenstein, man of the theatre as well as the cinema, described *mise en scène* in theatre as a process of montage: 'Mise-en-scène in which characters move from foreground to background and back again offers the equivalent of montage. We could call this latent montage' (1949: 15).

Vitez adds:

> Finally, there is another more subtle area in which theatre has been infected by cinema . . . From the end of the 1930s and under the influence of Central European and especially Russian directors, theatre decided to be as full of signs as

an egg . . . We [Patrice Chereau and I] imitated the cinema, investing the same amount of work in each play as one might in a film, or in a work not destined to be ephemeral. The real difference between theatre and cinema is that theatre is made to be destroyed by the rising tide, whereas cinema is made to be preserved and reproduced.

(Vitez 1980: 64–5)

Television ==› Radio

No technological influence.

Television — —› Radio

Radio necessarily occupies an inferior position with respect to television, since the latter can for the most part perform the tasks assigned to radio (reporting, news, broadcasting shows, etc.) with the added presence of the image that authenticates the message in the eyes of the audience. As a result, radio feels obliged to compete with television, multiplying its news and broadcasting sources, sticking to real events and informing the audience of them immediately by constantly repeating the same news (France-Inter (national public radio) every morning, also by allowing for listeners' questions and so forth. The 'realistic' character of the TV image appears to impose itself in the style of radio dramaturgy: radio plays stick too often to naturalistic notions of character, story, real places and chronology.

Radio ==› Television

Radio research has not yet been fully utilized for the TV apparatus, which is still a rather rudimentary music box.

Radio — —› Television

Television programs reproduce the same major categories as radio: news, fiction, variety, commercials, cut up into timed and relatively immovable segments. As for TV drama, the producers seem unable or unwilling to experiment as much as some radio playwrights. The reasons for this are many: TV drama looks in vain for its own way; it remains within the narrative domain of theatre

131

or cinema. Television addresses – or claims, driven by the ratings, to address – a larger audience than radio, and does not dare to displease them by too much formal experimentation.

Television ==› Cinema

For reasons of economy or efficiency video cameras are sometimes used for filming.

Television ——› Cinema

According to the experts, the influence of television on cinema is enormous and devastating. Alain Busson describes a transfer of the economically weakest consumers:

> An examination of customer structures shows that the eco-
> nomically weakest social groups have most changed their
> habits. Empty cinemas in the suburbs are connected with a
> more general refusal of collective consumption and a return
> to individual domestic activities, of which television is the
> fullest symbol.
>
> (Busson 1985: 103)

When we remember that 68.8 percent of the French watch tele-vision every day, 49.6 percent go to the cinema at least once a year, and only 10 percent go to the theatre (Busson 1985: 105), we can see that television dominates the other media, economically and aesthetically ravaging the theatre. Even the once dominant cinema is modified by this power relation. As the Malécot Report (January, 1977) notes: 'It is because the French have never seen so many films that cinema is in such bad shape' (quoted in Busson 1985: 104).

We have come to the point where films are currently made with the financial support of television, with a view to future use on the small screen. The result for film-making is a tendency to use television-specific thematics, cutting, editing and acting technique. This distortion is further aggravated when films made in this way are used for television: the image loses definition, the miniaturiz-ation makes it difficult to decipher the image. Cinema and tele-vision are thus both the worse for it.

132

Cinema ==› Television

Television has become the principal means for showing films, with some channels specializing in this kind of program.

Cinema — —› Television

Despite the current tendency to produce films which will be used as video cassettes and on television, TV drama is still made like miniature film, with the same cutting, the same excessive use of exterior shots and location changes, and the same kind of shot and narrative rhythm.

This 'nostalgia for the cinema' flatters the dominant public taste and limits what can pass for the technological specificity of television (video in the studio with tricks, insertions, reshaping of the image) to an experimental game without a future.

Radio — —› Video — —› Radio

This last relationship is the most surprising. It deserves special attention from the mass media industry. The pop video serves two masters: the record industry (radio) and the video market. It is in no way a referential illustration of the song or the music; it does not interpret or imitate anything.

Detached in this way from any textual reference, as theatre was 'once upon a time,' any interpretation (such as *mise en scène*), any classic cinematic narrative (such as television), the pop video uses music (particularly rock) in search of a visual rhythm that matches that of the music. Rock, which loves to play 'big bad wolf,' adapts perfectly to surprise shots and fantastic scenes. Given that a rock song does not tell a story, it does not tie down its visual accompaniment. The pop video must not bore the spectator with a fixed décor, but must rather offer a series of shocking visual ideas, marvelous events activated by friendly tricks, to make the singers and musicians little imps who are simultaneously the producers of the music and its first listeners/dancers, engaged in the marvelous fiction portrayed. As a product for immediate consumption and disposal, the pop video can at least be praised for forcing us to reconsider the relations among the media and leading to a new practice of visual representation.

In this overview of technological and aesthetic interference between theatre and the media, it has been shown, even if in a rather mechanical way, that theatre cannot be 'protected' from any media and that the 'work of art in the era of technical reproduction' (Benjamin 1936) cannot escape the socioeconomic-technological domination which determines its aesthetic dimension. Technological and aesthetic contamination is inevitable, whether as effective interaction of media techniques or as the frantic desire to maintain the specificity or poverty of theatre (Grotowski). The time has passed for artistic protectionism, and the time has arrived for experiments with different possibilities. The most marked influence of the media has been to found all aesthetic reflection on the notion of technological progress and mass diffusion; this reflection can thus be materially linked to production, diffusion and reception. Reflections of this kind on these practices of performance and visual representation cannot allow themselves to be overawed by the technical complexity of the media of the socioeconomic phenomena of the culture industry, but should rather examine, from the perspective of an aesthetic of form, the processes of semiotic transformation from one form to another, the emergence of meaning in these contaminations and the dynamism of practices of performance and representation in the media of our time.

NOTES

1. Translator's note: In order to maintain Pavis' implied distinction between the singular nouns 'médium' and 'média' (unavailable in English), I have used the English plural wherever possible.
2. This is the French TV studio where the first TV plays were broadcast.

BIBLIOGRAPHY

Abastado, Claude (1982) 'Culture et médias,' Le Français dans le Monde 173.
Barbier-Bouvet, Jean-François (1977) De la scène au petit écran, Paris: Ministry of Culture and Communication.
Baudrillard, Jean (1972) 'Requiem pour les médias,' Pour une critique de l'économie politique du signe, Paris: Gallimard; trans. Charles Levin (1981) For a Critique of the Political Economy of the Sign, New York: Telos.
Beckett, Samuel (1985) Letter, Modern Drama 27, 1.
Benjamin, Walter (1936) 'Das Kunstwerk im Zeitalter seiner technischen Reproduzierbarkeit,' Gesammelte Schriften 1, 2; trans. Harry Zohn

(1970) 'The Work of Art in the Age of Mechanical Reproduction,' *Illuminations*, London: Fontana.

Besenval, Patrick (1978) *La Télévision*, Paris: Larousse.

Bloch, Dany (1983) *L'Art vidéo*, Paris: L'image 2-Alin Avila.

Busson, Alain (1983) *La Place du théâtre dans le champ culturel*, Paris: Université de Paris.

—— (1985) 'L'Innovation et structuration du champ culturel,' *Théâtre/Public* 64/5.

Les Dossiers du petit ecran, CNDP (29, rue d'Ulm, 75005 Paris).

Duguet, Anne-Marie (1981) *Vidéo: la mémoire au poing*, Paris: Hachette.

Eisenstein, S. (1949) 'From Theatre to Cinema,' in Jay Leda (ed.) *Film Form*, New York: Harcourt Brace.

Eisler, Hanns and Adorno, T. W. (1947) *Music for the Film*, New York: Oxford University Press.

Enzensberger, H. M (1970) 'Baukasten zu einer Theorie der Medien,' *Kursbuch* 20; (1974) 'Constituents of a Theory of the Media,' *The Consciousness Industry*, New York: Seabury Press.

Esslin, Martin (1985) 'Drama and the Media in Britain,' *Modern Drama* 28, 1.

Flichy, Patrice (1980) *Les Industries de l'imaginaire*, Grenoble: Presses Universitaires.

Horkheimer, Max and Adorno, T. W. (1977) 'The Culture Industry: Enlightenment as Mass Deception,' *Dialectic of Enlightenment*, New York: Continuum.

Huser, F. (1975) 'La Vidéo et le temps,' *Revue d'Esthétique* 4.

McLuhan, Marshall (1964) *Understanding Media*, New York: Signet.

Maquerlot, J.-P. (1987) 'Le Téléfilm de théâtre,' *Shakespeare à la télévision*, M. Williams ed., Rouen.

Mattelart, A. and M (1979) *De l'usage des médias en temps de crise*, Paris: A. Moreau.

Modern Drama 28, 1 (1985), special issue on drama and the media.

Morin, Edgar (1958) *Le Cinéma ou l'homme imaginaire*, Paris: Minuit.

Piemme, Jean-Marie (1975) *La Propagande inavouée*, Paris: Union Générale d'Edition.

—— (1984) 'Le Souffleur inquiet,' *Alternatives théâtrales* 20–1.

Serror, Serge (1970) *Petit écran, grand public*, Paris: INA, La Documentation Française.

Vitez, Antoine (1980) 'Antoine Vitez, le signifiant et l'histoire,' *Ça Cinéma* 17.

Vitez, Antoine and Copferman, Emile (1981) *De Chaillot à Chaillot*, Paris: Hachette.

Williams, Raymond (1974) *Television: Technology and Cultural Form*, London: Fontana.

6

TOWARD SPECIFYING THEATRE TRANSLATION

Although the problems of translation, and of literary translation in particular, have gained some recognition, the same cannot be said of theatre translation, specifically translation for the stage, completed with a *mise en scène* in view. The situation of enunciation specific to theatre has been hardly taken into consideration: that is, the situation of enunciation of a text presented by the actor in a specific time and place, to an audience receiving both text and *mise en scène*. In order to conceptualize the act of theatre translation, we must consult the literary translator as well as the director and actor; we must incorporate their contribution and integrate the act of translation into the much broader 'trans-lation' that is the *mise en scène* of a dramatic text. The phenomenon of translation for the stage (my chief concern here) goes beyond the rather limited phenomenon of the interlingual translation of the dramatic text. In order to outline some problems peculiar to translation for the stage and the *mise en scène*, we need to take account of two factors: (1) in theatre, the translation reaches the audience by way of the actors' bodies; (2) we cannot simply translate a linguistic text into another; rather we confront and communicate heterogeneous cultures and situations of enunciation that are separated in space and time.[1]

PROBLEMS PECULIAR TO TRANSLATION FOR THE STAGE

The intersection of situations of enunciation

The translator and the text of the translation are situated at the intersection of two sets to which they belong in differing degrees

Figure 6.1

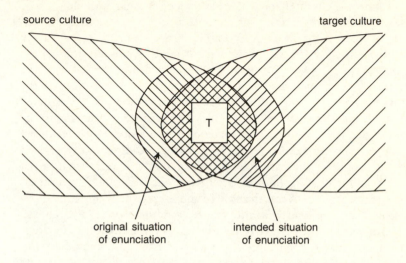

source culture

target culture

T

original situation
of enunciation

intended situation
of enunciation

(see Fig. 6.1). The translated text (rectangle T) forms part of both source and target text and culture, assuming that the transfer simultaneously involves the source text's semantic, rhythmic, aural, connotative and other dimensions, necessarily adapted to target language and culture. In theatre, the relationship between situations of enunciation must be added to this phenomenon 'normally' common to all linguistic translation: in other words, the text. The text T makes sense only in its situation of enunciation, which is usually virtual, since the translator usually takes a written text as point of departure. It can (rarely) happen that this text-to-be-translated is contained in a concrete *mise en scène* and is thus 'surrounded' by a realized situation of enunciation. But even in this case, as opposed to that of film dubbing, the translator knows that the translation cannot preserve the original situation of enunciation, but is intended rather for a future situation of enunciation with which the translator is barely, if at all, familiar. Hence the difficulty and relativity of the translator's work.

We can represent the source text's situation of enunciation as a part of the source culture (horizontal hatching). Once this text T (in its translated form) is staged for the target audience and culture, it is itself surrounded by a situation of enunciation belonging to the target culture (vertical hatching). The result for the rectangle T is the real or virtual intersection of these situations of enunciation in differing degrees in the text. We must take into account this concatenation of situations of enunciation while privileging the target situation of enunciation, distinguishing between: (1) the part of the situation of enunciation that belongs exclusively to the source (horizontal hatching) or target (vertical); and (2) the mixture of the two. In the case of an actual *mise en scène* of the translated text, we arrive at the situation of enunciation in the target language and culture. Going 'upstream,' the translator would find the situation more difficult, because in translating, he must adapt a situation of enunciation that he does not yet know. Before even broaching the question of the dramatic text and its translation, we must realize therefore that the real situation of enunciation (that of the translated text in its situation of reception) is a transaction between the source and target situations of enunciation that may glance at the source, but that has its eye chiefly on the target. The theatre translation is a hermeneutic act: in order to find out what the source text means, I have to bombard it with questions from the target language's point of view: positioned here where I am, in the final situation of reception, and within the bounds of this other language, the target language, what do you mean to me or to us? This hermeneutic act – *interpreting* the source text – consists of delineating several main lines translated into another language, in order to pull the foreign text toward the target culture and language, so as to separate it from its source and origin. As Loren Kruger has shown, translation does not entail the search for the equivalence of two texts, but rather the appropriation of a source by a target text:

> The reception of a particular translation as appropriate depends on the extent to which the situation of enunciation of the source text, the translator, and the target discourse can be said to correspond: this appropriateness is thus reflected in the apparent invisibility of the appropriation. The meaning of the translated text arises not so much out of what one can take over from it, as what one does to it.
>
> (Kruger 1986: I, 54)

The series of concretizations

In order to understand the transformations of the dramatic text, written, then translated, analysed dramaturgically, staged and received by the audience, we have to reconstruct its journey and its transformation in the course of these successive concretizations.

Figure 6.2   Series of concretizations

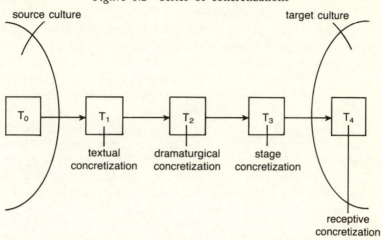

The original text (T_0) (see Fig. 6.2) is the result of the author's choices and formulations. As Jiri Levy notes: 'it is not objective reality that penetrates the work of art, but the author's interpretation of reality' (1969: 35). We shall leave aside the question of the work's textualization, pointing out only that the text T_0 is written and can be described in accordance with its auto-, inter- and ideotextual dimensions (Pavis 1985: 288–93). The text itself is readable only in the context of its situation of enunciation, especially in its inter- and ideotextual dimensions, that is in relation to the surrounding culture.

1 The text of the written translation depends, as we have seen, on the initial, virtual situation of enunciation of T_0, as well as on the future audience who will receive the text in T_3 and T_4. This text T_1 of the translation constitutes an initial concretization in the sense I have given that term following Ingarden (1931) and Vodička (1975) (cf. Pavis 1985). The translator is in the position of a reader and a dramaturge (in the technical sense): he makes choices from among the potential and possible indications in the text-to-be-translated. The translator is a dramaturge who must first of all effect a *macrotextual* translation, that is a dramaturgical analysis of the fiction conveyed by the text. He must reconstitute

139

the plot according to the logic that appears to suit the action, and (so) reconstitute the artistic totality (Levy 1969: 44), the system of characters, the time and space in which the agents develop the ideological point of view of author and period that show through in the text, the individual traits of each character and the suprasegmental traits of the author, which tend to homogenize their discourse, the system of echoes, repetition, responses and correspondences that maintain the cohesion of the source text. The macrotextual translation – possible only in a reading of the text – of textual and linguistic microstructures involves in return the translation of these very microstructures. In this sense, theatre translation (like any translation of literature) is not a simple linguistic question; it has too much to do with stylistics, culture, fiction, to avoid these macrostructures. As George Mounin rightly notes: 'a playable theatre translation is the product, not of linguistic, but rather of a dramaturgical act – otherwise, as Mérimée said of the translation of *Revizor*, 'one would translate the language well enough, without translating the play' (1963: 14). This initial translation or dramaturgical concretization is fundamental, because it *molds*, in Lotman's sense, and continues to constitute the text. Far from being an external 'expressive' formulation of an already known meaning, the translation breathes life into the text, constituting it as text and as fiction, by outlining its dramaturgy.

The dramaturgical analysis and stage T_2 of the translation process must incorporate a coherent reading of the plot as well as the spatiotemporal indications contained in the text, the transfer of stage directions, whether by way of linguistic translation or by representing them through the *mise en scène*'s extralinguistic elements. The dramaturgical analysis and the concretization which follows are all the more necessary when the source text is archaic or classical. In such cases, the translation will be more readable for a target audience than the source text (in the original language) would be for the same audience. Hence a paradox: Shakespeare is easier to understand in French or German translation than in the original, because the work of adapting the text to the current situation of enunciation will necessarily be accomplished by the translation. Shakespeare thus lives on in French and German, while being long since dead in English. The dramaturgical analysis consists of concretizing the text in order to make it readable for a reader/spectator. Making the text readable involves making it visible – in other words, available for concretization on stage and by the audience.

2 The dramaturgical text can thus be read in the translation of T_0. A dramaturge can also act as interpreter for translator and director (in T_2) and can thus prepare the ground for a future *mise en scène* by systemizing dramaturgical choices, both by reading the translation T_1 – which, as we have seen, is infiltrated by dramaturgical analysis – and possibly by referring to the original. From a theoretical point of view, it is not important whether this dramaturgical function is verbalized or not, separated from the work of T_2; what matters is the process of concretization (fictionalization and ideologization) that the dramaturge effects on the text (Pavis 1985: 268–94). In this sense, the dramaturge's translation is necessarily an adaptation and a commentary. The translator-as-dramaturge must provide in the text (or subsequently in the *mise en scène*) an array of information that the original audience needs to understand situation or character. When the commentary is too long or incomprehensible it is still possible for the dramaturge/translator to make cuts in his version destined for the target audience, where possible with the director's consent, since the latter can find theatrical means to make the same point. This procedure, which may seem an easy way out or a dismissal, often works better than incomprehensible allusions that would disconcert the target audience. Every translation – above all theatre translation, which must, as we tend to think nowadays, be clearly and immediately understood by the audience – is adapted and fitted to our present situation: 'In this way we hear the music of Bach or read Cervantes or Shakespeare: we fit the works of the past into the present, and in so doing, we partially erase their original intention and substitute our own. We continually adapt' (Vinaver 1982:84).

3 The following step – T_3 – is onstage testing of the text which was translated initially in T_1 and T_2: concretization by stage enunciation. This time the situation of enunciation is finally realized; it is formed by the audience in the target culture, who confirm immediately whether the text is acceptable or not. The *mise en scène* – the confrontation of situations of enunciation – whether virtual (T_0) or actual (T_1), proposes a *performance text*, by suggesting

141

the examination of all possible relationships between textual and theatrical signs.

4 The series is not yet complete, however, since the spectator has yet to receive this stage concretization T_3. We could call this last stage the *recipient concretization* or *enunciation*. This is where the source text finally arrives at its endpoint: the spectator. The spectator thus appropriates the text only at the end of a torrent of concretizations, of intermediate translations that reduce or enlarge the source text at every step of the way; this source has always to be rediscovered and reconstituted anew. It would not be an exaggeration to say that the translation is simultaneously a dramaturgical analysis (T_1 and T_2), a *mise en scène* and a message to the audience, each unaware of the others. We shall attempt in due course to demonstrate the connection between the various situations of enunciation, the individual body of the actor and the social body of a culture. It is already clear that the enunciation (and thus also the meaning of the utterance) depends on the way in which the surrounding culture focuses attention and determines the way characters (as carriers of the fiction) and actors (who belong to a theatrical tradition) express themselves. Several factors thus organize and facilitate the reception of a theatre translation. We shall review them quickly, focusing on the spectator's hermeneutic competence and command of rhythm.

The conditions of theatre translation reception

The hermeneutic competence of the future audience

As we have seen the act of translation concludes with the recipient concretization, which in the final analysis decides the use and meaning of the source text T_0. This stresses the importance of the target conditions of the translated utterance, which are specific in the case of the theatre audience who must hear the text and understand what has led the translator to make certain choices, to imagine a particular 'horizon of expectations' (Jauss) on the audience's part, while counting on their hermeneutic and narrative competence.[2] According to René Poupart, the translator represents himself and his discursive partners in a way that can correspond to the response that he gives to various questions he is supposed to ask: 'Where do I stand with respect to this translation procedure? For whom should I follow this procedure?' (Poupart 1985: 5).

In this evaluation of self and other, the translator establishes a more or less appropriate idea of his translation. This idea depends none the less on other factors.

The future audience's competence in the rhythmic, psychological or aural spheres

The rhythmic and prosodic equivalence or at least transposition of the source text (T_0) and the text of the stage concretization (T_3) is often treated as dispensable for a 'good' translation.[3] In effect, we need to take account of the form of the translated message, in particular of its rhythm and duration, since 'the duration per se of a stage utterance is part of its meaning' (Corrigan 1961: 106). None the less, the criterion of the playable or speakable (text) is valid on the one hand as a means of measuring the way a particular text is received, but it becomes problematic once it degenerates into a norm of 'playing well' or of verisimilitude. Certainly actors have to be physically capable of pronouncing and performing their text, which means avoiding euphonics, gratuitous play of the signifier, or multiplying details at the expense of a rapid grasp of the whole. This demand for a playable or speakable text can none the less lead to a norm of the well-spoken, or to a facile simplification of the rhetoric of phrasing or of a 'properly' articulated performance by an actor (cf. French translations of Shakespeare). The danger of banalization lurking under cover of the text that 'speaks well' (*bien en bouche*) lies in wait for the *mise en scène*. Furthermore, the works of those such as Vitez, Régy or Mesguish no longer acknowledge this criterion and instead consider every text playable, even those texts – and types of translation – that tend more toward the condition of babble (*discours-fleuve*), a dramatic poem or an *exercice de style*, than to the rapid, 'lively' dialogue of light comedy. What is much more important than the simple criterion of the 'well-spoken' is the convincing adequacy of speech and gesture, which we may call the *language-body*.

The corresponding notion of an audible or easily received text also depends on the audience and the faculty of measuring the emotional impact of a text and a fiction on the spectator. We shall see that contemporary *mise en scène* no longer recognizes these norms of phonic correctness, discursive clarity, pleasing rhythm, 'speakable' language or 'playable' text (Snell-Hornby 1984). Other criteria replace these excessively normative notions of a well-spoken text that is pleasing to the ear.

In examining the theatre translation's conditions of reception, we have already broached the question of the *mise en scène*, in particular the way in which the stage takes over from the linguistic text.

Translation and its *mise en scène*

Taking over the situation of enunciation

The translation (T₃) (already inserted in a concrete *mise en scène*) is linked to the theatrical situation of enunciation by way of an entire deictic system. Once it is thus linked, the dramatic text can relieve itself of terms which are comprehensible only in the context of its enunciation. This is accomplished by considerable use of deictics – personal pronouns or omissions – or by relocating descriptions of people and things in the stage directions and then waiting patiently for the *mise en scène* to take them up. The translation that is intended for the stage makes this economy even clearer, by trimming the source text even more. One might for example translate, 'I want you to put the hat on the table' by 'Put it there' accompanied by a look or gesture, thus reducing the sentence to its deictic elements.

This economy of the dramatic text and *a fortiori* of its translation for the stage allows actors to supplement the texts with all sorts of aural, gestural, mimic and postural means. Thus, at this point, actors' rhythmic invention comes into play; their intonation can say more than a long speech, their phrasing can shorten or lengthen tirades according to taste, structuring and deconstructing the text. All these gestural procedures ensure exchange between word and body (to which we shall return). What remains is the delineation of a debate, more normative than theoretical, on the inscription – or its absence – of the *mise en scène* in the translation.

Translation as mise en scène

Two schools of thought on the subject of the relationship between translation and *mise en scène* confront each other in the work of recent translators and directors; the polemic expressed in this debate may not make for an easy solution, but can be clarified within a theory of concretization in series.

1 For translators who jealously guard their autonomy and who often think of their work as publishable as it stands, unattached to any particular *mise en scène*, translation does not necessarily or completely determine the *mise en scène;* it leaves the field open for future directors. For Danièle Sallenave, 'neither translation nor direction comment on the text; one can comment only with words in the same language. Translation and direction rather involve transposition into another language or system of expression' (1982 20). There is therefore no interpretation *stricto sensu* of the text: 'one of the rules for theatre translation and for translation in general is never to appear as an interpreter of the text, but to keep oneself in check, so as to maintain its mystery.' It is true that it is criminal to remove an ambiguity or resolve any mystery that the text has especially inscribed in it. Can any reading, any translation, avoid interpreting the text? This would be a difficult position to maintain. Sallenave herself does not maintain it for long, in that she suggests that hearing voices or seeing bodies still does not entail thinking about *mise en scène:* 'Translating for the stage does not mean jumping the gun by predicting or proposing a *mise en scène;* it is rather to make the *mise en scène* possible, to hear speaking voices, to anticipate acting bodies' (1982: 20). Perhaps it is just a (false) conception of *mise en scène* that leads Sallenave to deny any organic link between translation and *mise en scène*. One would not want to hold against her the wish to preserve the text's mystery, if it is indeed a constitutive part of the source text. Other translators, like Jean-Marie Déprats, qualify positions like this one by making the translation not so much the *mise en scène à l'avance*, but a preparation for this *mise en scène:*

> the translation must remain open, allow for play without dictating its terms; it must be animated by a specific rhythm without imposing it. Translating for the stage does not mean twisting the text to suit what one has to show, or how or who will perform. It does not mean jumping the gun, predicting or proposing a *mise en scène:* it means making it possible.
>
> (1985: 72)

Sallenave and Déprats thus both reveal their concern not to encroach on the work of the director, and to allow him the freedom to produce his own concretization, the theatrical enunciation (T_3), which – according to our diagram, does indeed rewrite and go beyond T_0, T_1 and T_2. On the other hand, it would be difficult to make a move without T_1 and T_2, for the reasons I have already indicated. The very fact of leaving aside certain zones of indeterminacy or of not solving the mystery involves taking up a position with respect to the text, and leads to a certain kind of dramaturgical, theatrical and recipient concretization. Once uttered on stage, the text cannot avoid taking sides about its meaning possibilities. That does not necessarily entail, however, that the *mise en scène* is predetermined by the text (Pavis 1986).

2 For this reason, we shall give more credit to the opposing thesis, proposed by Vitez, Lassalle and Regnault, for example, who see translation as an operation which predetermines the *mise en scène*, or even is a kind of *mise en scène*. According to Vitez,

> because it is a work in itself, a great translation already contains its *mise en scène*. Ideally the translation should be able to command the *mise en scène*, not the reverse. Translation or *mise en scène:* the activity is the same; it is the art of selection among the hierarchy of signs.
>
> (1982: 9)

François Regnault, dramaturge and translator, has chosen as far as possible to subordinate the *mise en scène* to the text:

> The translation is destined to be performed in a particular *mise en scène* and is linked to a particular stage production. . . . The translation presupposes first of all the subordination of the *mise en scène* to the text, so that – at the moment of the *mise en scène* – the text is in its turn subordinated to theatre.
>
> (1981: 18)

For Jacques Lassalle, theatre translation and the theatrical enunciation in particular fill the gaps in the source text: in every text of the past there are points of obscurity that refer to a lost reality. Sometimes only the activity of theatre can help to fill the gaps – (1982: 13). A translation theoretician like Hans Sahl in fact uses

146

a theatrical metaphor to define translation: 'Translating is staging a play in another language' (1965: 105).

It would be easy to show how, in Claude Porcell's translation of *Der Park* by Botho Strauss for the *mise en scène* by Claude Régy (1986), the translation of a term as 'simple' as *tüchtig* in *tüchtige Gesellschaft* by 'société efficace' (efficient society) (Strauss 1986: 7), where one might have expected, given (French) stereotypical notions about Germany, something like 'société travailleuse' (industrious society), leads in the French version to a *mise en scène* of a hyper- or postmodern society, dedicated to electronics, to chilly bureaucratic efficiency. In Peter Stein's *mise en scène* at the Schaubühne (West Berlin), the focus was rather on the Germany of petit-bourgeois and working-class myth. The translation of *tüchtig* by 'efficace' sets the French translation on a track that orients the *mise en scène* in a one-way direction. In the same way, the fact of translating the semantic isotope *Streit, Streiten* ('quarrel,' 'to quarrel'), by varying the terms ('problèmes,' 'eternelles disputes,' 'se disputer') involves the French version in quite another isotope and loses the thematic coherence which 'Germanness' might offer, if not impose. In this sense too, the translation predetermines dramaturgical and theatrical concretization. How could it be otherwise once the translation, as a reading, interprets the source text T_0 and, as a translation, cannot but pronounce (judgment) on this source?

These then are some of the problems facing theatre translation for the stage. What remains to be seen is how this hypothesis of the series of concretizations, weighing more and more heavily on the meaning of the actually received text T_4, is established in relation to an exchange between spoken *text* and speaking *body* (see 'From text to body, from body to text,' pp. 147–55), and with respect to the interaction of cultures juxtaposed in the hermeneutic act of intercultural exchange.

FROM TEXT TO BODY, FROM BODY TO TEXT

We have described the successive phases of concretizations from T_0 to T_4, highlighting the series of enunciations. This done, we have barely outlined the way in which these enunciations confront the actor with the text, word with gesture. In order to grasp this confrontation, we need to reconstitute the passage from source text to target text, while examining the process of intersemiotic

147

translation between the preverbal [1] and verbal systems of the source [2] and target [3] texts.

Translation as *mise en jeu*

The little-known situation before the dramatic text is written is represented by [1]. This global situation is not yet semiotically structured; reality has not yet been captured in a cultural and semiotic system. We can speak of a hypothesis of a general picture, within which a situation and the fragments of a text are not yet clearly articulated. In this ante-textual magma, gesture and text coexist in an as yet undifferentiated way.

This preverbal element does not therefore exclude speech. Rather it contains it, but as speech uttered within a situation of enunciation, and as one of many elements in this global situation preceding the written text. Thus the preverbal is not limited to gesture, but encompasses all the elements of a situation of enunciation preceding the writing of the text: apart from gesture, this includes costume, the actor's manner, imagined speech, in short all the sign systems that make up the theatrical situation of enunciation.

In the dramatic source text [2], we are left with only the linguistic trace of the preceding gestural and preverbal processes. Speaking hypothetically, in order to get from source text [2] to target text [5], we must pass through [3] and [4]. We have to return to a preverbal (oral and gestural) situation, in the imaginary *mise en jeu* of the source text in a situation of enunciation within which the text would be confronted with the bodily gesture of the actor. Source [2] and target [5] texts are thus captured in this verbalization which takes the form of a written trace.

The *mise en jeu* of the source seeks an equivalence or a match for the gestural situation of enunciation and the linguistic utterance. We shall see in a moment that the exchange between [3] and [4] is effected by comparing and trying out word and object presentations in the two languages and cultures and in adjusting the language-body of the two systems accordingly. Once the *mise en jeu* of the target text [4] has been accomplished, it is transcribed in terms of a purely verbal system, that of the target text [5], moving away from word and object presentation in an attempt to reduce the *mise en jeu* [4] to a purely linguistic system. When this text thus translated is staged – placed within a theatrical and

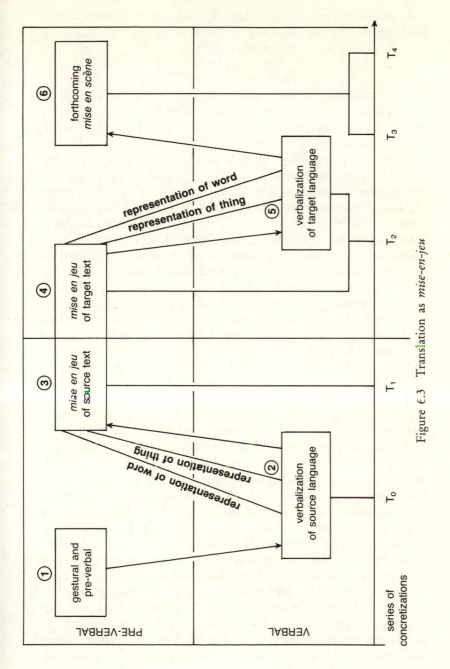

Figure 6.3 Translation as *mise-en-jeu*

recipient situation of enunciation (T_3 and T_4 in Figure 6.2) – it will return to a global situation of enunciation and will have actually arrived at its destination.

What remains is to refine the terms of this scheme. 'Word-presentation' (*Wortvorstellung*) and 'object-presentation' (*Objektvorstellung*) refer in Freud's work to two dimensions of the linguistic sign: word-presentation or sound picture (*Klangbild*) is the aural representation of the word, its auditive dimension, form of expression of the aural signifier. The object-presentation (*Objekt-* or *Sachvorstellung*) is the visual presentation ensuing from the object. We might call it the referent, which we associate with the object-presentation. According to Freud: 'the object-presentation is a combination of associations arising from the most varied representations: visual, aural, tactile, kinesthetic and others' (Freud 1953: IV, 296). These two kinds of presentation play a crucial and complementary role in the perception of an orally delivered linguistic text, particularly in the perception of its sub-stantives. What is at issue here is the signified of the word's reference on the one hand, and its aural signifying dimension on the other. Starting with the word, we can thus invoke the visual presentations that are associated with it and its aural, rhythmic, prosodic makeup.

Applying Freud to translation theory

In the exchange and the 'trial and error' in the *mises en jeu* between [3] and [4], we should take account of the word- and object-presentations in the two linguistic and cultural systems. We must transfer from the source to the target text both rhythmic and phonic signifier and some of the associations that are signified and conveyed by the source text. This double transfer is accomplished under varying conditions and according to varying proportions, since, as Freud remarks, 'object-presentation does not seem to be a complete representation and is unlikely to be completed, whereas word-presentation is apparently something complete, even if it can be expanded upon' (1891: 170). Applied to theatre translation, this would mean that the transfer between [3] and [4] takes place unevenly: the word presentations in the target language are not infinite in number and have a limited number of correspondences in [4] and [5]. As a result, the phonetic and rhythmic dimension of the text can be relatively well established and transferred. By contrast, object-presentation in the same text – its semantic dimension (concerning signified and referent) – is much more difficult to predict: the translation of signifieds and their linguistic signifiers in the two languages is very uncertain and difficult to predict or describe. We should remember that the Freudian distinction between word and object or thing allows us to conceive of the process of verbalization as conscious perception and its repression as a presentation that cannot be expressed in words. It is by recourse to the verbal image that the memory trace comes into consciousness:

> Conscious presentation encompasses thing presentation, followed by the corresponding word presentation, while unconscious presentation involves only thing presentation. The system of the unconscious contains the investment of objects (*Sachbesetzung der Objekte*, the initial and real investment; the preconscious comes into play when this object-presentation is completed by way of a link to corresponding word presentations.
>
> (Freud 1915: 160; 1952: XIV, 201)

What becomes of Freud's theory when applied to translation, in particular to this relationship between verbalization at the source [2] and at the target [5], via the double *mise en jeu* at the level of ⌈3⌉ and ⌈4⌉?

Let the Freudian analogy prompt us to differentiate between the verbal and the preverbal, the conscious from the preconscious and the unconscious:

At the level of the preverbal object-presentation are [1], [3], [4] and [6], where gesture and language are still undifferentiated. This is the exclusive province of the unconscious. Metaphorically speaking, one might say that the gestural/preverbal [1] element, the *mises en jeu* of source and target [2] and [4], and the future *mise en scène* [6] represent the unknown repressed part of the source and target texts [3] and [5], or the gestural and theatrical unconscious of the dramatic source and target texts. This provides a more or less precise picture of the situation of enunciation within which the linguistic text might be placed, having been enunciated in a way that (necessarily) limits its potential and adapts it to a concrete situation.

At the verbal level, that of word-presentation and the preconscious, are [2] and [5].

The relationship between these two levels, between [2] and [3] on
the one hand, and between [4] and [5] on the other, is that of
conscious presentation: the attempt to render conscious and
known both text and performance, word and gesture, to attach
linguistic utterance to gestural and situational enunciation, to
delineate the union of word and gesture, which we shall call the
language-body.[4] What we call the language-body, the union of
thing-presentation and word-presentation, would in the context
of theatrical enunciation be the union of spoken text and the
gestures accompanying its enunciation, in other words the specific
link that text establishes with gesture. Each *mise en jeu* and later
mise en scène would be characterized by a specific enunciation
that links text and gesture. Translating source *mise en jeu* into
target *mise en jeu* calls above all for the transfer of the language-
body of one system into another: we need to find equivalent
word-presentations (at the level of the verbal signifier) and object-
presentations that 'adequately' match the source text (level of
signified and referent). The language-body is the orchestration,
peculiar to a language and culture, of gesture, vocal rhythm and
the text. It is simultaneously spoken action and speech-in-action.
This resembles the notion of a 'dramatic unity between action and
language' (Snell-Hornby 1984: 113–14) that replaces the notion of
'equivalence.' We must grasp the way in which the source text,
following the *mise en jeu* of the source, associates a particular
gestural and rhythmic enunciation with a text; then we would
look for the language-body that fits the target language. In order
to effect the translation of the dramatic text, we must have a visual
and gestural picture of the language-body of the source language
and culture. This economy of the language-body cannot work
in the frameworks proposed by *word-movement*(*Wortbewegung*)
(Freud 1891: 170), 'empire of signs' (Barthes 1970: 18), *Gestus*
(Brecht), the 'pantomiming of the text' (Rivière 1971: 5),[5] '[eu]rhy-
thmics' (Jacques Dalcroze), 'the physique of a language' (Deprats
1985: 46), 'tempo-rhythm' (Stanislavski), 'rhythm' (Vinaver 1984),[6]
'moving word and body' (*Wort-* or *Fortbewegung*) (Morein 1985),[7]
'inscription of words in space' (Nemer 1982: 58).[8]

Examples of language-body: a few theories

Each of the following theories or theoretical intuitions attempts more or less consciously to define *language-body*. I shall therefore sketch a few of them, so as to examine their value for a theory of the translated gesture.

A. In his *L'Empire des signes* (1970) (*Empire of Signs* (1980)), Barthes evokes, from the western traveller's point of view, the way in which

> a conversation with the intent of making an appointment is conducted, not only by way of speech and voice, but by way of the entire body (eyes, smile, lock of hair, gesture, clothing), which engage in a sort of chatter purified by the perfect domination of the code of any regressive or infantile character. Making an appointment (using gesture, drawings, proper names) takes about an hour – to convey a message that could be dispatched in a moment if it had been simply spoken (at the same time essential and meaningless); one makes an acquaintance using the whole body, trying and receiving it: this body uses its own narrative, its own text (to no real end).
>
> (1970: 18)

The Japanese message is indeed conveyed by the speaker's body; its 'translation' into a gestural language is attempted, which could in turn be linguistically transcribed (in French).

B. In his theory of *Gestus*, Brecht is close to a gestural translation practice. His translation project – shared with the actor Charles Laughton – gave him the opportunity to put this theory into practice and to make performance a method of translation: 'We were obliged to do what linguistically better equipped translators ought to do: translate *Gestus*. . . . For language is gestic' (1967: XVII, 1120). Brecht's theory leads none the less to an ideological practice, since the gestic aspect of language should not only render the movement or rhythm of a speech, but also and above all, the 'attitude of the poet' (XIX, 404). In this context, the language-body would no longer be an account of meaning to be reconstituted, but an ideological norm which has more to do with reconstituting the ideological discourse to be emphatically inscribed in the

153

mise en scène than with the articulate and unique orchestration of text and gesture, of utterance and enunciation.

In the same way, Stanislavski's notion of 'tempo-rhythm' and the notion of playability used by Susan Bassnett-McGuire (1980: 172) or Mary Snell-Hornby (1984: 104) run the risk of degenerating into a norm of 'proper rhythm,' as if there were a performance rhythm or a *mise en scène* inscribed in the source text, which could be brought to light and reconstituted in the target text.

C. Common to all these approaches is the hypothesis of the text/body orchestration that is appropriate for a given text and culture, and that we ought to attempt to adapt, rather than copy exactly, in the transfer to the target language, while maintaining the relationship of the language-body. A number of translators try to preserve this language-body in their adaptations. Jean-Michel Déprats, translating Shakespeare, has set himself the task of 'limiting meaning, keeping the rhythm, preserving tone, metaphor and prosody, while avoiding the distortion of the poetic spirit.' He listens to an inner voice whose inflexion he tries to rediscover: 'the rhythmic impulse, whether full, or tense, flowing or jerky, that constitutes the song of each translation, its internal poetics,' while abandoning the irreplaceable quality of the 'physical shape of a language, its aural properties, the colours and movements of words' (Déprats 1985: 45–6). Carlson's concern is the relationship between the length of the enunciation and the meaning of the utterance (1964: 55). Corrigan sees in gesture a double indicator of the movement of speech and the movement of feeling thus induced in the spectator: 'Gesture is that meaningfulness that is moving, in every sense of the word, what moves the words and what moves us' (1961: 98).[9]

D. We could multiply examples from translators concerned with gestic and rhythmic aspects of language, who all point to the unnameable: the language-body of the dramatic text. The difficulty in this notion of the language-body lies in delimiting and measuring it in examples of translation. One of the easiest parameters to pick up is the pace of performance, which plays a role both in the unfolding of the text and in the formation of the actor's gesture. The pace of performance depends on the culture within which the dramatic text is inscribed. We might recall Meyerhold and Stanislavski's debate on the question of the 'best' pace for a

Chekhov play: the former reproaches the latter for slowing down the rhythm excessively, in order to create 'atmosphere,' a 'theatre of the unsaid,' furnishing pauses and silences with all sorts of noises and stage business. Transplanted in France, Chekhov has to be adapted to the pace of French actors and audiences. In addition, according to Jean-Louis Barrault, there is the fact that 'the French actor has the habit of relying on the text to regulate performance, since in French theatre the actor is most often enclosed within the text' (Barrault 1984: 58). The relationship between words and body is disturbed in a theatre such as Stanislav-ski's, whose tradition of performance relies more on silence and stage business than on the unfolding of the text. French actors tend to take the text as their point of reference and as an anchor for the language-body, upsetting the balance of the source text's language-body that had been based more on silence and silent action than on the unfolding of the text, while at the same time overloading the target text with a gestural weight that should have been shared more harmoniously between text and stage signification.

CONCLUSION

Reflection on translation confirms a fact well known to theatre semioticians: the text is only one of the elements of performance and, here, of *translating* activity, or, put in another way, the text is much more than a series of words: grafted on to it are ideological, ethnological and cultural dimensions. Culture is so omnipresent that we no longer know where to start investigating it. We are limited here to unmasking it in the series of concretizations, which vary according to the Social Context of the observer, and is complete only when a given audience finally appropriates the source text. The set of gestural moments and variations in the *language-body* have been used to show how the translation involves the transfer of a culture, which is inscribed as much in words as in gestures. We would have to broach the question of the actor shaping and finally interpreting his text and body; he can salvage the most ridiculous translation, but can also wreck the most sublime!

The phenomenon of intergestural and intercultural translation reminds us that culture intervenes at every level of social life, and in all the nooks and crannies of the text. Once again, we must comprehend the double movement that activates cultural theory. On the one hand, we are witnessing – as the case of the *Mahabharata* clearly reveals – a universalization of a notion of culture, a search for the common essence of humanity, which involves a return to the religious and the mystical, and to ritual and ceremony, in the theatre. On the other hand, it is the time to acknowledge the plurality of cultures, individualities, minorities, subcultures, pressure groups, and thus to refine socio-cultural methods of measuring the extent and effects of culture, which leads sometimes away from a global conception of the functioning of society, and towards solutions that are partial and technocratic. Even if this very contradiction in the notion of culture – which is not recent – is exacerbated with the problem of translation, it leads to a *'mythic'* conception of culture and translation. Culture thus becomes a vague notion whose identity, determination and precise place between infra- and superstructure we no longer know. Translation is the undiscoverable mythic text that tries to take account of the source text – all the while knowing that such a translation text exists only with reference to a source-text-to-be-translated. Added to this disturbing circularity is the fact that theatre translation is never where one expects it to be: not in words, but in the gestures, and in the 'social body,' not in the letter, but in the spirit of a culture, ineffable but omnipresent.

NOTES

1. I will not be discussing here the notion of translation as equivalence, which has been refuted by Loren Kruger (1986) and Mary Snell-Hornby (1984). The latter has written:

   The concept of equivalence, whatever the way in which it has been structured and interpreted, is essentially abstract, static and unidimensional; it ignores the changing dynamic of language and remains illusory. Its validity is limited to a few areas of technical translation, which depend on a conceptual identity independent of context, and employ a terminology linked to the establishment of objective norms.

   (Snell-Hornby 1984: 113)

   I will replace the concept of equivalence with that of *language-body*.
2. Narrative competence is one of the components of hermeneutic competence. In the case of the *Mahabharata*, the object was to adapt an Indian narrative for a public accustomed to more recent and less repetitive accounts.
3. The translation should restore the aural and rhythmic quality of the

source text. It is none the less self-evident that each culture appreciates and evaluates rhythmic and tonal qualities and syntactic construction in a different way, and thus that the transfer of the aural and rhythmic qualities is not mechanically applied to that of the source text and culture. (Cf. Gorjan 1965; Frajnd 1980.)

4. I have used the notation 'language-body' (*verbo-corps*) although the expression could also be written 'language em-bodied' (*verbe-au-corps*), which suggests another fundamental characteristic: in the theatre, the word is fixed (*vissé*) to the actor's body, so that s/he embodies language. (Translator's note: The analogy set up between *verbe-au-corps* and *diable au corps* is best left untranslated.)

5. The gap [between Racine and the performance text] does not arise out of a difference established between two series, the textual and the theatrical (there is no question of displacement 'stuck' on to the text), but rather constitutes itself by way of successive shifts or jumps between these two series in order to fashion out of the text, as collection of words, a *gesture* (a movement the detailed articulation of each *alexandrine* accentuates), which like the physical gesture of the actor (and in a dialectical relationship with it) contributes to the writing of this new text – the spectacle.

(Rivière 1971: 5)

6. To say that rhythm is primary in a theatre text implies that action takes place on the level of the very constitution of verbal matter. . . . In the theatre, when something happens, it is the action of words. How does it happen? To what does it owe this power? I call this quality rhythm, well knowing that the term lacks definition. . . . The rhythm of a theatre text is the indissoluble link between words and theatrical form, abolishing any distinction between content and container.

(Vinaver 1984)

7. 'The language-body (*Text-Körper*) as embodied language (*Körper-Text*). A practical introduction to the 'concrete interpretation of embodiment (*Verkörperung*)' (Morein 1985). For Morein, 'moving word and [one's own] body' (*Wort- und Fortbewegung*)'is the movement of embodied language inside the text, whatever the language, voice or verbs of movement in various texts.'

8. If the inscription of its own rhetoric in space is characteristic of theatre, then the inscription of space in theatrical rhetoric is no less characteristic. Without overemphasizing theatrical differences, we can pose the question of whether Shakespeare's poetic imagination is not structured in part by spatial representations that are also metaphors for a worldview. . . . Translating theatre [texts] is a multidimensional activity, since words, like the actor's body, are inscribed in space.

(Nemer 1982: 58)

9. As far as possible, we should guard against making language-body a

normative concept. Language-body does not imply the smooth translation that sits well in the actor's mouth and that the hearer grasps immediately: that would entail resurrecting the concept of the 'playable' translation and we know that translators, like directors today, prefer a focus on form and on an estrangement effect or a meaningful weight in the translated text (Vitez and Régy, among others). If we have occasion to complicate the actor's task, why not? No, language-body is the specific alliance of word and gesture that the translator notes in the source language and which he tries to imitate iconically in the target text.

BIBLIOGRAPHY

Banu, Georges (ed.) (1982) 'Traduire,' *Théâtre/Public* 44.
Barrault, Jean-Louis (1984) 'Pourquoi *La Cerisaie?*', *Théâtre en Europe* 2 (April).
Barthes, Roland (1970) *L'Empire des signes*, Paris: Flammarion; trans. Richard Howard (1980) *Empire of Signs*, New York: Hill & Wang.
Bassnett-McGuire, Susan (1980) *Translation Studies*, London: Methuen.
Benveniste, Emile (1974) *Problèmes de la linguistique générale*, vol. 2, Paris: Gallimard.
Brecht, Bertolt (1967) *Gesammelte Werke*, Frankfurt: Suhrkamp.
Brook, Peter (1985) 'Le *Mahabharata* ou les pouvoirs d'une histoire,' *Alternatives théâtrales* 24.
Carlson, Harry (1964) 'Problems in Play Translation,' *Educational Theatre Journal* 16.
Carrière, Jean-Claude (1974) 'Introduction du traducteur,' *Timon d'Athènes*, Paris: CERT.
—— (1985) 'Chercher le coeur profond,' *Alternatives théâtrales* 24.
Corrigan, Robert (1961) 'Translating for Actors,' in William Arrowsmith and Roger Shattuck (eds) *The Craft and Translation*, Austin: University of Texas Press.
Déprats, Jean-Michel (1985) 'Le verbe, instrument du jeu shakespearean,' *Théâtre en Europe* 7.
Frajnd, Marta (1980) 'The Translation of Dramatic Works as a Means of Cultural Communication,' *Proceedings of the International Comparative Literature Association*, Innsbruck.
Freud, Sigmund (1891) 'Zur Auffassung der Aphasien,' *Studienausgabe*, vol. 3, Frankfurt: Fischer; trans. J. Strachey (1953) London: Hogarth Press.
—— (1915) 'Das Unbewusste,' *Studienausgabe*, vol. 3, Frankfurt: Fischer; trans. J. Strachey (1952) 'The unconscious,' *Standard Edition*, vol 14, London: Hogarth Press.
Gorjan, Zlatko (1965) 'Über das akutische Element beim übersetzen von Bühnenwerken,' in Rolf Italiaander (ed.) *Übersetzen: Vorträge und Beiträge*, Frankfurt: Athenäum.
Ingarden, Roman (1931) *Das literarische Kunstwerk*, Tübingen: Niemeyer.

Italiaander, Rolf (ed.) (1965) *Übersetzen: Vorträge und Beiträge*, Frankfurt, Athenäum.

Jaques-Dalcroze, Emile (1919) *Le Rythme, la musique et l'éducation*, Lausanne: Foetisch.

Krejča, Ottomar (1984) 'L'infini tchékhovien est impitoyable,' *Théâtre en Europe* 2.

Kruger, Loren (1986) *Translating (for) the Theatre: The Appropriation, Mise en Scène and Reception of Theatre Texts*, Ann Arbor: University Microfilms International.

Lassalle, Jacques (1982) 'Du bon usage de la perte,' *Théâtre/Public* 44.

Lévi-Strauss, Claude (1973) *Anthropologie structurale*, vol. 2 Paris: Plon; trans. Monique Layton (1976) *Structural Anthropology*, New York: Basic Books.

Levy, Jiri (1969) *Die literarische Übersetzung*, Frankfurt: Athenäum.

Lotman, J. and Uspensky, B. (1977) 'Myth-Name-Culture,' in *Soviet Semiotics*, ed. D. Lucid, Baltimore: Johns Hopkins University Press.

—— (1978) 'On the Semiotic Mechanisms of Culture,' *New Literary History* 9, 2.

Morein, Andrea (1985) 'Der Text-Körper als Körper-Text,' unpublished MS, Universität Giessen.

Mounin, Georges (1963) *Problèmes théoriques de la traduction*, Paris: Gallimard.

Nemer, Monique (1982) 'Traduire l'espace,' *Théâtre/Public* 44.

Pavis, Patrice (1985) 'Production et réception au théâtre,' in *Voix et images de la scène*, Lille: Presses Universitaires.

—— (1986) 'Du texte à la scène: un enfantement difficile,' *Forum Modernes Theater* 2. English translation, 'From page to stage: a difficult birth,' is chapter 2 of this volume.)

Poupart, René (1985) 'Traduire le théâtre,' unpublished.

Regnault, François (1981) 'Postface à *Peer Gynt*,' ed. Beba, Paris: TNP.

Rivière, Jean (1971) 'La pantomime du texte,' *L'Autre Scène* 3.

Sahl, Hans (1965) 'Zur Übersetzung von Theaterstücken,' in Rolf Italiaander (ed.) *Übersetzen: Vorträge und Beiträge*, Frankfurt: Athenäum.

Sallenave, Danièle (1982) 'Traduire et mettre en scène,' *Acteurs* 1.

Schnapper, Dominique (1986) 'Modernité et acculturation,' *Communications* 43.

Snell-Hornby, Mary (1984) 'Sprechbare Sprache – Spielbarer Text. Zur Problematik der Bühnenübersetzung,' in R. Watts and U. Weidmann (eds) *Modes of Interpretation*, Tübingen: Narr.

Strauss, Botho (1986) *Der Park*, French trans. Claude Porcell, Paris: Gallimard.

Todorov, Tzvetan (1986) 'Le Croisement des cultures,' *Communications* 43.

Vinaver, Michel (1982) 'De l'adaptation,' in *Ecrits sur le théâtre*, Lausanne: L'Aire.

—— (1984) 'Traduire, écrire,' *Comédie française* 129–30.

Vitez, Antoine (1982) 'Le devoir de traduire,' *Théâtre/Public* 44.

Vodička, Felix (1975) *Struktur der Entwicklung*, Munich: Fink.

7

DANCING WITH *FAUST*: REFLECTIONS ON AN INTERCULTURAL *MISE EN SCÈNE* BY EUGENIO BARBA[1]

The first week of the International School of Theatre Anthropology (ISTA) in the Salento region of Italy took place under the sign of *Faust*. Eugenio Barba had brought together eastern performers (Japanese and Indian dancers and musicians) and western spectator-participants in a collective response to *Faust*, especially Goethe's *Faust* but also Marlowe's, as well as the whole western tradition of the popular character and of the myth. The work lasted five mornings, from 6 to 10 a.m. It was not supposed to lead to a finished performance nor was it to be presented to an audience outside the group. Was it then an exercise meant to explore a western director's engagement with Indian and Japanese dancers? Or was it a western production, however unfinished, which exhibited the characteristics of a *mise en scène*? I tend towards the second hypothesis, although Barba carefully sustained the ambiguity of his work and claimed rather to present a 'work in progress' trying out the possibility of a Eurasian theatre.

In any case, this quick sketch will permit us better to observe the growth and progressive consolidation of meaning in the gestural, vocal, textual, musical and spatial arrangement (*mise en place*) of the dancers and musicians.[2] I will describe stages of its development, working on the assumption that we are dealing with a western director and *mise en scène*.

In what follows, one of the participants – simultaneously judging and taking part and hence for ever contaminated by ISTA and deprived of his cherished neutrality – offered the Bari round table[3] not so much a description of Barba's method as a way of imagining how his work on *Faust* might be described with semiotic tools. The anecdotal circumstance of this *relazione* was once again the

160

challenge to semiotics – issued by theatre anthropology – to give an account of the activity of the performers and the *mise en scène*. The (tactical) response to this kind of challenge consists in saying yet again: semiotics has no particular use; it is the artist who makes use of semiotics: let us merely describe this use by examining the re-elaboration of Japanese and Indian gestural traditions through Barba's *mise en scène*.

If, as I have suggested elsewhere (Pavis 1989; see also Chapter 6) every (especially linguistic) translation is an appropriation of the source culture by the target culture, we might say, by analogy, that Barba appropriates oriental performance traditions by transforming and 'rewriting' them on the stage for a western audience. We could then identify a series of appropriations: (1) *semiotic*; (2) *ideological*; (3) *narratological* (in the broad sense). None the less, the term *appropriation* opens the way to an unfortunate misreading, if it suggests that the western director acts like a cultural imperialist expropriating (and destroying) oriental traditions, transforming them into a westernized by-product that no longer owes anything to its origins. In fact, the opposite is true: the re-elaboration of gestural and choreographic materials within a new frame (the plot roughly adapted from *Faust*) by a 'stage *auteur*' – a thoroughly western notion of the director – for members of an audience accustomed to stage discourse in which meaning is produced especially for them. This neutralized but somewhat insipid term – re-elaboration – only shows that the cultural and theatrical traditions of the source culture are transformed by the needs of the target culture's theatrical and cultural tradition, that of Barba and his target audience in this case, the performers, directors and theorists of ISTA.[4] We will follow the chain of gestural and cultural re-elaborations and reinterpretations that punctuate this stage (re)writing of *Faust*, in the hope of better understanding the links between cultures, practices and theatre traditions as well as their confrontation within the *mise en scène*.

PREPARATION OF THE MATERIALS

The choice of scenes depended on the ISTA participants, who were also the only spectators of this *Faust*. Five or six teams of five or six members were each asked to reread Goethe's play, to summarize the actions, to choose key scenes centered on the kernel of these actions, and finally to suggest a scenario that would start with simple situations in which the dialogue played only an accessory role in the service of clearly defined stage actions. Barba then made selections from these collective written suggestions, without explaining his choice explicitly or implicitly. We can only note that Barba kept the suggestions of actions and concrete situations and rejected philosophical or psychological reflections and literary commentary. He did not seem to be interested in a global dramaturgical analysis or in the text a priori. He did not try to adapt the whole work to remain faithful to the letter or the spirit of the myth or to give it a totalizing, coherent or consistent reading. He rather treated text and script suggestions as generators of situations and stage actions thematically linked to the plot of *Faust*.

This plot seems in many ways to be a myth that is profoundly and typically western, and this will be my main hypothesis. As André Dabezies has shown, it has crystallized, from the fifteenth-century legend to Goethe and beyond, the birth of individualism and individual freedom.[5] This evolution of the Faustian myth indicates the emergence of the individual from the familial, social or national group, the birth of individualism and the aspiration to freedom and knowledge. What is most 'western' about Faust is perhaps not so much the division of being as the active search for knowledge by an individual who feels himself to be sufficiently strong and detached from the group to deal with the devil as an equal (and no longer with a god in his own image), and to set out alone in search of truth. Confronted with this power of individualism, we might find it hard to imagine how Japanese (*buyo*) and Indian (*odissi*) dancers, both coming from national choreographic traditions that are rigidly codified, might particularize and individualize their performances, to the point of breaking with their own tradition, of entering into a 'gestural and cultural' dialogue with each other, and above all of formally reconstituting this individualist kernel of the Faustian myth. At ISTA, they first had to follow the instructions and themes of improvisations offered by Barba on the basis of their own tradition, while incorporating into their performance certain elements essential to the Faustian themes. None the less, these dancers were well acquainted with Barba, having worked with him on and off for eight years. Their *Faust* improvisations thus took place in the intercultural context of ISTA and represented the continuation of an experiment begun with the first ISTA in Bonn. The activities of

the Salento ISTA session were not new, except for the theme of
Faust.

THE DANCERS' INCORPORATION

The Japanese dancer Katsuko Azuma and the Indian dancer Sanjukta Panigrahi belong to two totally different cultural and theatri-
cal/choreographic worlds. It is difficult to link their art, and to
do so would be a very western simplification based on the facile
magic of the term 'oriental.'[6] The possibility of getting them to
work together is not self-evident, since the contrast in their presence, dynamic and gestural representation is striking. Moreover,
this 'Faustian' project, to confront them while imposing the plot
of *Faust*, is both perfectly arbitrary and completely legitimate,
since it forces the dancers and their director/choreographer to
adapt to a third term, to join their efforts in the construction of
a story that remains to be invented.

It is difficult to describe the way in which each dancer organizes
her improvisation based on the very general instructions given in
English by Barba. These instructions are only suggestions for an
action/improvisation on the basis of a concrete action, or for a
narrative frame within which the interpreters can freely improvise.
For example, Barba prompts Panigrahi (playing Mephisto) to
approach Azuma from a distance, hiding behind trees, while
waving her arms as if she wanted to attract Faust's attention. The
assimilation of materials derived from *Faust* thus occurs through
the dancing body, not through a psychological approach to character or a textual approach to the play. The choreography that
develops is not intended to elucidate character or to illustrate
various plot situations. The function of the dialogue is not to
explain character, or even to be fully comprehensible.[7]

It is not easy to measure the distance between canonical *odissi*
or *buyo* and the improvisations created by these dancers. Deviation from the codified traditional gestures does not seem to be
a threat, but rather a consciously assumed risk.[8] The director's
role, closer to Mephisto than to Faust, is essentially to provoke
the 'fall' of the oriental angel, and to destabilize the dancer, to
unbalance her in the sense of imposing a gesture or series of
gestures, an attitude foreign to the original codification. For example, Barba puts a glass bottle in Panigrahi's hands and asks her to
do drunken – and therefore rhythmically distorted – *mudras*,

163

to show the character's drunkenness. This process of voluntary deformation is immediately followed by re-formation, by moving to another type of codification. The dance of the drunken *mudras* becomes a parody of popular dance in which one dancer imitates the movements of the other, a joyful dance of two drunkards who end up synchronizing their drunkenness. This de-formation is not an elimination of the codified traditional form, but its re-formation into another kind of gesture, inspired by the tradition and preparing for the next stages of the re-elaboration.

The dancer incorporates into her performance and traditional codification those 'foreign bodies,' gestures and rhythms that she had automatically rejected. This appropriation is achieved by way of a sort of 'gestural graft,' which she must tolerate without rejection. As in the 'Eurasian' village which Barba (1982) conjures up, 'the performers (or a single male or female performer) not only analyse a conflict, are guided by the objectivity of the *logos*, telling a story, but also dance *with* and *within* it according to the *bios*' (Barba 1982). The two dancers' appropriation/incorporation of the *Faust* story is the first stage in the process of acculturation, the movement from eastern encoding to western decoding,[9] which turns out – as we shall see – to be recoding through the *mise en scène*. The dancers' improvisation constitutes the first shaping of the corporal materials, on the basis of which the *mise en scène* will effect a semiotic, ideological, narratological and cultural re-elaboration.

Concretely, what are the dancers doing? Panigrahi holds a bottle in her hands. She takes a few gulps, becomes drunk immediately. She staggers along, throws away the bottle, attempts a few *mudras*, which immediately seem uncertain and distorted by her intoxication. Azuma dogs her footsteps, imitating her, trying without much success to synchronize her gestures with Panigrahi's. They improvise a sort of *pas de deux*.

SEMIOTIC RE-ELABORATION: THE GESTURAL EXAMPLE

Semiotic re-elaboration in the strict sense involves the *mise en scène*'s manipulation of signs, which can be described and itself constitutes a set of pure semiotic operations. This claim will be tested briefly here.

Montage

Barba juxtaposes two choreographic traditions in the idiosyncrasies of the two dancers. He does not impose continuity in the 'gestural interaction.' He does not try to give the illusion of a transition, sequence or even a 'dialogic interaction' (question/answer). As in film montage, each dancer's gestural sequence maintains its autonomy; each unfolds and is perceived at the same time as the other's without the continuity, coherence or order that 'turn and turn about' in speech or gesture which would produce the plot in a continuous sequence. According to Barba, a performer's gestures can be compared to film montage, which is itself 'material for subsequent editing.' The director then edits these heterogeneous materials that the performers have provided: 'it is usually the director's work which combines the actions of several performers, whether in succession as though in response to each other or in simultaneous presentation, in which the meaning of both arises directly from their juxtaposition' (Barba 1985:179). Linking these gestural moments to establish coherence and continuity is up to the spectators, who are obviously guided by the system and the rhythm of the montage suggested by the *mise en scène*.

This technique can be seen in the sequence in which Azuma (Faust) briefly recapitulates the entire Faustian problem of origins ('in the beginning was . . .'): (1) she digs up a book; (2) leafs through it without understanding; (3) mechanically reads aloud the author and title; (4) throws it away and moves to a completely different action. These actions are run together to give the impression of an accelerated film.

Juxtaposition of emotional tonalities

The *mise en scène* not only juxtaposes the dancers and their sequences of gestures in montage, but also treats their gestural and emotional tonality in counterpoint, opening the gap and clearly differentiating their emotional worlds, displaying the absence of communication. In an extremely powerful scene, for example, we have Faust (Azuma) and Mephisto (Panigrahi) downstage, squatting face to face, unearthing the remains of a child, while behind them Margaret (played by the Onnagata Kan-Ichi Hanayaghi) goes through a series of emotions and states of mind which she (or he) demonstrates by showing each posture and its range of expressions. Three gestural keys, corresponding to three clearly distinct emotional tonalities, are thus presented 'in the same shot.'

The solitude of each character, the difference and originality of each but also the similarities within the differences, can be seen: the Danish actress Iben Nagel Rasmussen plays a Margaret who represents a consuming murderous madness, Azuma and Panigrahi repeat the same gesture (carrying and observing the child, perhaps) with finger positions and tensions both similar and different. Individual improvisation sometimes leads to interaction and correlation: Margaret turns her back on Faust, but remains within earshot, while Faust directs his gaze to the child whom Mephisto is carrying. The juxtaposition is sustained at particularly meaningful moments by its opposite, the interaction and the synchronization of emotion and gesture. The two dancers use little speech, but incorporate memory in a long series of gestures. Each dancer's language-body and language-culture is very different. Japanese language-body gives the impression of meticulously stitching together restrained and internalized cries, while Indian language-body is fairly externalized ('audible lips,' gesture underlining speech, stressing paralinguistic facial signs).[10]

Focalization

Juxtaposing and coordinating gestures clearly reveal the mobility and fragility of the performers' relationship. Furthermore, the body is never exposed as the body of an individual (i.e. as an indivisible whole), but remains a mobile montage of its separate parts. Each dancer has the power to focus the spectator's gaze on the part of the body judged pertinent at any moment. This technique of foregrounding a meaning or a part of the work, much praised by the Russian Formalists, leads to focalization, to the enlargement of a detail, to lengthening certain moments, to holding certain poses. Continual changes in focalization set up a narrative of the body, guiding reception by creating narrative continuity despite the fragmentation of the foregrounded shots, cut off from the overall structure.

Focalization magnifies or underlines a detail, eliminates signs judged secondary or irrelevant at a given moment, expands or concentrates time at will, 'dilates' or 'contracts' the performer's body, ensures the hierarchical arrangement of signs in performance.

This montage of gestural micro-actions makes sense only if it anticipates how spectators will receive the sequence (in the sense of receiving blows or caresses). We can see this focalization in Panigrahi's use of her hands. Her gaze, like that of her partner, is fixed on them: she uses her hands to distil the most obvious gestural variations, encouraging the spectator to make sense of these sequences.

Confrontation of gestural moments

The polarization of the roles of Mephisto and Faust and the clearly legible system of oppositions establish a hierarchy of signs. The casting is certainly not an accident, but Barba has not to my knowledge explained it, assuming perhaps that it is self-evident. The casting inscribes oppositions for the spectator (see Table 7.1).

Table 7.1 Semiotic oppositions

Mephisto (Panigrahi)	Faust (Azuma)
large	small
mobile	hieratic
comes from outside	already there
ease	obstruction
openness	closure
expressive face and arms	expressive bust and poses
activity	passivity
western masculine principle	western feminine principle

Comparing these two kinds of gestures and codification can be done only by way of a *tertium comparationis*, a third point of view that borrows from neither one nor the other, or from a referential system that seeks universality, a western obsession. In this search for transcultural categories, can we locate ourselves in what Barba calls the 'pre-expressive'?

We might rather say that we are faced with a narrative model, thoroughly influenced by a western ideological and cultural model. The opposition and the heterogeneity of gestural moments take on a dramaturgical significance that corresponds more or less to the traditional western image of the Faustian myth (from Marlowe and Goethe to Murnau and Valéry). Mephisto appears as the foreign element, disturbing and tempting, dominant and seductive, whereas Faust is linked to immobility and the hearth, to the passivity of a seduced victim: a stereotypical western opposition between masculinity and femininity, which makes of this couple of men (in the traditional *Faust*) or women (in this *mise en scène*), a homo-, a- or pansexual couple (whose sexuality is bracketed or elevated to the level of a universal principle). Thus it is possible to 'tell' this gestural dichotomy and gestural dialogue by bringing them together in a plot or anecdote, by projecting on to the plot the oppositions perceived on the level of formal and gestural rhythm. But isn't this a western view? Indeed, but how can we change our spots? We judge Barba's experiment according to our narrative habits that encourage us to 'translate' the performers into dramatic characters, then to compare and contrast these characters according to sex, age, activity and individual traits. The theatrical and choreographic codification here shifts to another much more subtle and implicit codification, that of culture, in which ideology is one component among many.

It is certainly artificial to set up an opposition between east and west and yet separate the Japanese from the Indian tradition. Let us note simply that, in Panigrahi's performance, due to its expressiveness in mime and attitude and its emotional externalization, the Indian tradition seems closer to the west than does the Japanese, and thus appears more 'legible' to a western audience. In other words, Mephisto is the western face of Faust, the one who questions and provokes the entirely eastern interiority of his consenting victim.[11]

Cultural dichotomy of gestural moments

This differentiation between Japanese and Indian culture is none the less reduced as soon as we contrast them with the tradition of Faust. Faust is an archetypal western Christian character and the fundamental figure of *Streben*, 'striving towards,' of elevation and the torturous quest, the original principle of dialogue and conflict and that of division of the soul. The conflict in Faust's character, induced by the devil himself, is difficult to transpose into a Japanese theatrical tradition which does not recognize western categories of psychology and inner conflict, choreographically represented by elevation, the rising movement of humanity and the soul toward God. On the other hand, as Watanabe (1982: 57) notes, the Japanese tradition differs from western dance that 'aspires upward'; the Japanese tradition 'is rooted in the ground and in the earth: it is a kind of celestial power, which descends to earth and stays there for a while, whose energy human beings would like to capture.' This *Faust* offers us a perfect illustration of the principle mentioned by Watanabe. Azuma 'plays' a Faust who is barely mobile and whose only gestural ventures are revolts that are quickly suppressed. In contrast, Panigrahi never stops moving, advancing or retreating, constantly changing her center of gravity, directing her piercing gaze at the other. In this sense, the inversion of signs produced by Azuma, tied to the ground by the powerful forces of the earth and by a rising, air-borne Mephisto, is as remarkable as the global inversion of the western myth of *Faust* in a choreography rooted in the earth by Japanese *buyo*. Paradoxically, the Indian tradition and Barba's *mise en scène* are allied in restoring to *Faust* some of its westernness.

Which semiotics?

Semiotics has some difficulty in describing this fragment of *Faust*, since it has not really decided whether to judge by the results of this acculturation-recodification that Barba and the dancers propose or the dynamic process of appearance and disappearance of these same codifications. In other words, it has to choose between a western semiotics following St Thomas, which believes only what it sees, or an 'energetic' semiotics (as Lyotard would say) that attempts to 'produce the greatest intensity (by excess or default) of what is there, without intention' (Lyotard 1973: 104), i.e. to imagine the direction of choreographic and cultural reinterpretation of the signs, which are themselves only the superficial traces, the discarded skin of a vanished snake. We ought to imagine this energetic semiotics that Barba and Lyotard dream of, a semiotics that would concern itself not with results and visible signs, but with the cultural reinterpretation in which we can still see the old under the new, the 'rough sketching which indicates traces of other movements and features all around the fully worked-out figure' (Brecht 1977), like the traces in which one sees both what has just been expropriated and what is appropriated, deculturation as well as acculturation. In order to read this kind of semiotics, one would have to be an 'ideal' spectator, who should be, according to Barba (1982), capable of following or accompanying the performer in the dance of 'thinking in action': a moving subject *par excellence* who has to describe an evolving object. This is perhaps the new challenge to semiotics: to shift perspective on an object itself in motion, without giving up the notion of sign and pertinence, but allowing sufficient play and fluctuation.

Western semiotics is naturally aware of this principle of concatenation, of the syntagmatic and metonymic organization of signs. But it ought to become a little 'oriental' and try to understand the simultaneous actions, their paradigmatic and metaphorical organization, to follow the 'thought-in-action.' Ideally, semiotics ought to follow this 'thinking in action' (Barba 1982), and the theorist, like Barba's ideal spectator, ought to be able to 'follow or accompany the performer in the dance of thinking in action' (Barba 1988: 129). Semiotics ought to be able not only to pin down the already perceived meaning, but also to anticipate its direction, to imagine what Indian theatre theory calls the spectator's *nritya*, i.e.

> the combination of dance and emotional expression accompanied by meaningful gestures, modes of speech or a lyric poem. It is so carefully wrought, so perfect, that it is enough to keep the spectators alert and able to follow all the unexpressed thoughts and the conception of a character.
> (Panigrahi 1983: 87)

This 'energetic semiotics' would no longer – as is still the case in western semiotics or *mise en scène* – have to recognize and describe the pertinent features of a sign, but rather hide and reveal signs in the same moment and the same movement of denegation.

IDEOLOGICAL RE-ELABORATION

The semiotic control and re-elaboration of gestural moments by the *mise en scène* are so clear only because they correspond to certain familiar ideological and emotional categories of the western audience – namely that human action, motivation and comprehension must be easily understood, identified and accepted. The action of Barba's *Faust* conforms to the spectator's horizon of expectation. This often leads to a universalizing of values and gestures, which translates sometimes into a humanist universalizing of diverse cultures and sometimes into a uniformity induced by the combined effect of simplification and the influence of technology and the mass media.[12]

Pathos

Certain situations are particularly apt to generate pity and terror, the good old categories of Aristotelian tragedy: for instance, exhuming all that remains of the child, the swaddling clothes that Mephisto slowly unearths with malicious pleasure. Barba prolongs this scene by slowing down its rhythm, accompanying it with melodramatic music composed by Jan Ferslev for guitar, flute and four female voices situated behind the performance area; in the background, Margaret's emotional reaction. Barba creates pathos that must deeply touch every spectator. In the same spirit, the scene with the knife is played in the cathartic register of a theatre of cruelty, which clearly appears, even in Artaud's rebellion, as the culmination of the entire western tradition.

Melodrama

The systematic and insistent expression of universal feelings (fear, despair, suffering, sense of injustice, etc.) relates to the technique of emotional manipulation characteristic of melodrama. This reminds us of Murnau's magnificent silent film of *Faust*, which also makes abundant use of universal feelings, pauses and poses of joy and despair, playing on all the nuances of melodrama. Barba uses western music to underline the melodramatic atmosphere of the text, which highlights in an altogether different way a text as crude and grotesque as the ballad of Margarethe ('Meine Mutter, die Hur, die mich umgebracht hat!') ('My mother, the whore, who killed me'). To the extent that melodrama is a typical form of western theatre (in the eighteenth and nineteenth centuries), it is not surprising that it works especially well for the re-westernization of the Faustian myth.

Burlesque

On the other hand, several scenes employ the comedy of burlesque, Faust's and Mephisto's drunkenness for example. The pact with the Devil is celebrated in an unconventional and sympathetic way: by getting the signatories roaring drunk. This turn of the drunken lurching actor is one we have seen a hundred times in popular comedy or silent film. It gives us the immediate and sensual pleasure of recognizing a dramatic *topos*. It is also the pleasure, almost relief, of seeing the drunken and suddenly uncontrolled bodies of the dancers, freed of constraints, codification and prohibitions, very similar to those of western spectators; these bodies are provisionally at the mercy of physiology, since alcohol has no bounds. But the bodies remain full of culture, since one lurches differently if one has received the gestural education of *odissi* or *buyo*.

Ideological adaptation in this *Faust* does not occur by neutralizing formal or philosophical options of theatre traditions, or through praising some virtue of the western soul, but rather through fine-tuning some great universal feelings, by appealing to fundamental categories of reception (pity, terror, comedy, melodrama). The function of this adaptation is to erode codified theatrical or choreographic forms that are too specifically honed to single cultures and performance traditions, the better to adapt to the audience's universalizing demands. Thus, the human and dramatic situation becomes immediately comprehensible, without the mediation of the artistic codes of specific theatrical forms. This flattening is the price paid for the spectator's comfortable reception of what Barba calls the pre-expressive, what we could also call a psychologizing ideology of the universal.

The semiotic and ideological reinterpretation of this *Faust* improvised by Azuma and Panigrahi can be particularly clearly seen in the way Barba chooses to *tell* the story, and one can see the gestural and rhythmic narrative as the backbone of the *mise en scène* and thus speak of a complete narratological restructuring.

NARRATOLOGICAL RE-ELABORATION

This narratological restructuring takes place in the wings, as it were, since there are two significant absences at ISTA: the erotic body and structural narratology (and if you had seen our long undivided dormitory, you would understand that we had no desire to practice structural narratology). Barba does not appear to pose the question of narrative in his writings: is there a universal, transcultural way of telling stories or are there on the contrary narrative techniques peculiar to each cultural tradition? There is furthermore a danger, which neither Barba nor Grotowski escapes, of limiting narrative to *logos*, instead of seeing it as a structural principle which manifests itself in several substances (verbal language, gestural movements, painting, cinema, etc.). For example, Grotowski opposes *logos* to *bios*, instead of envisaging them as parallel ways of telling (*lexis*), whether verbal or gestural:

> We have *logos* and *bios*; *logos* is linked to descriptive and analytical discourse. In a different way, the problem of *logos* even arises in case of the eastern performer. In that tradition, the eastern performer uses his or her body to express words, sentences, discourses, i.e. *logos*. But it is as if this *logos* has, because of the performer's strong tradition, retained certain principles of *bios*; for this reason, the eastern performer seems alive to us.
>
> (Grotowski 1982:56)[13]

It is questionable to assert, as does Grotowski, that the body of the eastern performer expresses words, i.e. *logos*, even if the performers, especially in Kathakali, do indeed have at their disposal a repertory of signs – *mudras* – referring to objects in the real world and if they tell their story according to an implicit sentence, which specialists can practically 'hear' as they follow the performers' hand movements. The Kathakali actor offers a gestural narration, a story told not with words (*logos*), but with gestural narrative units, which can certainly be identified or described with words, but are not themselves words (*logos*).

> In this [professional Eurasian] 'village', it often happens that the performers (or a single performer) not only analyse a conflict, allow themselves to be guided by the objectivity of *logos* and tell a story, but also dance *in* it and *with* it according to *bios*. This is not a metaphor: this means concretely that the performer does not stay yoked to the chariot of the plot, does not interpret a text, but rather creates a context, moves around and within events.
>
> (Barba 1982)

Barba also takes up the opposition between *logos* and *bios*, mistakenly limiting the story told to verbal language (*logos*), but at the same time he attempts to overcome this opposition. The dance *with* and *within* the story redefines the relationship between the 'physical' performer and spoken text: one is not reduced to the other, but they form the 'dance,' an interaction between what the performer does with gesture and what the text says. The performer should not reduce or interpret the text, but rather invent (together with the director and the *mise en scène* as a whole) a situation within which the text makes sense.

Once this model has been established, it is easier to understand how Barba reappropriates the (western) myth of *Faust* using the improvised material that the dancers provide. He transposes the original microstructures of *buyo* and *odissi* into a gestural and narrative macrostructure. This narratological retotalization is not, however, an adaptation in the western sense: Barba does not feel obliged to restore the proportions and complexity of Goethe's text. He does not start from a global outline of the play or a preconceived idea or Brechtian dramaturgical analysis. He treats *Faust* rather like an argument for a ballet, or a possible story.

From micro- to macrostructures

Buyo and *odissi* use gestures to tell stories. The gestural narrative is made up of a very large number of microsequences, each of which corresponds to an episode or a detail of the story. Only specialists can analyse, identify and paraphrase these codified microsequences. We do not need to recognize them, however, in order to appreciate the dance. As director and reorganizer of these microsequences, Barba has to take the ignorance of his western audience into account.

On the other hand, in the western tradition, meaning is not established analytically from myriad gestures and codified episodes, but from a narrative macrosequence, which sums up a whole scene, or even the whole play. Brecht, for example, bases his *mise en scène* on a search for the fundamental (*Gestus* of key scenes, 'extracting' the story of the play, i.e. the 'theatre's great operation, the complete fitting together of all the gestic incidents, embracing the communications and impulses that must now go to make up the audience's entertainment' (Brecht 1977: 200). The *Gestus* is a synthetic narrative macrostructure that includes a long series of episodes, but can be divided up only a posteriori, once one examines the actions in detail.

In his re-elaboration of *Faust*, Barba indeed uses materials available to him through the dancer's improvisation, but he edits and integrates them into a larger structure: a situation, a scene or a gest. He had advised the 'scenario writers' not to enslave themselves to the letter of Goethe's text, but rather to suggest global actantial narrative situations, broad frames in which action and situation would be clearly readable. Once Barba had selected and defined the general narrative framework, the dancers could concentrate on inventing and fixing the details of plot and text. Due to this synthetic procedure, in the adaptation as in the performance options, the dancers and then the spectators normally and easily identify the overall situations and the unfolding of the narrative, as the dancers inscribe the detail of their improvisation within the broad and firm framework of the narrative macrosequences. Barba's narratological appropriation thus involves restructuring the analytical, gestural codification into a narrative macrostructure with large units, and dissociating, in the *mise en scène* as well as in the spectator's mind, the analytic and coded reading of word and gesture from the global reading of the story. Because the adaptation and the *mise en scène* propose large units of situation and action, the spectator succeeds in locating and *linking* (as well as *reading*) (*lier/lire*) the episodes of *Faust*'s story. Inevitably, this process involves some simplification, since each tradition must adapt to the other and can only enter into dialogue with the other if it simplifies its narrative arguments.

A classical narratology

This dissociation of narrative macrostructure and gestural microsequences is reinforced by Barba's narratological model. This model is binary, transitive, active and thus classical in its simplicity. It is of the type, Subject + Verb + Direct Object: Paul eats an apple; Faust sells his soul; Faust loves Margaret; Barba likes ISTA.

The actants can be easily identified and are engaged in a simple action, in which the one influences the other actively and directly. Modeling (which influences action) or metatextual reflections are avoided or postponed or reduced to some microsequences, without loss of overall legibility. Everything abstract, intellectualized, or diluted by philosophical commentary is eliminated in the interests of concrete and univocal action. The suggestion of our group to adapt the passage in Goethe in which the issue is knowing what came first, the word, meaning, power or action – a key passage for the philosophy of the work – is concentrated in a few seconds and 'translated' into a visible and explicit action: Azuma holds a copy of *Faust*, mechanically reads everything written on the cover, and then throws the book away: a very explicit way to get rid of the text's philological subtleties and to translate Goethe's lucubrations by a series of actions. Exit the Book!

From epic to dramatic

The western macrostructural narrative logic efficiently compensates for the partial unreadability of the traditional eastern microstructures. Dancing according to their traditions, Azuma and Panigrahi speak with their bodies: the story is told in an epic fashion by the dancers' actual bodies. They do so by focusing on the details of their facial expressions or postures.

In contrast, classical western narrative logic, which Barba imposes through the improvisations, infiltrates and restructures the material according to an encompassing dramatic action conveyed by the two actants: the story is acted out in a dramatic fashion by the characters' fictional bodies.

Labeling meaning

The narratological transfer brought about by Barba is possible only to the extent that spectators are in a position to identify and differentiate the units of the narrative, thanks to this encyclopedic competence. The choice of the title *Faust* immediately suggests to a spectator with some degree of sophistication a certain expectation of themes, actions and characters, which are more or less recognized and confirmed. Western culture functions by labeling, naming, appraising.

Western subtitles

Labeling would still not be enough to guarantee an approximate deciphering of the story of *Faust*. What is necessary is some kind of subtitling, as in a silent or foreign film in the original language. The words pronounced in Italian (by Cesare Brie) clarify the Sanskrit or classical Japanese. The (German) choir of the cries of 'Heinrich' function as intermediaries, 'fixing' meaning as indices open to the intelligence and the culture of ISTA's western audience. The subtitles complete the narratological re-elaboration and western adaptation of the choreography inspired by *Faust*.

CULTURAL RE-ELABORATION

Does the conjunction of semiotic, ideological and narratological re-elaboration suffice to describe and explain the genesis as well as the reading of this *Faust* montage? An analysis would not be complete without examining the overall view of the director who takes up and synthesizes a certain number of typical cultural practices of western *mise en scène* (see Pavis 1988).

The unifying subject

It is the director's responsibility to select and edit the improvisations. As the stage *auteur* 'signing' the production, the western director, Barba, does not have to justify his choices other than by way of a subjective search for expressiveness, coherence and formal clarification, a search which never completely reveals its own logic. The *mise en scène* is the site on which bricolage becomes structural. Western *mise en scène* – and thus the appearance of a third party, the director, alongside author and actor – is linked to the historical development of western culture: the decline of classical performance traditions, the disappearance of a strong form, the culmination of a bourgois individualistic tradition, the formation of a theory of the subject and the author, in this instance the stage subject (a theory which, barely constituted, explodes under the pressure of Marxist and psychoanalytical deconstruction).

The director's cultural re-elaboration of these Faustian fragments is indispensable if this Italian-German-Indian-Japanese encounter is not to produce the most explosive mix. Here Barba is both a conflicting subject (preserving the diversity of forms proposed by the dancers) and a unifying subject (bringing together all these centripetal forces back to the western story of *Faust*). His *Faust* returns finally to its point of departure: a western vision conveyed by eastern traditions is reworked by a western director, ending up with a sketch which bears all the distinguishing features of western *mise en scène*.

A metacultural vision

This unification is realized also by the neutralization of one theatrical and cultural tradition by another, by the discovery of transcultural values, by 'the constant factor in cultural variation' (Grotowski 1982: 56). These transcultural values are very general: quest (Faust), temptation (Mephisto), fall (Margaret), melodramatic sentiments. The neutralization is also achieved by frequent parodies of one codification by another: when, for example, Azuma/Faust drunkenly attempts *mudras* imitating Panigrahi/Mephisto. The parody of one form by another implies the ability to imitate, but above all to quote, rewrite, in short to appropriate. This parody can easily become metatextual, since it implies a reflection on forms and the means of surpassing them. As Juri Lotman remarks, the 'twentieth century has produced not only scientific metalanguages, but also metaliterature and metapainting, and is now apparently creating metaculture, a metalinguistic system to the second degree that encompasses everything, (Lotman and Uspensky 1978: 229). For this kind of activity, we need a metacultural (not simply transcultural) vision that could confront forms and dramaturgies. Parody does not exclude interaction between the parodist and his object; it reveals their mutual influence. In the above-mentioned example of the semantic opposition between Panigrahi/Mephisto's externalized and aggressive and Azuma/Faust's internalized and passive gesture, for instance, we can observe the interaction between the two dancers' gazes. The more Panigrahi is present in her gaze, the more Azuma internalizes hers, her suffering, her body, the more she reduces her movements, giving way to the demon tempter.

Their interaction and the 'montage by attraction' that Barba establishes do not amount to a simple semiotic or narratological operation. They engage an entire ideology and culture as a montage of antagonistic forces. They also bear witness to Barba's refusal completely to expropriate 'foreign' theatre codification and his determination to maintain cultural 'transparency,' i.e. to let cultures be seen through cultures. There is always a double displacement of the Japanese or Indian source cultures. Barba's western spectator must see, on the one hand, that these cultures are foreign (easy enough), but also that these cultures diverge from their usual codification and norms as a result of the work of the *mise en scène*. The codes of oriental theatre are both as foreign and as displaced in our direction. Awareness of difference remains intact. This confrontation never results in ideological or transcultural uniformity, but is rather a relativizing practice conducted by the actual spectators discussed by Barba and who, east or west, are few in number, but 'for whom theatre may become a necessity.' For them, Barba says: 'Theatre is a relationship, which is not based on a union, does not create communion, but rather ritualizes the reciprocal foreignness and the laceration of the body social hidden beneath the uniform skin of dead myth and values' (Barba 1982).

Does Barba get to a Eurasian theatre at the end of this engagement of *Faust* with Japanese and Indian traditions? The term is not without ambiguity and contradiction. That is in fact its *raison d'être*. But can we go beyond Barba's observation (1982) that 'the seduction, imitation and exchange are reciprocal in this eastern/-western encounter'? It is almost impossible to think the 'inter' in the 'intercultural,' except in terms of concentric metaphors: exchange, sharing, contact, barter, revitalization, appropriation, a stealthy imperialism that has swapped the gun for theatre interculturalism? The danger certainly exists, but isn't there something a little ridiculous and demagogic in the concern of someone like Bharucha (1984) who warns intercultural directors not to exploit 'donor' countries by appropriating their substance like cunning western vampires, when these artists make the effort not to reduce one culture to another, while assembling the theoretical and meta-cultural bridges that allow us to observe a give-and-take between them, when Japanese and Indian culture have abundantly drawn from the western technology for better or worse? How could we reproach Barba, for example, for having re-elaborated a western vision and *mise en scène* of *Faust*, when we easily accept the idea that the dancers help themselves without reservation to the argument and the materiality, the letter and the spirit, of 'our' *Faust*? Doesn't the value of this intercultural *mise en scène* lie in the way it confronts oriental codification and choreography and the typically western organization of *mise en scène*? The conflict is still intact.

'Zwei Seelen wohnen, ach! in meiner Brust' ('Two souls, alas, are housed within my breast'), lamented old Faust. But if he had known that his breast would one day be a theatre of interculturalism, God knows whether he would have agreed to sign a pact with the Devil!

NOTES

1. This chapter first appeared in *The Drama Review*, 123 (Fall, 1989).
2. I will not discuss the question of defining the performers here as

actors or dancers. The distinction is far from being as distinct in Japan or India as it is in Europe: I prefer the term 'dancer' as a way of focusing on the very gestural codification of the performers. Deciding whether this is a theatrical dance (using speech) or a theatre codified like choreography is not very important. (Translator's note: The English term 'performer' provides the semantic suppleness that the French chases after here; I have therefore translated 'acteur' and 'actrice' by 'performer' except in cases where the gender of 'actress' is essential to the argument.)

3. 'Primo Incontro Internazionale fra Semiologia e Antropologia Teatrale' (First International Convention of Semiotics and Theatre Anthropology), Bari, September 12, 1987. The Odin Theatre has a video of the rehearsals, which was made by Italian television.

4. Barba likes to speak of a 'new elaboration,' borrowing Richard Schechner's term, 'restored behavior': restored behavior is a living action treated as a film-maker treats a sequence of film. Each sequence has to be edited and reconstructed. It is independent of the set of causes (social, psychological, technological) which have given it birth: it is behavior in its own right (*un comportement propre*). The original truth or intention of this action may be lost, unknown or hidden, engendered or deformed by the myth constituting the initial materials of a process used in the course of rehearsals to get a new elaboration, the performance itself; these visual sequences of the action are no longer processes, but rather objects, materials (Barba 1985: 179).

5. Dabezies (1972) identifies three stages and variants of the myth: (1) 'the Christian myth of sin and the risks of freedom' (p. 312); (2) 'the risks of greatness and freedom,' of the 'quasi-metaphysical aspiration to the infinite and the ideal' (p. 314); (3) 'triumphal freedom,' which cultimates in the view that Oswald Spengler offers in *The Decline of the West* of Faustian man: 'the mythic figure of the West as a whole' (Dabezies 1972: 316).

6. 'The popular slogans about individualism and realism in the west opposed to the mass mentality and mysticism in the east reveal their absurdity as soon as we analyse them seriously,' as Goetz notes (1960). Likewise, to speak of 'oriental theatre' (as Artaud does in his essay 'Occidental and oriental theatre') can be a source of simplification.

7. Cf. Artaud:

> Furthermore, I am well aware that the language of gestures and postures, dance and music, is less capable of analyzing a character, revealing thoughts, or elucidating states of consciousness clearly and precisely than is verbal language, but whoever said that the theater was created to analyze a character, to resolve the conflicts of love and duty, to wrestle with all the problems of a topical and psychological nature that monopolize the contemporary stage?
>
> (Artaud 1958: 41; translation modified)

8. Panigrahi created her dances from the songs written in another lan-

guage in her native region, Orissi. Her work at ISTA gave her the opportunity to expand her repertoire; 'I asked Barba if I might work with him to discover new possibilities. I do not believe that this work could threaten my traditions. If that were the case, I would stop at once.' (Panigrahi 1982: 68).

9. Barba describes his 'good advice' for western and eastern actors in the following way:

> Contemporary western actors have no organic repertoire of advice on which they can rely and on the basis of which they orient themselves. In general, their point of departure is a text or the director's instructions. They lack these rules governing action, which would aid them without constraining their artistic freedom. Traditional eastern actors, on the other hand, base their work on an organic and tested body of 'absolute advice,' that is, rules similar to the laws of a code. They codify a self-enclosed style of action to which every actor of that genre must conform.
>
> (Barba 1985: 4)

10. For the notion of 'language body,' see Chapter 6, 'Toward specifying theatre translation.'

11. The Japanese director, Moriaki Watanabe, notes that Panigrahi's dance appears close to western art:

> If Sanjukta's demonstration seems strange to you westerners, from the Japanese perspective, there are many things in her performance that are closer to western art, based on her way of codifying the performance, similar to your ballet. In the four traditions of eastern theatre [Indian, Japanese, Balinese and Chinese], there are common elements, but also great differences. Indian dance's proximity to western dance, for example, can be seen in Béjart's ballets, such as *Le Sacre du Printemps* that makes good use of Indian techniques (the *tribanqi*, for example); but when Béjart imitates Japanese dance, the result is catastrophic.
>
> (Watanabe 1982)

12. Marcel Mauss, in his presentation of the Première Semaine Internationale de Synthèse, *Civilisation, le mot et l'idée* (Paris: La Renaissance du livre, 1930) (reprinted, Mauss 1969) identified progress and a 'general acquisition by societies and civilizations' (478) and an 'increasing uniformity of civilizations' (481).

> Just as, at the national level, science, industry, art, even 'distinction,' are no longer the exclusive patrimony of a minority and become, in the major nations, a sort of common privilege, the best features of these civilizations will become the common property of more and more social groups.
>
> (478)

It certainly seems that we are heading towards increasing uniformity in civilization. Cinema is one of the instruments: from one end of the world to the other, filmic mimicry and scenes exercise a suggestive power, encouraging imitation.

Mauss wrote this in 1929, during the era of silent film, which tended to emphasize facial expression and which had not yet invaded and westernized the world. Thus he observes that this growing tendency to uniformity has not yet reached Japan: 'None the less, Japan appears immune to our Western films and vice versa. For Japanese laugh at scenes that make us cry and conversely' (Mauss 1969: 481).

13. For a thorough discussion of the relationship between body and language in Grotowski, see Bernard 297–312).

BIBLIOGRAPHY

Artaud, Antonin (1958) 'Metaphysics and the mise en scène,' *Theatre and its Double*, trans. Mary Caroline Richards, New York: Grove Press.

Barba, Eugenio (1982) 'Le théâtre eurasien,' *Bouffonneries* 4. (English version: 'Eurasian theatre,' *TDR* 32,3.)

—— (1985) 'Montage,' in Eugenio Barba and Nicola Savarese (eds) *Anatomie de l'acteur*, Cazilhac: Bouffonneries Contrastes.

—— (1988) 'Quatre spectateurs,' *L'Art du Théâtre* 10.

Bernard, Michel (1976) *L'Expressivitié du corps*, Paris: J.-P. Delarge.

Bharucha, Rastom (1984) 'A collision of cultures: some western interpretations of the Indian theatre,' *Asian Theatre Journal* 1.

Brecht, Bertolt (1967) 'Kleines Organon für das Theater,' *Gesammelte Werke* vol. 6, Frankfurt: Suhrkamp; trans. John Willett (1977) *Brecht on Theatre*, New York: Hill & Wang.

Dabezies, André (1972) *Le Mythe de Faust*, Paris: Armand Colin.

Goetz, Michel (1960) *Inde – Cinq millénaires d'art*, Paris: Albin Michel.

Grotowski, Jerzy (1982) 'Lois pragmatiques: Entretien avec Jerzy Grotowski par Franco Ruffini,' *Bouffonneries* 4.

Lotman, Juri and Uspensky, Boris (1978) 'On the semiotic mechanism of culture,' *New Literary History* 9, 2.

Lyotard, Jean-François (1973) 'La dent, la paume,' *Des dispositifs pulsionnels*, Paris: Union Générale d'Edition.

Mauss, Michel (1969) 'Représentations collectives et diversité des civilisations,' *Oeuvres*, Paris: Editions de Minuit.

Panigrahi, Sanjukta (1982) Article in *Bouffonneries* 4.

—— (1983) 'La danse Odissi,' *Bouffonneries* 9.

Pavis, Patrice (1988) 'Du texte à la scène, un enfantement difficile,' *Théâtre Public* 79. (English translation, 'From page to stage: a difficult birth,' is chapter 2 of this volume.)

—— (1989) 'Problems of translation for the stage,' trans. Loren Kruger, in Hanna Scolnikov and Peter Holland (eds) *The Play out of Context*, Cambridge: Cambridge University Press.

Watanabe, Moriaki (1982) 'Entre l'Orient et l'Occident. Entretien avec Moriaki Watanabe et Franco Ruffini,' *Bouffonneries* 4.

8

INTERCULTURALISM IN CONTEMPORARY *MISE EN SCÈNE*: THE IMAGE OF INDIA IN THE *MAHABHARATA*, THE *INDIADE*, *TWELFTH NIGHT* AND *FAUST*

There is something presumptuous or at best naïve in proposing a theory of interculturalism in contemporary *mise en scène*, given the complexity of the factors at stake in all cultural exchange and the difficulty of formalizing them. Every typology of cultural relations requires a metalanguage that would be, as it were, 'above' these relations, encompassing them all: it is hard to imagine where theorists would find this metalanguage, especially since they are themselves caught up in a language and culture from which it is difficult to disengage. Furthermore, there is no general theory of culture that correctly integrates historical, social and ideological factors without being reduced to them. Cultural studies have had the merit of rehabilitating phenomena that are not situated in the socioeconomic infrastructure and that cannot be described in purely economic or sociological terms. Conversely, however, they sometimes tend to dissolve all socioeconomic political and ideological factors in culture, to present the cultural as the social element in individual behavior, foregrounding the influence of the individual unconscious on cultural phenomena. We must avoid two exaggerations: that of a mechanical and unreconstructed Marxism that neglects the importance of cultural phenomena and their relative autonomy,[1] and that of a culturalism that turns the economic and ideological infrastructure into a form of unconscious discursive superstructure.

183

What remains is to imagine a theoretical model that would describe in as detailed a manner as possible the way in which the *mise en scène* presents and transmits a foreign culture to the public, and what operations come into play in this cultural transfer using theatrical means. Since a general theory of this intercultural transfer has yet to be established, we will begin with an outline, using concrete and contrasting examples. This allows us to compare the manipulatory factors at each stage of the transfer. The four *mises en scène* were chosen because, in varying degrees, they have India as a common reference point in the source culture and because they all address a French or western audience. They are (a) the *Mahabharata*, adapted by Jean-Claude Carrière and directed by Peter Brook (1986); (b) *L'Indiade ou l'Inde de leur rêves* ('Indiade or the India of their dreams') (1987) written by Hélène Cixous and directed by Ariane Mnouchkine at the Théâtre du Soleil; in these two cases, an aspect of mythical and historical India is transmitted through text and performance. To complete this prestigious diptych, we have two other *mises en scène* in which the thematic and formal connection is more tenuous: (c) *La Nuit des Rois (Twelfth Night)* staged by the Théâtre du Soleil (1984); and (d) Eugenio Barba's study of Goethe's *Faust*, developed during the course of an ISTA workshop in the Salento region of Italy (September, 1987).

On the basis of these examples, we hope to see what reaches the spectators (the target audience) after the interventions of author, adapter, translator, director, actor and, finally, spectator. We can represent this cascade of interventions by a series of filters or by an hourglass (see (Fig. 8.1) whose upper bowl, the source culture, empties into the lower one, passing through a series of screens or filters and arriving at the recipient only as a fragment of the source culture, (1) and (2), thoroughly reworked by operations (3) to (8). We thus assume the position of the audience (10) receiving a foreign culture that has gone through a series of operations and transformations, which facilitate its transfer and adaptation. This model thus refers to the intercultural transfer of a certain number of cultural facts (belonging to the source culture) to a different audience and culture. We will see which elements of Indian culture pass from (1) to (10) and how they are transferred in a series of operations ((3) to (8)), which are crucial if they are to reach the target audience and culture.

Our 'hourglass' thus includes:

(1) and (2), the 'superior' bowl of the source culture, as it is conceived and formalized before the actual work of adaptation begins

(3) to (11), the 'inferior' bowl, which we can divide into the following:

(3) to (8): the theatrical production (which none the less anticipates reception)

(9) to (11): reception by audience and target culture.

Figure 8.1 The hourglass of intellectual exchange source culture

(1) cultural modeling (*modélisations*), sociological, anthropological codification, etc.
(2) artistic modeling
(3) perspective of the adapters
(4) work of adaptation
(5) preparatory work by the actors, etc.
(6) choice of theatrical form
(7) theatrical representation/performance of culture
(8) reception-adapters
(9) readability
(10) reception in the target culture
A. artistic modeling
B. sociological and anthropological codification
C. cultural modeling
(11) given and anticipated consequences

(1) CULTURAL INSCRIPTION; IDENTIFICATION OF THE CULTURAL REFERENT

In order to describe the course of cultural transfer from (1) to (11), we must try to reconstitute the entities and the operations within which the cultural object is identified and elaborated, arising in the source culture and transmitted to (10). But we must also determine which form this cultural object takes and which aspect of it is shown or signified. The source culture reveals itself through the mediation of a form, that is a semiotic system and model, which Lotman calls a 'secondary modelling system' (*modélisation*). In this way, social or ritual practices, techniques of the body (Mauss), philosophical, religious, literary or mythic systems, are textualized, are modeled into a structured texture of significations or texts in the semiotic sense of the word. Culture can be grasped and described only in the form of a semiotic system whose mode of functioning must be established; without this, we will pick up only superficial and isolated traits, which would not have the complexity of a cultural system and would not deserve the name of culture. These diverse modeling systems take the form of (more or less precise) codifications, whether sociological, ethnological, or expressed by systems of evidence and values or implicitly ideological judgments (sometimes called ideologemes) (see Pavis 1985: 290–4).

These modeling systems rarely emerge in a state of perfect codification; we have to complete them, or even establish them, on the basis of textual indications and our knowledge of the context.

In (1) and (2), we are located in the source culture or, more precisely, secondary modeling systems within the culture. We need to specify the relationships postulated among these systems (sociological, ethnological, anthropological, etc.), i.e. how we understand the dimensions and meaning of the culture. This necessitates an epistemology of anthropology which can show how we gain knowledge of different cultures, especially if we want to avoid the trap of ethnocentrism. During the process of adaptation ((3)-(8)), there is a real danger of projecting ways of thinking, schemas and categories (9), (10), (11) belonging to the target culture on to the source culture. We cannot completely efface the systematization and the connection between anthropological and sociological perspectives inherited from our own culture. This ethnocentric deviation[2] is further reinforced by the need to render the source culture relatively comprehensible and readable for the target audience, so as to prepare the ground by drawing a sort of grid on it from a point of view that does justice to the specificity of the source culture as well as the reading powers of the projected audience, and thus to see intercultural transfer as a process whereby the target culture appropriates the source culture. We thus run the risk of projecting our own western categories on to the foreign culture and of defining modeling systems which are not always specific to the source culture (for instance, western notions such as autonomy of codes, authenticity, aesthetics, or the opposition between art and craft).

Let us examine the inscription of India and its cultures within these secondary modeling systems.

a) In the *Mahabharata*, we have access to a mythical India, that of an epic narrative (in 100,000 stanzas), the saga of the Bharata, one of the two great Sanskrit epics, whose composition extends over several centuries and which has been transmitted orally by bards. This is an imaginary India, but one that has a tangible connection to past and present; Brook (1987: 161) also shows aspects of contemporary everyday culture and sees Indian culture as a codification of human experience:

> The Indian has indefatigably explored every possibility. If it is that most humble and most amazing of human instruments, a finger, everything that a finger can do has been explored and codified. If it is a word, a breath, a limb, a sound, a note – or a stone, a color, or a cloth – all its aspects, artistic and spiritual, have been investigated and linked together.

Brook takes into account all the potential artistic modelings of Indian civilization, but he integrates them into a vision of rural India at once eternal and contemporary. It is not India, but it has all the flavor of India! The set designer and costume designer have no geographical, economic or ethnological pretensions. India is suggested by the beaten earth, the sea-green water, the fires lit to attract the protection of the gods; it is both the real earth of the Indian subcontinent and the symbolic terrain of humanity as a whole. Brook looks for a balance between rootedness (as in the *Iks*) and a universalizing imaginary (as in *The Conference of the Birds*). The acting style of this 'immediate theatre' creates a direct link with the audience. No cultural references are essential to an understanding of the performance, or rather – since cultural references cannot be avoided – the references to the source culture are easily understood by the audience because universal transcultural factors have been considered.

b) The *Indiade*, on the other hand, is situated in a precise historical context: the period from 1937 to 1948, immediately preceding independence and partition. Thus, contemporary history represents the cultural referent here; its codification is not at all obvious, even if Hélène Cixous treats the subject as a chronicle that claims to be objective, including most of the political leaders and alluding to the principal events. But India is signified above all by the body techniques of various characters: gait, posture, gaze, skin color; everything must contribute to the illusion of an

187

ethnological reconstitution of the Indian mosaic. The vast frontal space made of bricks and marble, covered with carpets and cushions, evokes an exterior location – one thinks of the Taj Mahal, because of the reflection of the marble tiles – and an interior one, where the political negotiations take place. A few details of behavior are enough to give us a variety of images of the Indian people: instead of a totality or a totalizing schema, the *mise en scène* chooses a few indices, traces of the inexhaustible reality of this continent: 'It is not India; it is only an Indian molecule, a footprint' (Cixous 1987a: 16).

c) We can find no allusion to India in the text of *Twelfth Night*, which refers to a mysterious Illyria. The presence of India is not thematic, but simply linked to the search for an atmosphere and emotional coloration. It corresponds to the artistic modeling system (2): Indian or Persian miniatures representing erotic scenes. The allusion to India in the scenography, music and actors' gesture is never clear. What is important is that the country seems far away, or imaginary, that 'it has the colors, smells, and femininity of India: carnival images impregnated with heady powder and insistent sounds which lap around the house of Olivia.' The cultural reference is effected through an ideological code, a western vision of the east connoted by exotic commonplaces: the erotic painting, music punctuated by an eastern timbre, the languid and effeminate carriage of the men (the Duke).

This emotional décor of an ethereal and sensual India completely suppresses an Elizabethan era and culture necessarily inscribed in Shakespeare's text which, since we still hear the text, continue, despite the Indian covering, to convey their own socio-cultural values. All the same, the dramaturgical analysis and historical references are so weak in this *mise en scène* that the anchoring in India remains the dominant cultural characteristic.

d) In his 'adaptation' of Goethe's *Faust*, Barba uses an Indian and a Japanese dancer. The image of India is thus very marginal; it is expressed only through the artistic modeling of *odissi* dance, which is thoroughly reworked in Sanjukta Panigrahi's improvisations. Here also, the medieval culture of *Faust* and the classical culture of Goethe are obliterated and replaced only partially by a choreography vaguely inspired by *odissi* and *buyo* dance. The only thing that is Indian is the extraordinary behavior of the *odissi* dancer, the acculturation produced in learning the dance. The connection with the culture is thus quite indirect; Barba is not interested in comprehending a foreign culture or in making it comprehensible. He is only interested in foreign forms of behavior, which he modifies by juxtaposing foreign gestures with the original *odissi* codes.

(2) ARTISTIC MODELING SYSTEMS

Certain cultures produce theatre genres and performance traditions that are codified in an immutable form. It is often difficult to understand why a particular culture at a particular moment in its historical evolution should engender a particular codification, all the more so because, once established, codifications enjoy a relative autonomy and evolve according to their own internal logic, without an absolute mimetic connection to the social and cultural context within which they are inscribed. It is none the less true that in the first instance, it is the social content of an era and a culture that generates artistic modeling systems.

Let us recall, as does Francastel (1965: 237–8) that 'it is not the form which creates the thought or the experience, but the thought, as an expression of the common social content of an era, that creates the form.' Despite relative autonomy (at least from a western point of view), codification may also evolve. Even the traditional forms of performance may be modernized, influenced by the west or 'restored' (Schechner 1983: 95–108). They do not exist in a vacuum, but are already influenced or subject to influence by other cultures, including the recipient culture, which sometimes forgets that it has already encountered these traditions.

In each of these performances, the artistic modeling system to which the *mise en scène* refers is more or less clearly modified and 'autonomized' into a strictly organized code.[3]

a) The epic poem, the *Mahabharata*, did not produce a codified dramatic form, but the secular tradition of popular story-tellers constitutes a minimal form of theatrical presentation and innumerable adaptations of the *Mahabharata* are staged nowadays. The adapter, Jean-Claude Carrière, and the director, Peter Brook, simultaneously take up the text of the poem and the popular tradition of its recitation, which gives them direct access, without being solemn or reverential, to this monument of Hindu culture. The connection to the literary text is thus facilitated by its mode of enunciation, which is both authentic and well adapted to Brook's performance style.[4] Brook does not need to copy a foreign theatrical tradition.

b) The *Indiade* was written in 1987 to document recent history. The text thus belongs to western culture; it is not intended for a particular theatrical codification, since the genre of the chronicle that inspired Cixous has not produced a particular performance style. The fact that the play's subject is contemporary India does not require the use of Indian performance techniques. Mnouchkine is interested in Indian culture as presented by the simulacrum of actors trying hard to imitate the body techniques of various ethnic groups.

c) In *Twelfth Night*, the link with Indian culture and artistic modeling is once again different. We should take care to distinguish: 1. the codification that the Shakespearean period would have proposed, and which we seek in the text and performance traditions; 2. the codification, borrowed from Indian artistic traditions, which Mnouchkine uses freely in this *mise en scène*.

1. The Elizabethan performance style has not been preserved by a living tradition and is difficult to reconstruct, all the more because this form, now dead, would appear both out of place and too mimetic and simplistic. In Mnouchkine's opinion, this form has not produced any impressive codification and there is no point in trying to restore it. For this reason, Mnouchkine substitutes without regret an entirely different form, inspired by other traditions, eastern and western: Kabuki, classical Indian theatre, *commedia dell'arte*, etc.

2. The artistic codification that vaguely inspires the *mise en scène* is that of classical Indian theatre. The silk used as backcloth gives a whole range of colors that correspond, in traditional Indian theatre, to the principal emotions. The actors display all the signs of their emotions according to the system of four manners (gracious, grandiose, violent, verbal). The languid gait, the panting breath, the distracted look: such is the representation of the lover possessed by an unhealthy passion. The *mise en scène* is thus freely inspired – i.e. without the formal restraint of traditional

codification – by Indian theatrical models, which obviously color the atmosphere of the Shakespearean comedy.

d) Barba's adaptation of *Faust* is much more radical. He is not at all interested in the artistic modeling created by western culture which could permeate *Faust*. It is only later, on the level of adaptation (4) and on that of reception and legibility (8), (9) that he intervenes in a western manner. Abandoning any cultural analysis of *Faust*, he has an Indian dancer improvise on *odissi* dance forms. She modifies her performance, adapting it to her Japanese partner according to Barba's instructions. Paradoxically, this Indian choreography is both a product of Indian culture and completely recast by the *mise en scène*.

We have just seen the inherent difficulty in recapturing the cultural reference and modeling system within artistic codifications: the difficulty is also due to the confusion between: 1. the *original* or 'natural' culture that has produced the dramatic text or artistic modeling system; 2. the *thematized* culture that the text deals with thematically; and 3. the *referred* or imposed culture, which the *mise en scène* chooses as reference culture as well as the original culture.

Having clarified this question of origins, we must ask ourselves from which perspective and in what spirit this recourse to several cultural contexts can be effected. At the outset, this poses the question of the adapters' perspective (3), of the context of their intervention, of their ideological and artistic project. Out of the response to this question flows a series of further questions ((4)–(9)) concerning the activity of adaptation, the actors' preparation, the choice of a form, the establishing of an enunciative framework (*dispositif*).

(3) THE ADAPTER'S PERSPECTIVE

The adapter can be the linguistic translator of the text as well as the director, designer, actor, or all those who have a mediating function, adapting, transforming, modifying, borrowing, appropriating source text and culture for a target culture and audience. All these artists necessarily adapt the source culture to the target culture, i.e. mediate or act as a bridge between two poles. This process of adaptation is all the more important as it often takes place subconsciously. Adapting involves setting up meaning that is not self-evident, by facilitating its reception and comprehension, by intervening in the mediation between cultures and connections between cultures. The adapter can perceive the difference between his culture and the foreign one, without setting up hierarchies or attempting to reduce one to the other. This perception of otherness is the condition of any cultural exchange: 'Only the experience of one's own culture and of a foreign culture as different entities and as systems that are perceived as correct within their own domain creates the basis of reciprocal interpenetration' (Lotman 1974: 434). But this perception of otherness is not enough: the adapter must choose tactics; he will judge culture sometimes from within (including himself) and sometimes from without (excluding himself), choosing to bring it closer or to distance it from the target public, to accentuate the differences from his/her culture or to erase them, to individuate or particularize it or to look for universals, to clarify and simplify, or to quote the culture in all its complexity. All these are tactical choices; in the final analysis, they are ideological and political choices, linked to the adapters' inscription in the target culture (10A,B,C).

The adapter is a ferryman conveying a poorly identified cargo from one side of the river to the other, a *traduttore/traditore* caught between the devil and the deep blue sea. Adapters differ from linguistic translators in that they have at their disposal the whole theatre apparatus as an aid to expression and clarification as much as complication. At this level we can best perceive the ideological dimension of cultural transfer and the political conception that determines choice: for example, Cixous and Mnouchkine's naïve universal humanism, or Brook's quest for a universal theatrical language since his research on language for *Orghast* or Barba's skepticism about any notion of cultural identity and his interest in professional identity.

a) In the *Mahabharata*, Brook's intention is above all to bring India and its culture closer to the western audience, to produce signs that facilitate the identification of a reality that is unfamiliar to this audience. This universalizing connection and the echoes of humanity as a whole do not exclude an Indian rootedness, an accumulation of details – smells, clothing, music, voices – that suggest contemporary rural India. Hindu philosophy, which inspired the work, is thus filtered through the contemporary Indian public, which has assimilated the text to all the circumstances of its everyday life. It is extended by the effect of familiarity which the French- or English-speaking public feels in the presence of the actors. The polarity between universality and rootedness corresponds to Brook's desire to find a balance between the particular and the general, the concrete and the abstract (see Brook 1985a: 33–5).

b) The *Indiade* by Cixous and Mnouchkine likewise tries to bring closer the history of India and its partition, to the point where this political chronicle becomes a parable of the divided and torn human heart. India is only a pretext (or at least an opportunity) for speaking of the multiplicity, suffering and dislocation of the human soul: Cixous' text is intended to remind us of these universal conclusions. Parallel to this monologic discourse, the representation of the Indian people is very rich in detail, accentuating variety and individuality in the body techniques, so that the audience feel they grasp the variety and the anthropological and emotional unity of humanity.

c) In *Twelfth Night*, as in *Faust*, it is difficult to evaluate the distance of proximity that the *mise en scène* sets up with respect to the public. The point in both cases is not to identify a culture but to give it an exotic image, as in *Twelfth Night*, or to make use of one of its theatrical traditions to indicate a pre-expressive universality, according to Barba's anthropological theory. Nevertheless, Mnouchkine's perspective conflicts with Barba's. We can see this in their respective distancing from their source text. For Mnouchkine, Shakespeare is not our contemporary; he is 'as far from us as is our deepest self.' She therefore feels at liberty to impose a foreign theatre form on Shakespearean culture and our own. On the other hand, Barba is interested in Japanese and Indian dance solely in so far as they confirm the existence of a pre-expressive universality. He does not try to recover the medieval German culture that 'produced' *Faust*.

These different perspectives evidently produce an image of India that is different in each case: a land of meditation and wisdom in Brook's *mise en scène*, it gives us a peaceful and reconciliatory image of humanity despite war; for Cixous and Mnouchkine, it is synonymous with richness, diversity and division; in *Twelfth Night*, Mnouchkine treats it in the minor mode of embellishment and erotic miniature, while Barba is interested only in the artistic convention of a form, both stable and evolving, which he would have in universal dialogue with other traditions. It is at this level of the image, or the stereotype, that we find the determinants of this perspective: an eminently ideological construction that predisposes the judgment of those involved in a culture.

Once the perspective is established – and with it the ideological presuppositions and implications are unveiled – the work of adaptation is nothing more than a practical application, to transfer forms and content from one context to another, whether in the case of an original text, a dramaturgical analysis, an adaptation or revision, a stage commentary or a gestural montage.

(4) THE WORK OF ADAPTATION

a) Carrière and Brook have divided up the task by working in apparently opposite directions, even if the result is a balance between distance and closeness. Carrière read the text of the *Mahabharata* in an academic French translation: he did much more than translate or adapt it; he added entirely rewritten scenes while keeping the proper names and the tonality of the epic poem. He chose an adaptation that would at all costs avoid the reproach of colonizing appropriation; he thus kept Sanskrit terms (like *dharma*) to prevent any unconscious colonization in the use of vocabulary, since 'to say that we can find equivalents for every Indian word implies that French culture could in a single word appropriate the most profound and pondered ideas of Indian thought' (Carrière 1985). But he falls none the less into the elitist trap – doubtless preferable to the colonization trap – since this text can be perfectly understood only by a Sanskrit specialist.

Fortunately, Brook compensates for the remoteness of Hindu culture and this religious respect for philosophical concepts by proposing a direct acting style that would be familiar to the spectators; this 'immediate theatre' would thus be received as universal, easily translated into the cultural referents of a European audience.[5] In the dramatic text as in the acting style, Brook and Carrière meet under the auspices of Shakespeare. This is clear in the constant movement from one stylistic level to another, the links between the everyday, the fantastic and the metaphysical,

194

the contradiction between an Indian literary form and universal themes of conflict, the complexity of characters at once epic and dramatic, the immediacy of conflicts and situations, the use of rupture: all characteristic of Shakespeare.[6]

b) Hélène Cixous explicitly invokes Shakespeare as a model: she takes up the architectonic structure, the scene and act divisions, the oscillation between historical chronicle and individual tragedy, the collective and individual levels of the plot, the chain of metaphors. If Brook sees in Shakespeare an author close to us, 'our contemporary,' Cixous and Mnouchkine are more taken by his poetry and by the mixture of proximity and distance, of individuality and collectivity. Theirs is a Shakespeare seen through Joyce and Freud, for instance in the reworking of history and dream: 'In a historical play, the historical work resembles dream work: our dream epics last five minutes, thanks to condensation and displacement. We have only enough time to play 'at life and death' (Cixous 1987: 22).

c) Curiously, *Twelfth Night* seems to be the least Shakespearean of the four plays, since the *mise en scène* dilutes the plot, which is already meandering and romantic. This 'undoing of Shakespeare' is not, however, due to the 'Indian' style, but to the loss of the meaning of the architecture and the textuality of the play. Since the 'Indianization' of the play is not thematically motivated, it appears what it attempts to be: an aestheticizing phantasmagoria that offers no rereading of the play, but confirms its 'escapist' tendency. As a result, one no longer bothers to examine the reasons of the modalities of the highly successful intercultural transfer. The furtive and fragile reference to India remains on the decorative level without engaging with the culture it is supposed to represent.

d) In Barba's case, the adaptation is not fixed in the text but rather offers a montage of actions, situations and gestural sequences which claims to be neither faithful, nor exhaustive, nor a classical narrative, at least at the start, since Barba ends (in (8) and (9)) by imposing a thoroughly western ideological and narratological grid, which facilitates reception for a European audience. The adaptation thus brings together an artistic modeling system (2), cut off from its culture (1), and reworked according to western theatrical modeling systems (10A); it thus passes quickly through the usual cultural transfer, which takes into account aesthetic and ideological representations of the two cultures, source and target, and which passes through a dramaturgical analysis (from (6) to (7), (8) and (9)). This dramaturgical analysis constitutes a key link in the chain to which everything else, including the *mise en scène*, can be articulated.

(5) PREPARATORY WORK BY THE ACTORS, (6) CHOICE OF FORM

Extensive preparation on the part of the actors is indispensable for this stage-by-stage cultural transfer. This preparation forms an integral part of the performance once the acculturated techniques of the actors have become inseparable from their bodies. This preparatory work can be seen in the actors in all the performances, which share a view of theatre as transformation, although differently inflected: naïve and alienating in Mnouchkine, philosophical and mystical in Brook.

This preparation makes sense only once it is accompanied by the choice of an overall form for the *mise en scène*, a form which is borrowed from a culture other than that of the target audience. Such a form revitalizes the natural structure of the work, concentrating attention on its novelty and strangeness, so as to produce an effect of defamiliarization (*ostraniene*), which de-automatizes habitual perception and highlights the value of theatrical codification.

a) Brook's actors trained in Kathakali in India and Paris, not for the purpose of reproducing this technique in the performance, but to 'open themselves to new ways of using their bodies and to understand the reason for the development of these forms. Having grasped the essential meaning of a particular form, the next step is to leave it' (Brook 1986a: 19). This training is essentially the heightening of awareness of performance techniques foreign to the culture of the actors themselves; it should not lead to an 'external imitation of Indian dance or theatre techniques' (Brook 1986a: 19). The actors begin by improvising in their native languages, trying out the scenes prepared and then rewritten by Carrière. They try to maintain direct and straightforward communication with the audience, guarding against any exotic effects or intimidating virtuosity. This is why Brook does not seek the outward form or the tradition of the foreign culture in order to assimilate it. He appears to distrust any purely decorative use of forms; he prefers to comprehend the form in depth, but does not want to synthesize the diverse cultures of his troupe or to exchange techniques and know-how. He attempts to understand what animates forms at their source:

> We are looking for whatever breathes life into a culture. Instead of taking up a cultural form as it stands, we try to discover what enlivens that form. The actors should try to get out of their own culture and stereotypes, as much as possible.
>
> (Brook 1973)

This warning of Brook's is valid for any intercultural *mise en scène*: we have to find out what the form hides, what aspect of it we keep, how it is transformed when it is transplanted in the target culture. With good reason, Brook objects to a purely 'cultural' conception of theatre, which pays attention only to the aesthetic of forms, without seeing the 'invisible' event that sustains all these forms.[7]

In performance, this preparation leads to an atmosphere of interiority and meditation. But the actors take care not to be overly influenced by or locked into tradition or any codification external to their culture by respecting this period too religiously. The popular view of the *Mahabharata* 'from below' and according to the 'carpet show' resembles the 'rough' and 'immediate' quality of their usual performance style,[8] tried out in Africa and used in the *mises en scène* of Shakespeare, Jarry and Bizet.

b) The preparation of the Théâtre du Soleil actors does not revolve around an apprenticeship in Indian techniques or in their universalization as in Brook's company. It begins with the investigation of the character by way of an absorption of body movement techniques from different ethnic and religious groups. Mnouchkine and Cixous entertain a mystique of actors offering themselves to the role and losing their identity in the process, etc. This preparation is psychological rather than technical or choreographic: once the spirit is willing, the flesh tries to follow.

And it follows more or less well, even if it is not supported by a major theatre form (as in the 'Shakespeares' which were enlivened by Kabuki or reminiscences of classical Indian theatre). Instead of returning to already existing, highly codified artistic modeling systems, Mnouchkine and her actors offer a mimetic characterization of historical figures and popular characters. All the formal theatre research has given way to a rather sterile exercise in imitation and identification of historical figures and ethnic groups. The political and artistic message is dissipated in this tour de force of imitation. The politics lacks the sustaining power of a major form, as it attempts the theatrical coding and performance of world conflict; we are far from *1789* and *L'Age d'or*.[9]

Mnouchkine might have been intimidated by the wealth of Indian cultures to the point of not daring to impose a larger 'eastern' form on them, which might have seemed either redundant or less than real, or displaced in the case of a non-Indian eastern culture. It is certainly much easier to use a 'strong form' to enrich a cultural context that has lost a clear traditional identity. The mimetic demands of a historical chronicle certainly do not facilitate the theatricalization and codification of events, as the actors feel obliged to do their best to copy historical figures and so to avoid any form that might have come between them and the historical referent.

c) In *Twelfth Night*, on the other hand, the actors were not called upon to reconstitute part of a historical referent; they could avail themselves freely of the forms and codes foreign to Shakespeare's. In rehearsals, they began by experimenting with costumes made from bits of cloth, piecing together a jigsaw of colors and passions. Without ever achieving the formalization or the rigor of a tradition such as the Kabuki used in *Richard II*, the decoratist reference to an exotic bazaar-like India gradually took the shape of an imaginary Illyria, a 'faraway country belonging to the depths of our unconscious where all dreams, desires, fears, premonitions, repressions dare to speak, where everything is possible' (Moscoso 1984: 6).

A comparison of *Twelfth Night* with *Richard II* or *L'Age d'or* (1975) clearly shows the evolution of Mnouchkine's aesthetics. In the latter two productions, the research on major theatrical forms was obvious and approved as a way of avoiding aesthetic realism: 'Pure theatrical forms allow us, *inter alia*, to escape from the constraints of aesthetic realism. . . . Most of the time in theatre, everything is meaningful except the actors and what they have to say. . . . True realism is a transposition' (Mnouchkine 1975: 5). The recourse to traditional forms is not a direct borrowing, but an inspiration; everything in them has been reworked and reinvented by the actors. In *Twelfth Night*, the *mise en scène* did not take up a major theatrical form such as Kabuki; it was inspired by images of Indian culture, which it then diluted in an atmosphere of sensuality and haziness.

d) In Barba's case, the outlines are more clearly defined and the preparatory work codified by the dancers' daily practice. The only – and radical – preparation consisted of taking or being taken by surprise: the dancer had to be prepared to deconstruct her gestural program, so as to integrate the director's improvisations and instructions as well as the suggestions of the other (Japanese) dancer. Barba's 'transcultural pedagogy' establishes its own theatre tradition by measuring it against foreign traditions: 'it discovers our own center in the tradition of traditions' (Barba 1988).

In the preparatory work, the actor is placed at the meeting point of two plot principles: 1. the concatenation of cause and effect in time and action; 2. the simultaneous presence of several actions. The dancer or actor must reconstitute a synthesis of these effects of concatenation and simultaneity.

> The actor, for example, obtains simultaneous effects as soon as he breaks the abstract schema of movements, just as the audience is about to be able to anticipate them. He composes his actions (in the sense that 'compose' derives from *cumponere*, to put together) into a synthesis which is far removed from a daily way of behaving. In this montage he segments the actions, choosing and dilating certain fragments, composing the rhythms, achieving an equivalent to the 'real' action by means of what Richard Schechner calls the 'restoration of behavior.'
>
> (Barba 1985: 77)

The codified form of *odissi* dance is thus restructured and deformed by the foreign bodies that it has absorbed. Barba edits together microsequences of gestures, rather than episodes of the plot. The cultural transfer is linked not to a translation of images, meanings or values, but to a translation of codification according to pre-expressive elements, considered transcultural and universal.[10] These formal displacements may seem tiny, even imperceptible to the western eye, but the accumulation of deviations ends up producing a choreography that is at once faithful to its origin in tradition and completely rejuvenated.

By definition, the addition of a strong theatre form that is foreign to the target culture or even to the source is surprising and distancing; it introduces a contradiction between form and theme, expectation and reception. Each of our four examples justifies this sort of contradiction, which it resolves more or less well: the contradiction in Brook's *Mahabharata* has to do with the *distance* of Carrière's adaptation as opposed to the intimacy established by the *mise en scène*. The *Indiade* inscribes its contradiction in the space between the text's universalizing humanist moral and the restoration of a typically Indian ethnology: we can also see this contradiction in the relationship between a western neo-Shakespearean text and a figuration of India, in *Twelfth Night* as well as the *Indiade*. In Barba's case, a contradiction exists between the content of the western myth of *Faust* and the eastern (Indian and Japanese) codification set up to evoke this myth. This contradiction tends to resolution in the synthesis of Eurasian theatre (Barba 1988), which reduces cultural differences thanks to the valorization of cultural universals.

One might think that the choice of theatrical form depends only on the will of the director. This is only partly true. It must take into account the abilities of the target audience, of their competence in recognizing codification, of their taste for universality or specification of the transferred culture. We need also to understand how the *mise en scène* uses specifically theatrical means to convey its meaning, how culture is theatricalized so as to move from one side to the other.

(7) THEATRICAL REPRESENTATION OF CULTURE

Choosing a theatrical form involves choosing a type of theatricality, a status of the fiction *vis-à-vis* reality. Theatricality offers specific means for transferring a source culture to a target audience: only in this context can we speak of a theatrical interculturalism. We may certainly doubt whether culture can really be represented by theatrical means or even performed. Perhaps only the most external and superficial features of culture can be represented; in any case, we must look for specific theatrical means to express or perform this (foreign) culture.

a) Brook sees in theatre a means of transmitting what no other medium can communicate: 'Here lies the responsibility of the theatre: what a book cannot convey, what no philosopher can truly explain, can be brought into our understanding by the theatre. Translating the untranslatable is one of its roles' (Brook 1987: 164). Translating the untranslatable means finding the gestures, atmosphere, the symbolic actions, which concretely enact a concept as abstract and untranslatable as *dharma*, using a series of actions showing people caught in the conflict between the possible and its negation.

b) In the *Indiade*, this implies that the *mise en scène* sets out to simulate a situation in which the actors are supposed to behave as if they inhabited the culture on stage; they ought to go so far as to embody the traits of their role. None the less, it is clear that, despite these good intentions, their performance is only a simulation, since we are still in the theatre and not in India. As a result their mimetism is only a product of their theatrical skill. The denegation characteristic of this sort of naturalism, the fundamental ambiguity of the actors' personalities, blurs the signs: we are no longer sure what belongs to mimesis and what is deliberately exaggerated and theatricalized. Since Cixous' and Mnouchkine's conception of history is close to the Shakespearean *theatrum mundi*, in which kings are only fools and the world's a stage, and great men are at once on the stage of history and on that of the Cartoucherie, political reality is already theatrical and its staging becomes theatre within theatre. We thus receive information about the foreign culture as much through the effects of the actors' imitative immersion as through the theatricalization of their acting styles.

But we are nevertheless hard put to connect this theatricalized culture to our own, since reality and theatricality continually interfere with one other as if to scramble the signals. We penetrate Indian history gradually. First, in the foyer, we have the pleasant welcome of Indian food: we are in the midst of the referent, since we eat it; second, we enter a half-fictional, half-real world of the dressing rooms where the actors themselves are putting on the attributes of their roles; third, we see an anonymous crowd on stage polishing the floor: we appear to be in a museum of applied ethnology; fourth and finally, the performance begins and Cixous envelops us in the whirlwind of history, trying to persuade us that she is only turning the pages of an objective chronicle. The confusion of these levels produces a certain hallucination, because it presents us with culture, or rather fragments of culture, in motion and process. It is no longer a matter of representing (imitating, showing) this culture, but of 'performing' it. Theatre becomes the means of transferring and translating a foreign culture:

> Intercultural exchange takes a teacher, someone who knows the body of performance of the culture being translated. The translator of culture is not a mere agent, as a translator of words might be, but an actual culture bearer. This is why performing other cultures becomes so important. Not just reading them, not just visiting them, or importing them – but actually doing them.
>
> (Schechner 1984: 217)

For Schechner, Barba, Brook or Mnouchkine, theatre does not only represent foreign cultures, but it also performs them, displaying a number of its operations. The power of theatre lies in its ability to represent a culture theatrically, which no commentary or analysis could do. Hence a very specific use of theatricality.

a) For Brook, the actors are involved in a performance, almost a ritual search for authenticity, and their means are self-willed, poor and non-realistic: they do not attempt to imitate the world, but try to preserve the sacred quality of their performance.

b) Mnouchkine's actors in the *Indiade* use a naturalist acting style in their attempt to become their roles, but everything that surrounds them – space, the plot, sometimes their costumes – is false because it is visibly theatrical. They appear all the more inauthentic as they attempt to behave like Indians; they speak, think and dream like products of western humanism.

c) In *Twelfth Night*, text, delivery and acting style present themselves as hypertheatrical and thus false; paradoxically, this theatricality or artificiality reveals an underworld of phantasms and desires that are real enough.

d) In Barba's terms, the question of theatricality is not posed in terms of fiction/reality. Dance does not pose the problem of verisimilitude and fiction, but rather that of a performance technique and the universality of a pre-expressive dimension.

In every case, the spectator is in a position to evaluate the status of theatricality by following a route parallel to the actors performing this culture, and is thus 'able to follow or accompany the actor into the dance of thought-in-action' (Barba 1988).

(8) RECEPTION-ADAPTERS

This dance that Barba mentions cannot simply be taken for granted. In order to effect the cultural transfer smoothly, the director must be familiar with the target culture and be able to predict the audience's reaction. He must therefore arrange the source culture's reception and predict those arrangements that will facilitate communication between cultures. Certain adapters, established in relation to the perspective of the 'dramaturgical' adapters (3), assure readability (9) and reception (10).

a) Brook is particularly careful to move the *Mahabharata* closer to a western audience, through the choice of a popular theatre form but also in the way of narrating the epic. He gave two French actors the roles of narrator and intermediary between myth and audience: Alain Maratra played the role of Vyasa as a troubadour and Maurice Bénichou the role of Ganesha, who in turn incarnates Krishna. The latter is accompanied by a child to whom he tells the story. Using all these narrators simplifies the transmission of the epic and encourages the spectators to adapt the myth to their own personal stories. 'We know that for the child that is in each of us there is a very direct lesson to be learned from these fabulous adventures from another era' (Brook 1985c: 9).[11]

b) Mnouchkine does not use a narrator in the strict sense of the term, but she delegates a member of the lower classes, Haridassi, to welcome the audience, comment on the action, act as a witness to the historical figures. Haridassi assures the link between the Indian people and the theatrical event to which they invite the Paris audience. But, in contrast to *1789* and *L'Age d'or*, historical events are not presented from the people's perspective, but from a king's eye view, which corresponds to that of Cixous and a philosophy of great destinies. The roles of great men become themselves reception-adapters thanks to the effect of recognition (figures such as Gandhi or Nehru). This greatly facilitates the identification of the characters, just as the details of costume or behavior help the perception of groups. By contrast, there is no longer any dialectic between big and little, the heroes and the people: each group is cut off from the other, without any dialectical relationship between high and low.

c) The importance of these adapters (or structural devices of adaptation) is particularly clear if we compare the *Indiade* with *Twelfth Night*, which does not use any framing device or selection principle: one had better reread the play before the performance if one hopes to follow the plot and understand its dramaturgy. This cultural blurring rebounds on the readability of the plot, but at the same time it achieves its aim: using the phantasmatic image of India so as to combine the vagueness of the plot, the artistic and erotic haziness of the representation, and the modern notion of unconscious desire and daydreams.

d) In the final analysis, it is always the *mise en scène* that guarantees the adaptation and the communication of cultural worlds. We can clearly see this in *Faust*. Barba imposes – we might almost say he 'tacks on' to the dancers' improvisations a series of western dramaturgical devices: an easily decipherable classical narrative; 'subtitles' of Sanskrit or Japanese words provided by a narrated Italian translation; songs borrowed from Goethe as a musical emphasis of the pathos, etc. (See Chapter 7, 'Dancing with *Faust*').

(9) CONSEQUENCES FOR READABILITY

In appealing to a 'productive' spectator, all these *mises en scène* bear witness to the wide and adaptable range of readability. There is as yet no general theory of the readability of literary and cultural texts, still less of levels and modes of legibility: narrative, ideological, hermeneutic, etc. We need to know at what level the text is to be read and how its linguistic, ideological or cultural transposition sometimes entails a change in its general readability as well as its particular level of readability. At the moment everything implies that the target culture can impose its way of 'seeing and reading' the texts.

Faust compensates for its relative thematic unreadability – the difficulty of understanding words and cultural allusions – by the readability and cohesiveness of gestural sequences and their organization within a *mise en scène* that a western spectator can easily decipher.

The *Indiade* has a high readability in ethnological and geopolitical terms, but it pays for this directness with an extremely oversimplified conception of history and an 'unreadability' of the socioeconomic forces and contradictions that criss-cross Indian society.

The *Mahabharata* cannot be easily read at the level of detail in the actions and their religious and philosophical motivation, but the universalizing perspective allied with a direct acting style allows one to follow the actions in their physical, mythical and universal dimensions. The narrative and philosophical unreadability of the Indian poem is thus transmuted into a mythical and 'atmospheric' readability that remains with the spectator well after the performance.[12]

In cultural transfer, we have to decide what mode of readability we ought to highlight and in what proportions: immediate or lasting, thematic or formal, synthetic or analytic, particularizing or generalizing, etc. Intercultural communication is often possible only at the price of changing the mode of readability from one culture to another.[13] The history of a text or a culture is nothing other than the history of the successive ways in which it has been read.

Readability implies an act of communication between an *I* who reads and a *you* (what is read by and written for that *I*). Every mode of readability implies a mode of alterity. But this alterity can take very different forms. The other can be: distant or close in space; distant or close in time; unknown/familiar; strange/familiar; conform or not conform to my opinions.

Most of the time, several criteria are combined, so that it is very difficult to take a position *vis-à-vis* the other in the knowledge of what distinguishes us from it.

(10) RECEPTION WITHIN THE TARGET CULTURE

Having finally (or almost) arrived at its destination in the target culture, the transcultural *mise en scène* confronts the last obstacle, the audience, which opens and identifies this cargo that has been more or less clandestinely transported from one side to the other. The audience can simply accept it (take for granted that *Twelfth*

Night takes place in India) or reject it and refuse to recognize it, for several reasons: they may refuse from the outset the culture that is the vehicle of the transmission (rejecting Shakespeare done in the style of Kabuki, for example), or contest the appropriateness of the chosen cultural reference (preferring Korea as a setting for *Twelfth Night*), or object to the fact that other considerations – such as the political perspective in the *Indiade* – have been sacrificed to a purely culturalist and decorative transfer.

Whatever these reactions might be, specators will always be tempted, even constrained, to compare cultural and artistic modeling systems in the source ((1) and (2)) with those in their own culture or to observe differences and justify transformations: the comparison is all the easier, in that it involves not vague cultural images, but well-established modeling systems and codifications ((1), (2) and (10A), (10B), (10C)), which the audience judge as consumers of their own culture, as specialists competent in familiar and strange forms and as private individuals marked by their ideological and aesthetic presuppositions. I will limit myself to my own immediate impressions here: a) I was touched in the *Mahabharata* by the universalizing immediacy of the performance, but its narrow register too much resembled High Mass; b) despite its textual and stage virtuosity, the *Indiade* wearied me with its repetitive effects of plaintive speeches and sentimental politics; c) *Twelfth Night* had the perfection of an opera, which was just as well, since the words and plot were profoundly boring; d) *Faust* surprised me, since I could no longer decide whether it dealt with the western myth or the gestural re-elaboration of Asian codes.

Intercultural communication obviously involves more than such personal impressions or blank refusal, or on the contrary unconditional acceptance, of the aesthetic object. It makes more sense to 'calmly' analyse the reception codes of the target audience. We might return here in (10) to the categories and subdivisions set out in (1) and (2), and to examine in particular the difficult relationship between anthropological and sociological codification, observing how this relationship could have developed from one culture to another and what shifts or balances have resulted.

In sociological codification, we adopt the context of a culture in the ideological sense of the term. Culture here is no longer an anthropological concept or a means of integration or communion, but 'the instrument used by one subgroup against the others in the social conflict' (Camilleri 1982: 26). What we have to determine is how the audience, in whole or in part, appropriates in a hegemonic or ideological way an element of the source culture for its own 'selfish' ends. For example, we might observe that part of the so-called progressive audience of the *Indiade* takes pleasure in its rejection of a Marxist conception of history and the pseudo-humanist confusion that results. A 'cultivated' subgroup of this Cartoucherie audience uses the spectacle of India in the play as a means of confirming its own cultural supremacy and knowledge (however superficial) of India or Gandhi's non-violence, as well as its conviction that we are now in an era of post-history and there is no more point in analysing cultures in militant political terms.

The target audience's reception is by definition subject to any change in the audience. Every modification in the context of reception *ipso facto* modifies the impact of the *mise en scène* and the functions of the principal elements of its structure ((3), (4), (6), (7), (8), (9)), which it thus restructures and reorganizes. The choice and the connotations of a form, the presumed intention of the adaptations, the function of theatricality, the mode of read-ability – everything is called into question, that is concretized and read in a different way. The *mise en scène* can be seen as a series of open choices, strategies, propositions, which will be differently received by future audiences.

One last – risk – factor remains: the way in which the work proceeds and undergoes modification in the spectator's conscious-ness. To access this – an almost impossible and dangerously subjec-tive task – we would have to take account of the last link in this intercultural chain: 'given and anticipated consequences' (11) both for the stage and symbolic future of the work and for the history of the individual spectator – the 'missing link' in theatre studies.

(11) GIVEN AND ANTICIPATED CONSEQUENCES

Only Brook claims explicitly that the *mise en scène* has a trans-formative effect on the spectator, which is the counterpart of the actors' work on themselves (5).

> The final reconciliation is for me much less an anecdotal reconciliation between characters, than an internal reconcili-ation that ricochets on to the audience: the audience should

leave the theatre having lived all this and, at the same time, reconciled with themselves, liberated.

(Brook 1986b)

Reconciled with themselves, the spectators are also reconciled with each other, in so far as the performance has succeeded in making them share a common experience, which reflects the search for new cultural links between spectators and between cultural traditions, which the *mise en scène* reunites and universalizes in an ephemeral way.[14] This is the point of Brook's interpersonal and intercultural quest: 'It was by making the act of theatre inseparable from the need to establish new relations with different people that the possibility of finding new cultural links appeared' (Brook 1987: 239).

From this loosely defined area, open to the audience's memories and to cultural connections in and beyond the performance, it is still possible to ponder the linkage of intercultural transfers and to check whether this operation that has been more or less consciously achieved from steps (3) to (10) still corresponds to the final result and the 'working' of the performance in collective and individual memory. The analysis of interculturalism thus remains in a state of permanent evolution and the boundaries between the various layers in this model must be kept open to interpenetration. And we must not forget to turn the hourglass from time to time.

But before doing so – and to avert this vague impression of anticipated reception – we can predict certain reactions from a spectator confronted by cultural *otherness*. First of all, we should relativize the optimistic view that we can understand our own culture while remaining impervious to foreign cultures. Do we really understand our own culture? Are we not after all caught in the obviousness of the ideology that constitutes our culture and the rules that determine it? Are we not equally caught in the unconsciousness of the roots and origins of our own culture? And, conversely, do we not notice elements of a foreign culture that the 'natives' no longer notice? Does the distance not add emphasis? Wasn't the goal of Brecht's 'alienation effect' to make strange what had too long been familiar?

Cultural otherness provokes a number of different reactions in the spectator. The question is what 'receiving a foreign or strange culture' means; it might be severally or simultaneously: linguistic understanding; rational understanding; understanding in detail and overall; aesthetic understanding (at the price of an aestheticizing or exoticizing attitude); being moved by something that the foreign activity reveals at the pre-expressive level (Barba); understanding the 'methodological code' (Camilleri 1982: 25) which allows us to decipher the performance and to produce other cultural events of the same sort (i.e. to be cultivated in Lotman's sense, in which culture is also a productive synthesis making possible the continuing production of information); seeking reinforcements of our image of the foreign culture or, on the contrary, disruption of that image and production of a new one.

Having compared the image of India and its culture in these *mises en scène*, we may certainly wonder whether the performances deal with the same thing or if they have the least reference in common. This fragmented and elusive image is perhaps proof that it is impossible fully to grasp a culture – even with theatre's mimetic means – and *a fortiori* impossible to compare evidence of cultures in artifacts that completely rework the referent by making it imaginary and unrecognizable. Further, this rather simplified theoretical model does not take account of every possible schematization. We are still far from a general theory of interculturalism, founded on a semiotic model that could be compared, in precision, to the theory of intertextuality. As with linguistic texts, it is tricky to make out what belongs to quotation, borrowing, rewriting, collage, re-elaboration or appropriation, especially since these operations are often combined.

However, it is within this semiotic model of exchange, like rewriting or intertextuality, that we would best be able to formulate the theoretical model of interculturalism. In this sense, this model fits easily within the general model of the *mise en scène*, conceived as intermediacy, as an economical way of rehashing languages, influences, different realms of fiction: a way of rehashing which the director knows as well as the cook. Ingredients, raw material, signs of various and sometimes doubtful sources must be mixed, so that the audience ends up by finding them to their taste and homogenizing by their gaze these still heterogeneous elements. The relationship of this intercultural model to that of translation is undeniable, since we can simultaneously understand interculturalism as a kind of translation of one culture into another and translation as an intercultural exchange in the broad sense of the term.

Whatever the semiotic model chosen to integrate these diverse questions, we need to be able to evaluate the ideological function of interculturalism within contemporary *mise en scène*. Why has interculturalism become a sort of categorical imperative for a good number of contemporary directors? Is it really because it appears to be the new dominant theatrical aesthetic, a new well-meaning ethics of understanding between peoples? Is it not rather because it corresponds to a need of the theatre apparatus and fulfills an ideological function of whitewashing under cover of a democratic openness to all the cultures of the world? Our four examples speak eloquently on this subject: *Twelfth Night* ties up with a pre-Brechtian 'culinary' way of staging the classics, a refusal to analyse how Shakespearean dramaturgy or a culturalist rereading of it may be made productive for us here and now. In the *Indiade*, we have a 'postmodern' way of dispensing with a critical and political approach to history: despite a hallucinatory ethnological representation, the heated and moralizing humanist discourse returns us to a romantic picture of the people and their suffering. This question-mark over any critical historical vision, and *a fortiori* any Marxist analysis, corresponds to a turn which the Théâtre du Soleil probably had to take to maintain the feeling of still being 'in.' Brook has not had to perform similar about-turns, since he has remained true to his investigation of theatre's ritual function, without claiming (as the Soleil once did) to grasp culture in its political and ideological dimension as well. As before, he is concerned only with the 'culture of links ... between man and society, between one race and another, between the microcosm and the macrocosm, between humanity and machinery, between the visible and the invisible, between categories, languages and genres' (Brook 1987: 239). Barba's investigations are inscribed in a current of anthropological research which no longer compares cultures in terms of theme or socioeconomic background, but which faces the area of performance codification and the universal principles of pre-expressivity. In each case, the intercultural approach corresponds to insistent demands made on the theatre and ideological apparatus by the institutions within which it functions.

It is striking to note that there is a parallel and harmonious development of intercultural and postmodern theatre and that there is neither rivalry nor symbolic conflict between the two tendencies, to the point where the theatre of Robert Wilson has come to represent the perfect synthesis of the two because he has the art of quoting cultural and historical details by grounding them in an aesthetic that does not differentiate between them within a vast 'collage of cultures' (Fischer-Lichte 1987: 232). Our era and our western guilty conscience encourage both an alliance with foreign cultures and a functional transformation of all signs into a postmodern 'supracultural' product that is icily but fatally beautiful.

Thus we gain on two fronts: culture becomes both a quest for foreign sensuality and for coded abstraction.

1. The *culture of sensuality*, with the desire to nourish itself at bargain prices at the foreigners' expense, makes an effort to revitalize western forms and traditions by adding or substituting extra-European forms. Faced with its own loss of flavor, sensuality, any link to reality at home, western culture reacts with the secular reflex of importing rejuvenating raw materials.[15]

2. But western consciousness does not so easily give up the *culture of abstraction* that has become its own. The quantification of knowledge and language, which according to Lyotard characterizes the 'postmodern condition,' leads to an aesthetic of technocratic and computerized efficiency excluding every relationshp with the world of objects or moral and philosophical values. The result is a theatrical culture of abstraction and technological precision, an internal machine that moves by itself without a hitch, whether in Wilson's case or that of postmodern authors such as Heiner Müller, Michel Vinaver or Bernard-Marie Koltès. Culture thus conveyed no longer bears any resemblance to reality; it bypasses any reference to nature or humanity; it has become a coded, abstract language, whose value resides in its syntax and programming, but which says literally nothing about the phenomenal world. This is a phenomenon of normalization and internationalization (rather than interculturalism) that facilitates the exchange of theatrical products, once they have been frozen in a visual phantasmagoria so powerful that it dispenses with the text or cultural allusions, as with an anxiety of origins or any concern for ideological determination.

As a result, we can legitimately doubt the creation of a world culture,[16] in which very different cultures would participate, but which would also succeed in respecting and enhancing the particularity of each culture (Fischer-Lichte 1987: 239), since such a culture would first have to reconcile the irreconcilable, sensuality and abstraction.[17] Of course, this is exactly the program of many intercultural aesthetics, which would like to bring together specificity and universality, but there are no convincing examples of this quest except perhaps Brook's work. Unfortunately, we seem to be heading toward a two-tiered culture and interculturalism: a consumable culture for a large audience or even for a targeted group from the conservative middle class, a culture of easy access that is neither controversial nor radical, which provides ready-made answers to big questions, cavalier views on history (Cixous) or pleasing embellishments (Mnouchkine), preaching an end to cultural differentiation under the cover of 'an all-purpose culture'; or, on the contrary, an elite culture that is radical and irreducible, that abandons spectacular performance to work at the microscopic level, almost in secret, and whose results are never immediate and often obscure.

Theatrical interculturalism does not escape the historical contradictions of our age, even if, in making its own theory and producing its most delicate fruits, it would like to put those contradictions in brackets for a moment, to find out how two cultures meet and to see what they have to tell us and how they might love each other.

NOTES

1. An even more primitive version rejects cultural anthropology as bourgeois and maintains that this sort of anthropology 'does not contribute to understanding between people or to a cultural exchange in the sense of peace and progress,' but presents instead the 'anti-historical anti-humanist and reactionary political nature of this tendency' (Wessel 1980).

2. For a definition of ethnocentrism, see Preiswerk and Perrot (1975: 49):

> Ethnocentrism is defined as the attitude of a group which accords itself a central place in relation to other groups and positively valorizes its achievements, while projecting its values on to outsiders who are interpreted according to the in-group's way of thinking.

3. This notion of modeling systems is relevant for theatre which necessarily creates a microcosm of reality. Hence its specificity, according to Brook: 'What is remarkable about theatre and what separates it from other forms of expression is that it enables us to create a true

microcosm. Other art forms are individual expressions. Theatre, on the other hand, is a mini-cosmos' (Brook 1982a).

4.   By nature, theatre even ancient theatre, is always a modern art. The phoenix which must be continually helped to rebirth. . . . In five years a production is past its prime. We must therefore completely abandon the idea of a theatre tradition, since that idea carries its own contradiction.

(Brook 1980: 121)

5. We know Brook's taste for texts and symbols that are not tied to any particular culture but form a part of human culture, accessible to everyone. In *The Conference of the Birds*, for example, the bird is an accessible symbol, even it remains inexplicable:

The bird is one of those symbols that are not tied to any particular culture. Indeed, every culture, probably for the same reason, has a bird myth deeply embedded in it. But the bird itself is part of human culture and a symbol of humanity; it is a simple thing, which affects even a child, but which is at the same time difficult to understand or to grasp.

(Brook 1983b: 118)

6. See Brook (1985b); also *The Empty Space*:

Shakespeare is our model. In this respect, our work on the Shakespearean productions is always to make the plays modern, because it is only when the audience comes into direct contact with the play's themes that time and conventions vanish. . . . The problem is always the same: where are the equivalents of Elizabethan strengths in the sense of range and stretch.

(Brook 1968: 107)

7.   I believe that the great misunderstanding, the decadence of the European tradition – and this is also true of Africa and Asia, at least as we see them – arises because we see theatre only in terms of 'culture,' in terms of formal art. This art is not theatre. It is a way of applying external plastic criteria to the theatre event.

(Brook 1983a: 16–17)

8. Brook thus simultaneously seeks a highly developed theatre form (the poetic text of the *Mahabharata*) and a popular approach to this form. This combination confirms his desire to be universally accessible, despite cultural differences. That was already the point of choosing *Carmen*: 'No other opera is as well known as *Carmen*, all the more because it contains universal elements that move any one despite cultural differences' (Brook 1982a). What is at issue is the reconciliation of serious and popular forms, 'the richness of the content expressed in a popular way,' 'profound, but accessible meaning.'

9. We are far from the use of *commedia dell'arte* and Chinese theatre in earlier productions such as *L'Age d'or*, for example. In that

213

production, these forms were used to deepen the relationship among actor, plot and spectator, to impose on the performance a highly developed form that transcended mere imitation: 'we have not treated these forms as old forms; we have taken up these forms at a level below which we do not want to fall' (Mnouchkine 1975: 5).

10. Barba always looks at eastern theatre with the eyes of a western director:

> I believe that my way of working in theatre has led me to discover the hidden aspect of theatre underneath the skin of conventions. . . . Western theatre has enabled me to examine Eastern theatre, to look at it with different eyes. I have begun to see that actors in Eastern theatre use similar principles to the Odin actors, even if the forms are different.
>
> (Brook 1982b: 48)

11. In all his productions, Brook has taken care to manage the relationship between stage and audience with an eye on the constant 'changes in distance.' He mentions two kinds of movement:

> the one circulates between the social and the personal point of view, or between the intimate and the general. . . . The other is a vertical movement. It is the contact between the superficial aspects of life and those hidden aspects that are more subtle and more intense.
>
> (Brook 1982a)

12. In this sense, Brook's *mise en scène* fulfills the conditions and virtues of his own version of theatre. As he writes: 'The primary virtue of a theatre performance is that it is living, and the second, that it can be immediately understood' (Brook 1980: 118).

13. We must also take account of performance traditions that belong to a nation or culture and what makes a *mise en scène* part of that context. In receiving this tradition within a quite different cultural context, we must take into account the residue of the foreign culture and transpose it into the target culture.

14. 'There ought to be a meeting, a dynamic relationship between a group which has had special preparation and another group, the audience, which is not so prepared' (Brook 1980).

15. One example among many: the performance of *The Tempest* in Balinese by Murdoch University in Australia. 'Our original interest in the play was to see whether inspiration from another culture could effect a revival of the play's original power – whether Indonesian theatre could restore to us one of our own classics' (George 1988: 22).

16. In a sense, this one-world culture is the antithesis of interculturalism, which refuses to reduce the gaps between cultures and cultivates cultural peculiarities. I would ask Andrej Wirth who distinguishes between an interculturalism aimed at understanding between cultures and one (like Wilson's) that is content to distance cultures one from another: who decides if interculturalism really helps understanding

between peoples? I would also ask Erika Fischer-Lichte, who contrasts the historical avant-garde (of the early twentieth century) that shamelessly exploited exotic cultures with a postmodernism that respects other cultures and integrates them in a utopian world culture: what guarantees the purity of postmodernism's intentions?

17. It is certainly not impossible for a theatre like Wilson's to succeed in maintaining the misunderstanding and in reconciling sensuality and abstraction, prolonging in *modern* (and not *post*modern) fashion the classical opposition between reason and sensuality. As Annette Hornbacher has pertinently remarked:

> This stage abstraction, which Wilson has highlighted against any emotionalization, is the same western misunderstanding that we see in his most enthusiastic followers, whose merely formalistic sound and light shows promise only *sensuous pleasure*. Both sides reproduce the typically new age – and therefore in no way *post*modern – impression that there is in fact an opposition between intellect and meaning on the one hand and sensuality and feeling on the other.
>
> (Hornbacher 1987: 12–13)

BIBLIOGRAPHY

Barba, Eugenio (1982) 'Le paradoxe pédagogique,' *Bouffonneries* 4.
—— (1985) 'The Nature of Dramaturgy: Describing Actions at Work,' *New Theatre Quarterly* 1.
—— (1988) 'Théâtre eurasien,' *Bouffonneries* 4.
Brook, Peter (1968) *The Empty Space*, London: McGibbon & Kee.
—— (1973) 'Rencontre avec Peter Brook: interview de Denis Bablet,' *Travail théâtral* 10.
—— (1980) *Le Fait culturel*, Paris: Fayard.
—— (1982a) 'Interview with Yutaka Wada,' *Kabana Sagetsu* 142.
—— (1982b) 'Le paradoxe pédagogique,' *Bouffonneries* 4.
—— (1983a) 'Des apparences porteuses d'invisible,' *Recherche, Pédagogie, Culture* 61.
—— (1983b) 'Ein Gespräch mit Peter Brook,' *Kreativität und Dialog*, Berlin: Henschelverlag Kunst und Gesellschaft.
—— (1985a) Interview with Herbert Mainusch, *Regie und Interpretation, Gespräche mit Regisseuren*, Munich: Fink.
—— (1985b) 'Shakespeare et le *Mahabharata*,' *Théâtre en Europe* 7.
—— (1985c) 'Le *Mahabharata* ou les pouvoirs d'une histoire,' *Alternatives théâtrales* 24.
—— (1986a) 'Interview,' *Nouvelles de l'Inde* 248.
—— (1986b) 'Interview,' *Vogue* (February).
—— (1987) *The Shifting Point*, New York: Harper & Row.
Camilleri, Carmel (1982) 'Culture et sociétés: caractères et fonctions,' *Les Amis de Sèvres* 4.
Carrière, Jean-Claude (1985) 'Chercher le coeur profond,' *Alternatives théâtrales* 24.

Cixous, Hélène (1987a) *L'Indiade ou l'Inde de leurs rêves*, Paris.
—— (1987b) 'Sur *l'Indiade*', *Acteurs* 29.
Fischer-Lichte, Erika (1987) 'Das eigene und das fremde Theater. Inter-kulturelle Tendenzen auf dem Theater der Gegenwart,' in Wilfried Floeck (ed.) *Tendenzen des Gegenwartstheaters*, Tübingen: Francke Verlag.
Francastel, Pierre (1965) *La Réalité figurative*, Paris: Gonthier.
George, David (1988) '*The Tempest* in Bali,' *New Theatre in Australia* 3.
Hornbacher, Annette (1987) 'Robert Wilsons Theater: Ornamente aus Menschen, Requisiten und Dekorationen,' *Die Deutsche Bühne* 11.
Lotman, Jurij (1974) *Kunst als Sprache*, Leipzig: Reclam.
Mnouchkine, Ariane (1975) 'Première ébauche: entretien avec Ariane Mnouchkine,' *Théâtre/Public* 5–6.
Moscoso, Sophie (1984) 'Notes de répétitions,' *Double Page* 32.
Pavis, Patrice (1985) *Voies et images de la scène*, Lille: Presses Universitaires.
Preiswerk, Roy and Perrot, Dominique (1975) *Ethnocentrisme et histoire: l'Afrique, l'Amérique indienne et l'Asie dans les manuels occidentaux*, Paris: Anthropos.
Schechner, Richard (1983) 'Du comportement reconstitué,' *Bouffonneries* 9.
—— (1984) 'A reply to Rustom Bharacha,' *Asian Theatre Journal* 1, 2.
Wessel, B. (1980) *Kultur und Ethos: Zur Kritik der bürgerlichen Auffassung uber die Rolle der Kultur in Geschichte und Gesellschaft*, Berlin.

INDEX